WHAT IS MAN?

Adam, alien or ape?

Edgar Andrews

BSc, PhD, DSc, FInstP, FIMMM, CEng, CPhys.

ELM HILL

A Division of
HarperCollins Christian Publishing

www.elmhillbooks.com

What is Man?
Adam, alien or ape?

Published in Nashville, Tennessee, by Elm Hill, an imprint of Thomas Nelson. Elm Hill and Thomas Nelson are registered trademarks of HarperCollins Christian Publishing, Inc.

Elm Hill titles may be purchased in bulk for educational, business, fund-raising, or sales promotional use. For information, please e-mail SpecialMarkets@ ThomasNelson.com.

All Bible quotations are taken from the New King James Version, Copyright © 1988 by Thomas Nelson Inc. Used by permission. All rights reserved.

Library of Congress Cataloging-in-Publication Data

Library of Congress Control Number: 2018930396

Prelaunch edition ISBN: 978-1-595556844

ISBN 978-1-595542991 (Paperback)
ISBN 978-1-595558466 (Hardbound)
ISBN 978-1-595543035 (eBook)

OTHER BOOKS BY THE AUTHOR

From Nothing to Nature
God, Science and Evolution
Christ and the Cosmos
The Spirit Has Come
Free in Christ (Galatians)
A Glorious High Throne (Hebrews)
Preaching Christ
Who Made God? Searching for a Theory of Everything

ENDORSEMENTS
WHAT IS MAN? ADAM, ALIEN OR APE?

Edgar Andrews has a way of making the profound accessible. His scholarship informs the reader about key questions of our time, offering wise guidance and illumination.

— PAUL COPAN, *PLEDGER FAMILY CHAIR OF PHILOSOPHY AND ETHICS, PALM BEACH ATLANTIC UNIVERSITY, USA.*

This winsome new work by Professor Andrews sets forth a cogent answer to one of the most pressing questions of our day: "What is Man?" It demonstrates the utter failure of the pervasive worldview of Darwinian naturalism to provide a satisfying answer to this question, and why we must turn to an ancient source, namely the Bible, to find the ultimate answer. Based on solid scholarship both scientific and theological, and robustly argued, I highly recommend it!

— MICHAEL A.G. HAYKIN, *PROFESSOR OF CHURCH HISTORY, THE SOUTHERN BAPTIST THEOLOGICAL SEMINARY, LOUISVILLE, KY.*

I found *What Is Man?* informative and hard to put down. Understanding the biblical teaching on this subject is essential for developing a Christian worldview. Dr. Andrews' reader-friendly writing style, combined with his scientific and theological expertise, make this book unique. I would highly recommend it for pastors and laymen alike. If you are a Christian, it will stretch your mind, bless you and aid you in defending your faith in a world that is increasingly hostile to the gospel of Jesus Christ.

— ROBERT L. DICKIE, *AUTHOR AND SENIOR PASTOR, BEREAN BAPTIST CHURCH, GRAND BLANC, MICHIGAN, USA.*

What Is Man? brings together insights from the many current philosophical views of man, detailing for the layperson their meaning and ramifications. The reader will be uplifted by Dr. Andrews' deep knowledge of faith and science, and believer and seeker alike will enjoy this book. While some of the topics are complex, the writing style makes this book accessible, informative, and educational. I highly recommend it to anyone, regardless of their faith or education, because the issues discussed will become more and more relevant in an age that is questioning the very meaning of reality.

— SCOTT SCHROEDER, *GRADUATE, MICHGAN STATE UNIVERSITY, USA.*

It's a really great read. Edgar Andrews' work is both deeply informed and very enjoyable—a wonderful combination of virtues for an author. We will happily promote *What Is Man?* on *Books At a Glance* with high recommendations.

— FRED ZASPEL, *PASTOR AT REFORMED BAPTIST CHURCH OF FRANCONIA; ASSOCIATE PROFESSOR OF THEOLOGY AT THE SOUTHERN BAPTIST THEOLOGICAL SEMINARY; EXECUTIVE EDITOR AT "BOOKS AT A GLANCE," USA.*

Dr Andrews combines humor, wit, and convincing arguments in *What Is Man?*—an articulate masterpiece that defends the biblical worldview while competently refuting the evolutionary perspective.

— NATE HERBST, *MASTER PLAN STUDENT MINISTRIES AND* THE GOD SOLUTION *RADIO SHOW, USA.*

Down the centuries, a galaxy of thinkers have given their answers to the Psalmist's deceptively simple question, *What is Man?* asked three millennia ago. Most have fallen wide of the mark; a few have come nearer the target. Here, with honesty, erudition, and a sure but light touch, Edgar Andrews leads his readers, through the maze of conflicting ideas, to the answer that surely captivates the intellect and satisfies the spirit.

— ROGER W. FAY, *PASTOR AND EDITOR OF* EVANGELICAL TIMES, *UK.*

This engaging book, written by an accomplished scientist and easily digestible by a general readership, succeeds splendidly in breaking down into "bite-sized" pieces complex ideas about the origin, constitution, significance, and final destiny of mankind—offering a sometimes humorous but still profound critique of the claims of secularists. Apt analogies taken from everyday life are an outstanding features of the book.

— MARTIN ERDMANN, *THEOLOGIAN, AUTHOR, AND DIRECTOR OF THE VERAX INSTITUTE.*

In *What Is Man?* Dr Andrews, boldly addresses one of the preeminent questions of our generation. The debates regarding the nature of man are scientific, theological, philosophical and cultural, just as starters. The implications are legion. Andrews' treatment is pointed, comprehensive, humorous, sound and (most critically) thoroughly informed from a biblical worldview centered on the wonderful gospel of Jesus Christ.

— JOE FLEENER, *HUSBAND, FATHER, PASTOR, BIBLE COLLEGE LECTURER, CONFERENCE SPEAKER, NEW ZEALAND.*

It was both delightful and edifying to read Professor Andrews' earlier book *Who Made God?* on the evidences for the existence of God. An excitement in the staid ranks of Christians greeted its publication. Everyone was reading it. Now he has produced a sequel answering the next most fundamental question people are asking: What is Man? Who am I? Where did I come from? What is my purpose in my brief and uncertain life? Begin your search here!

— GEOFF THOMAS, *PASTOR AND CONFERENCE SPEAKER, UK.*

In *What Is Man?* (a sequel to his excellent book *Who Made God?*), Prof Andrews tackles another great question we all ask. Next to a true knowledge of God, a true knowledge of ourselves remains critical. With his usual combination of reliable and helpfully explained science, biblical knowledge, cultural awareness, good humor and rapier-sharp reasoning, the author covers virtually every important aspect of the question. Would that every young person could read this book, which offers such clear direction amidst the many voices calling for their attention.

— STEVEN BOWERS, *DIRECTOR, EUROPEAN MISSION FELLOWSHIP AND FORMER PASTOR.*

Two of life's most important questions are, "Who is God?" and "What is Man?" Our answers to these two questions shape our worldview and how we live our lives. In his previous book, *Who Made God ?* Dr. Andrews gave us answers to the first question; in this follow-up book, he answers the latter— in a poignant, accessible, and often humorous manner. As a scientist and theologian, Dr. Andrews has a unique way of presenting complex scientific and philosophical ideas in a way that laymen such as myself can understand. In our increasingly secularized Western world of thought, *What Is Man?* offers thought-provoking reasons, to both skeptics and believers, as to why this trend should be rejected.

— GREGORY S. WEST, *RATIO CHRISTI CAMPUS APOLOGETICS ALLIANCE; FOUNDER AND EDITOR OF THE POACHED EGG CHRISTIAN WORLDVIEW & APOLOGETICS NETWORK.*

The question of human identity is one of the most pressing issues facing this generation. Edgar Andrews employs his scientific understanding to respond to some of the key humanistic and evolutionary answers provided to that question, and then sets out the biblical case for humanity as made in the image of God, with Jesus Christ as the perfect exemplar. Professor Andrews has a rare ability to make complex scientific issues plain to nonspecialists without dumbing down his explanations, and that ability is on full display in this book.

— ROBERT STRIVENS, *FORMERLY PRINCIPAL OF THE LONDON THEOLOGICAL SEMINARY.*

AUTHOR'S PREFACE

In 1906, American humorist Mark Twain published a sixty-page essay entitled "What Is Man?" Consisting of a tedious dialogue between a senior citizen (who believes that man is just a machine) and a young man (who believes nothing in particular but is open to persuasion), it wasn't one of his finest books. But at least he tried. Authors since then seem to have avoided the subject like the plague. Jewish theologian Abraham Heschel published a collection of lectures in 1965 under the title *Who Is Man?* while Waller Newell (2001) and Joaquin Molina (2013) wrote books bearing the title *What Is a Man?* But that's about all I could find, and these books[1,2,3] address what it means to be *male* rather than what it means to be *human*. When the psalmist asked, "What is man?" (Psalm 8:4) he was, I think, seeking an altogether more profound answer.

The avoidance of the subject is all the more strange because there has never been a time like our own, when curiosity about man's origin and destiny has been greater, or the answers on offer more hotly disputed. It's a safe bet that any attempt to give the "big picture" on the origin, nature, and "specialness" of mankind will be contentious, and that might explain why writers have generally fought shy of it. Yet at heart it is the question most of us really do want answered, because the answer defines that precious thing we call our identity, both personally and as a race.

The Psalmist did, of course, offer his own answer three millennia ago. Man, he claimed, was created by God for a clearly defined purpose—to exercise dominion over planet Earth and (by implication) to ultimately share something of the glory of the divine nature. The rest, as they say, is history, but it's not a happy tale. As Mark Twain says in another essay, "I can't help being disappointed with Adam and Eve."

Not surprisingly, then, a large proportion of humanity today is looking for alternative solutions, accepting the challenge of the Psalmist's question without embracing the optimism of his answer. In this book we are going to consider the alternative solutions on offer by considering man in the contexts of cosmology, biology, and psychology—before returning to the biblical context and discovering that, after all, the Psalmist got it right. Don't let the science-sounding stuff put you off. I'm writing in a reader-friendly and often humorous style, specifically for the nonexpert.

ACKNOWLEDGEMENTS

No book of this nature would see the light of day without the encouragement and advice of others. I therefore want to extend my warmest thanks to the many friends who have read the draft manuscript and made helpful suggestions for its improvement. I am not going to list their names lest I inadvertently omit some of them, but I must mention just one person, Eddy Maatkamp, who translated my earlier book *Who Made God?* into Dutch and has now published a Dutch version of *What Is Man?* He has supported the present project with unfailing wisdom, care and enthusiasm and I owe him a special debt of gratitude.

REFERENCES

Each chapter has numerous endnotes. In the past I have tried to avoid using internet websites in references because they often lack permanence and many links disappear over a period of time. However, situations change and much original work is now published on the internet and is not available in hard copy forms. Even when it is available in university and similar libraries, other important reference material is inaccessible to most readers except on the internet. No doubt some of my internet links will be lost over time, but parallel sources can often be found by searching for authors or subjects, and the alternative would be to have no reference at all. Wherever possible, of course, I do provide hard-copy references.

Edgar Andrews
Welwyn Garden City
2018

ENDNOTES:

[1] Abraham Joshua Heschel; *Who Is Man?* (Lectures; Stanford University Press, 1965).

[2] Waller R. Newell; *What Is a Man? 3,000 Years of Wisdom on the Art of Manly Virtue* (Harper Collins, 2001).

[3] Joaquin G. Molina; *What Is a Man?* (Spring of Life Fellowship, 2013).

CONTENTS

Author's Preface, Acknowledgements and References   *viii*

PART 1. MAN AND THE COSMOS

Ch.1. Who Do You Think You Are?   1
(What is Man? A summary)

Ch.2. The Cheshire Cat Cosmos   21
(Can a universe create itself from nothing?)

Ch.3. Small Flat Bugs   39
(Where is Man?)

Ch.4. The Cosmic Cookbook   63
(A fine-tuned universe)

Ch.5. Deutsch's Dauntless Dinosaurs   91
(Exploring the mega-multiverse)

PART 2. MAN AND THE BIOSPHERE

Ch.6. Death And Taxes   113
(Human uniqueness)

Ch.7. The Devil In The Details   133
(Digging deeper into genes and genomes)

Ch.8. Dem Dry Bones   157
(What fossils really tell us about the rise of Man)

Ch. 9. Aristotle And The Snowball   181
(On human consciousness)

PART 3. MAN AND THE BIBLE

Ch.10. Worldviews At War   205
(On the nature of reality)

Ch.11. Adam And The Apple   227
(The historicity and fall of Adam and Eve)

Ch.12. The Image Of God   251
(Why Man is unique)

Ch.13. The Second Adam   275
(Jesus Christ, the perfect man)

Ch.14. The Resurrection: Fact Or Fiction?   295
(The claim, the evidence, and the implications)

CHAPTER 1

What is Man? The poet Alexander Pope proposed that Man is "the glory, jest and riddle of the world." But that's a restatement of the question rather than an answer to it. The purpose of this book is to find answers, and in this opening chapter we review the main theories popular today about the origin and nature of mankind. We'll see that these ideas fall into four main categories; Man is either (1) a superior ape, (2) an evolved animal embellished with an emergent spirit, (3) an evolved animal endowed with a divine image, or (4) an unevolved special creation made by God in his own spiritual likeness. What evidence exists for each of these options, and are they mutually exclusive?

Although the whole book is devoted to resolving these issues, this chapter provides an overview of the subject before we plunge into deeper waters and consider how we relate as human beings to the cosmos, the biosphere (the world of living things), and the Bible. Be prepared to smile, frown, and ponder.

WHO DO YOU THINK YOU ARE?

What is Man? A summary

> *What is Man that you are mindful of him, and the son of Man that you visit him?*
>
> PSALM 8:4.

What is Man? The subtitle of this book offers three options: Adam, alien, or ape. By "Adam" I mean the biblical view that human beings are made in the image of God. I use "alien" to reflect the popular idea that humanity is not the only intelligent life form in the cosmos and may even have arrived on Earth from somewhere else. By "ape" I mean the common belief that you and I are simply superior simians.

Let's start by making clear what we mean by "man." The word is used in three ways. It can mean a male member of the human race (man = male). It can mean the human race itself (man = humanity).

And it can mean a member of the human race regardless of gender (man = person). A manhole can be used by women as well as men, and a man-eating tiger isn't bothered about the sex of its victim.

This third use of "man" is today often considered politically incorrect, and I apologize in advance to anyone who is offended by it. But in writing this book, I found it unavoidable for two reasons. Firstly, there is no alternative when discussing the *essence* of the human condition. To give just one example, the phrase "the spirit of man" cannot be replaced by "the spirit of humanity" because "humanity" is a collective noun and its use would change the meaning. Secondly, this third use of "man" is common historically, and without it I could neither quote the Bible accurately nor offer you the wisdom of Alexander Pope's poem, "The proper study of mankind is man" cited below. In this book, therefore, I shall make use of all three meanings of the word "man" but I trust that the context will always make it clear which is intended. For clarity I will capitalize the first letter to read "Man" whenever the reference is to humanity as a whole.

THE RIDDLE OF THE WORLD

Writing in 1734, the poet Alexander Pope described the contradictions of human nature with eloquent clarity. Man is, he writes[1]:

"In doubt to deem himself a god or beast;
    In doubt his mind or body to prefer;
    Born but to die, and reasoning but to err;
    Alike in ignorance, his reason such,
    Whether he thinks too little, or too much;
    Chaos of thought and passion, all confused;
    Still by himself, abused or disabused;
    Created half to rise and half to fall;

> Great lord of all things, yet a prey to all,
> Sole judge of truth, in endless error hurled;
> The glory, jest and riddle of the world."

The depressing fact is that everything Alexander Pope said nearly 300 years ago is still true! As a race we continue to notch up amazing achievements in the arts, science and technology, counterbalanced by uncertainty about what it means to be human and apprehension about where mankind is heading. To an impassioned observer we are indeed "the glory, jest and riddle of the world."

Whether we accept it or not, the Bible has a clear explanation for this state of affairs, this confusion and inconsistency. Made in the image of God, Man retains a nobility of nature and purpose that leads to great achievements. But as a race in rebellion against its Creator, we can and frequently do plumb the depths of wickedness and depravity. This book contends that we can never really understand ourselves—our triumphs and our failures—without this biblical perspective on human sin and our need of redemption.

Digging up roots

British TV presenter Natasha Kaplinsky went to Cape Town, celebrity chef Rick Stein to China, and actress Zoë Wanamaker to Ukraine. What were they looking for? The answer is their "roots." The long-running British TV series *Who do you think you are?* helps various celebrities construct their family trees, discovering secrets and surprises from the past—along with the skeletons lurking in their ancestral cupboards.

Most people are intrigued by their own ancestry. When Alex Haley's book *Roots* was published in USA in 1976, it became a sensational best seller. More than a mere book, it tapped deeply into the

hunger of black Americans to know more about their African ancestral home. According to commentators, Haley's quest for his roots
changed the way black people thought about themselves and how
white America viewed them. Why? *Because our origins ultimately
determine who and what we are.*

But no amount of world travel or searching dusty archives will
reveal what *really* ought to excite our curiosity—the origin of humanity itself. The question "Who am I?" can only be truly answered when
we know the solution to the larger riddle: "What is Man?" When a
young child asks, "Where did I come from?" the child isn't asking for
a lesson in reproductive biology. Rather, the question relates to self-
consciousness—the child's awareness of his or her own individual
"selfhood." Neither chickens nor chimpanzees, I suspect, worry about
such things. These concerns are unique to Man and that is nothing
new. Addressing the biblical God some 3000 years ago, King David
put it thus:

> "When I consider your heavens, the work of your fingers,
>> The moon and the stars which you have ordained,
>> What is Man that you are mindful of him,
>> And the son of Man that you visit him?
>> For you have made him a little lower than the angels
>> And you have crowned him with glory and honor"

PSALM 8:3–4.

DAVID OR DARWIN?

There are, of course, some zany answers to the question, "What is
Man?" The famous physicist Enrico Fermi seriously discussed the idea
that we might be an alien race that colonized the Earth from space[2]. A

more philosophical but equally strange idea is that we are computer-generated simulations—the products of a "matrix" set up by powers beyond out comprehension for their own entertainment. I'll let James Berardinelli tell the story.[3]

> "Thomas Anderson is leading a double life. To most people, he's a hardworking computer programmer who holds down a nine-to-five job for a major software corporation. But, in the privacy of his home, he's a hacker named Neo.... Neo is dissatisfied with his existence, and while he's groping for a meaning to it, he is contacted by a mysterious computer presence known as Morpheus ... [who explains that] the reality he is used to is a fabrication, the product of a sinister race of intelligent machines that use human beings as power supplies, to be discarded at will."

Bizarre though they may be, such speculations are not easy to refute, but I will pass them by and move on to what most people would consider more solid ground.

Today we are presented with several plausible answers to the question, "What is Man?," answers typified by two extremes—by David in his psalm and Charles Darwin in his theory of "evolution" or "common descent" (in so far as it seeks to explain the origin of Man without reference to God). However, there are other alternatives that lie between these extremes, so in this chapter we shall briefly introduce not two but four "models of Man." Using "image" terminology throughout for the sake of consistency, these four views see mankind as being made, respectively, in (1) the image of the apes, (2) the image of an emergent spirit, (3) the image of an implanted spirit, or (4) the image of God. I use the word "spirit" here simply as a shorthand to describe the qualities of mind and self-awareness that separate Man so completely from even the most intelligent animals.

IMAGE OF THE APES

Under this heading we need to consider two distinct themes that underlie what Raymond Tallis calls "aping mankind"[4] (of which more later). There is, of course, the familiar biological narrative of neo-Darwinian evolution, but this is only one side of the coin. The other side—less obvious but probably more powerful—is a *philosophical* narrative called "positivism" which claims that "all knowledge is ultimately based on sense experience."[5] Why does this matter? Because the biological story, nourished by this hidden philosophical stream, proudly proclaims itself to be the only show in town. It isn't, of course, as this book seeks to demonstrate. But positivism's total denial of God, metaphysics, spirituality and the soul, dominates twenty-first-century Western thought to an amazing degree. Even if your eyes glaze over at the very mention of the word "philosophy," be warned—your understanding of both yourself and the world around you is almost certainly affected by positivistic thinking.

Here we'll do little more than identify this hidden stream because it will become a major topic later in the book when we consider the mind and consciousness of Man, but let me give one or two recent examples to whet (or spoil?) your appetite.

In their 2010 book *The Grand Design*, famous cosmologist Stephen Hawking and his coauthor rename this philosophy "scientific determinism" and explain: "This book is rooted in the concept of scientific determinism which implies ... that there are no miracles or exceptions to the laws of nature."[6] The laws of nature are, of course, derived exclusively from our *physical observations* of the natural world around us, observations that are ultimately recorded by our physical senses (aided where necessary by instruments like microscopes, telescopes, and so on). A second example is the search for extraterrestrial life that often hits the headlines in the popular press. We shall examine this in depth in Chapter 3, and see that the whole hugely expensive enterprise is based on the idea that life and intelligence have arisen on Earth by natural processes and must therefore exist (or have existed) on a multitude of Earthlike planets throughout the universe. Any suggestion of creation by God is rigorously excluded, not by the science involved but by the underlying positivist philosophy. So more of that later; let us now consider the biological narrative.

Biology after Darwin

In *The Descent of Man* Charles Darwin traced Man's origin back to apelike ancestors and beyond, believing that all living things (the whole "biosphere") originated from a single primal organism—an idea called "common descent." His original theory published in his famous book *On the Origin of Species by Means of Natural Selection, or the Preservation of Favored Races in the Struggle for Life,* has, of course, been significantly elaborated over the years into neo-Darwinism, the so-called "modern synthesis" which incorporates genetic evolution. Briefly stated, the theory claims that organisms evolve by a dual process consisting of (1) random genetic mutations (changes in the organism's DNA produced by a variety of causes) followed by (2) "natural selection" of those members of a population to which mutations have imparted superior reproductive capacity. Although it is admitted that genetic mutations are overwhelmingly damaging or neutral in their effect, it is held that favorable mutations (that is, those that improve reproductive success) do occasionally take place. These beneficial mutations then spread through the population because their owners reproduce more successfully than others.

One seldom mentioned problem with this scenario, as it is applied to mankind, is that if it is true, humans are seriously overevolved. That is, we have acquired characteristics that far exceed any conceivable value in increasing our reproductive capacity. According to the neo-Darwinian narrative, no capacity should arise in an organism that does not improve its ability to reproduce, but humans possess powers that flatly contradict this. An interesting example was reported in the London *Times* newspaper ("Think big—your brain can store 4.7 billion books")[7]. Terry Sejnowski, professor of computational neurobiology at the Salk Institute in California, has found that the part of the brain that deals with memory has a capacity ten times bigger than previously thought and could store data roughly equivalent to the entire contents of the worldwide web. He states,

> "Our new measurements of the brain's memory capacity increase conservative estimates by a factor of 10 to at least a petabyte, in the same ballpark as the World Wide Web.... We discovered the key to unlocking the design principle for how hippocampal neurons function with low energy but high computational power."[8]

If we could use this enormous memory storage capacity, of course, it could be interpreted as the outcome of "survival-value" Darwinism, but we can't. We regularly forget the names of acquaintances and where we put the car keys—and I doubt whether many of us could memorize even one book, let alone 4.7 billion. In other words, we have failed to evolve any means of accessing this huge potential memory capacity, which therefore can do nothing to help us reproduce. So why do we possess these potential powers of memory? Why have they (allegedly) evolved? No naturalistic theory of evolution can answer this question. I might add that there are many other human characteristics that have no plausible reproductive value such as the ability to handle and enjoy musical, aesthetic, philosophical and mathematical concepts. Humble bacteria reproduce far more efficiently than human beings.

DOUBTING DARWINISM

I devoted several chapters in my book *Who Made God?* to a step-by-step critique of evolutionary mechanisms and will not repeat it here. However, the conclusion was that although Darwinian processes can and do produce minor changes in the characteristics of populations ("microevolution"), it is incapable of creating the major changes required to transform one kind of creature into another ("macroevolution"). Evidence from centuries of artificial selection by human intervention, as practiced by plant and animal breeders, supports this conclusion. While many new varieties and breeds (of, say, cats or dogs) have been generated, artificial selection never produces new kinds of organism (like breeding bears from cats or goats from dogs). There are natural barriers to macroevolution that no amount of human ingenuity can overcome. Some of these barriers may well be surmounted using "genetic engineering" in which scientists deliberately "edit" the DNA of an organism to produce, for example, disease-resistant crops or bacteria that manufacture medically useful compounds. But genetic engineering requires the skilled and purposeful manipulation of organisms by intelligent human agents; it doesn't happen by chance or accident.

Furthermore, the emergence of the hypothetical first living organism from nonliving starting materials (a process often called "chemical evolution") is today commonly attributed to fortuitous but entirely undirected physical and chemical processes which are as yet unknown. Such *undirected* processes have never been observed in the laboratory and are never likely to be observed, in spite of decades of effort by origin-of-life researchers. It is true that artificial life of a kind has been created by chemists such as Craig Venter[10] using sophisticated techniques to imitate the DNA found in nature. But this has only been achieved under the most precise control and direction of skilled scientists. The creation of artificial life forms, if achieved, will not occur without the careful direction of highly intelligent people—never by undirected natural processes.

Though technically not part of neo-Darwinism, the theory of chemical evolution completes the picture for the evolutionist by reducing the origin and development of life, and thus of Man, to purely natural processes accessible to scientific study. Most people today assume that Darwin's "scientific" account of human origins must be right and the Bible's "religious" teaching must be wrong or at best mythological. Man is not God's creation, we are told, but simply an animal that happens to have climbed further up the tree of evolution. Like every other form of life, he is an accident of evolution. But the urgent and ongoing search for "missing links" between apes and Man (considered later) bears witness to the huge biological, intellectual, and existential gap that separates humans from our closest supposed relatives such as chimpanzees.

Criticism of common descent is not tolerated in educational establishments, in spite of its gaping scientific inadequacies and the fact that many well-qualified scientists reject it. Alternatives to Darwinism are vigorously suppressed, not least in Western nations like the UK, where the teaching of evolutionary theory is mandated in schools and "creationism" is effectively banned and ridiculed, both by the establishment and the mass media. This unwillingness to allow an open public debate of evolutionary theory is rather curious, given that its proponents claim to have overwhelming scientific evidence in their favor. We shall develop this debate later but here's a final thought: in spite of the adulation heaped upon it, Darwinism makes virtually no contribution to modern biological research! Philip S. Skell, Emeritus Evan Pugh Professor at Pennsylvania State University, and a member of the USA's National Academy of Sciences, writes;

> "The modern form of Darwin's theory has been raised to its present high status because it's said to be the cornerstone of modern experimental biology. But is that correct? While the great majority of biologists would probably agree with Theodosius Dobzhansky's dictum that "nothing in biology makes sense except in the light of evolution," most can conduct their work quite happily without particular reference to evolutionary ideas."[11]

Professor Skell also points out that A.S. Wilkins, editor of the journal *BioEssays*, wrote in 2000, "Evolution would appear to be the indispensable unifying idea and, at the same time, a highly superfluous one."

IMAGE OF AN EMERGENT SPIRIT

In a spirited attack on the unvarnished molecules-to-Man scenario, British physician and neuroscientist Raymond Tallis sets out his opposition to much modern thinking about the nature of Man in his book *Aping Mankind; Neuromania, Darwinitis and the Misrepresentation of Humanity*.[12] The book is described on the flyleaf as "a devastating critique ... [that] exposes the exaggerated claims made for the ability of neuroscience and evolutionary theory to explain human consciousness, behavior, culture and society." This is particularly interesting because Tallis describes himself as "an atheist and also a humanist" but completes the sentence, "I believe that we should develop an image of humanity that is richer and truer to our distinctive nature than that of an exceptionally gifted chimp" [p.10]. Tallis makes it clear that he accepts neo-Darwinian evolution for all life forms bar one, but underlines Man's distinctiveness in the following terms.

> "Humans woke up from being organisms to being something quite different: embodied subjects, self-aware and other-aware in a manner and to a degree not approached by other animals. Out of this, a new kind of realm was gradually formed. This, the human world, is materially rooted in the natural world but is quite different from it. It is populated by individuals who are not just organisms ... [but] inhabit an acknowledged, shared public sphere, structured and underpinned by an infinity of abstractions, generalizations, customs, practices, norms, laws, institutions facts and artifacts unknown to even the most social of animals" [p.11].

Tallis then spends the rest of his 361 pages presenting his detailed case, arguing that the nature of Man cannot be reduced to neurons and brain states or explained as a simplistic Darwinian fallout.

The key term in the last quotation is, of course, the expression "woke up." It is this awakening that Tallis believes transformed mankind from being a mere animal to being something else. But as a self-confessed atheist he is, of course, unable to credit this awakening to God and must instead devise some wholly new and naturalistic explanation for it. He does make an effort to find such explanations as we shall see later. But his attempts to do so fail and he is forced in his final chapter ("Back to the drawing board") to write,

> "Okay, you might say, you have told us what is wrong with the biological account of human beings, but isn't this only the beginning, not the end, of the matter? Now tell us what you will put in its place. The truth is that I don't know; but I am sure that no one else knows either."

Under the heading "Conclusion" he quotes Jerry Fodor, Emeritus Professor of Philosophy at Rutgers University and an authority on philosophy of mind and cognitive science. Writing on the "hard problem" of human consciousness, Fodor admits;

> "We can't, as things stand now, so much as imagine the solution to the hard problem. The revisions of our concepts and theories that imagining a solution will eventually require are likely to be very deep and very unsettling ... there's hardly anything we may not have to cut loose from before the hard problem is through with us"[13]

There is, of course, only one *kind* of answer that atheists can offer to the "hard problem" of human consciousness, namely, that it has somehow *emerged* from the tangle of neurons, synapses, chemical fluxes and electrical impulses we call the brain. This alleged process is often modeled by the idea, fuelled by science fiction writers, that as computers become more complex, powerful and sophisticated they will at some stage acquire consciousness and begin to match the minds of humans. But even if this were to happen (which is highly unlikely), it could only do so as a result of the labors, intelligence, and ingenuity of human computer architects and software writers. Emergent consciousness isn't something that can just happen by accident. We will return to the question of human consciousness in Chapter 9.

IMAGE OF IMPLANTED SPIRIT

Even those who side with King David offer two very different scenarios—"special" (that is, miraculous) creation or theistic evolution. The latter view subscribes to neo-Darwinian evolution and common descent but insists that it was and is directed in some manner by God. In effect, "theistic evolution" holds that God used the process of evolution to bring mankind into existence (along with all other life forms, of course). C. S. Lewis describes one such scenario in the following words;

> "For long centuries, God perfected the animal form which was to become the vehicle of humanity and the image of Himself. He gave it hands whose thumb could be applied to each of the fingers, and jaws and teeth and throat capable of articulation, and a brain sufficiently complex to execute all of the material motions whereby rational thought is incarnated. The creature may have existed in this state for ages before it became Man; it may even have been clever enough to make things which a modern archaeologist would accept as proof of its humanity. But it was only an animal...."[14]

At first sight this scenario offers an attractive option, since it seems to sidestep the need for any *physical* miracle. It thus embraces the scientific claims of evolutionary theory and yet (by thoughtfully keeping God in the loop) avoids the philosophical bleakness of atheism. However, a little thought shows that the matter is not so simple. The God-implanted consciousness appealed to here would necessarily entail *miraculous* changes in brain structure and function—otherwise there would be nothing to distinguish the humans from their animal progenitors. And by rejecting emergent consciousness and substituting divinely implanted consciousness, this narrative necessarily appeals to a nonnatural process as the creative step that separates Adam from the apes. A small invisible miracle in the brain might seem easier to swallow than a dramatic dust-to-Adam creation, but once *any* miraculous origin for Man is allowed, it is hard to see what size has got to do with it.

But this is not the only problem with the implanted consciousness theory. Firstly, of course, any arguments for or against the scientific validity of common descent apply equally to this idea—at least up to the point of implantation—and we shall look at these arguments in due course. Secondly, the scenario has somehow to account for the complete disappearance of the prehuman race that, in terms of biological development, was indistinguishable from humanity. What with their opposable thumbs and tool-making skills, these prehumans would have been endowed with huge evolutionary superiority over other animals, yet they died out while less advantaged lower animals survived. Lewis suggests, of course, that fossil remains of these prehumans would be physically indistinguishable from those of *Homo sapiens* and would be mistaken for humans by paleontologists. But these *human-looking-but-not-human* fossils should greatly outnumber genuine human fossils, so where are they hiding? And with such close resemblance between humans and prehumans, would there not have been interbreeding to further confuse the picture? Again, we'll look more closely at these things in due course.

IMAGE OF GOD

The final view of human origins considered here is that Man is made in the image of God as stated in the book of Genesis;

> "Then God said, 'Let us make Man in our image, after our likeness. And let them have dominion over the fish of the sea and over the birds of heaven and over the livestock and over all the Earth and over every creeping thing that creeps on the face of the Earth.' So God created Man in his own image, in the image of God he created him; male and female he created them."[15]

Now, I am well aware that many who adopt the "implanted image" view of Man offered by theistic evolution also believe that Man is made in the image of God, but I am here distinguishing an implanted image from a created image. That is, I am using the image of God to describe the nature of a specially (that is, miraculously) created being, concerning whom Genesis also says, "The Lord God formed Man from the dust of the ground and breathed into his nostrils the breath of life; and Man became a living being."[16]

Many years ago I appeared in the British late-night TV magazine program *Newsnight* along with the naturalist and TV presenter David (now Sir David) Attenborough and astronomer Chandra Wickramasinghe, currently professor and director of the Buckingham Centre for Astrobiology at the University of Buckingham, UK. Chandra had recently coauthored a book with astrophysicist Sir Fred Hoyle entitled *Evolution from space*[17] and the discussion centered on this book's proposal that life arrived on Earth from space (a process known as "panspermia"). I was arguing for the creation of life on Earth by God, advancing as evidence the immense information-content of living things. David Attenborough, a champion of common descent, asked me scornfully if I believed that God took a handful of mud and fashioned it into a man. I didn't get the chance to answer because the presenter Jon Snow broke in at that point. But what I would have said in reply to David's question was, "But isn't that exactly what macroevolution teaches, except that it took 4000 million years to happen by random mutations?"[18]

Looked at in this way, I suggest, all our explanations call for miracles of one kind or another, whether we are evolutionists or creationists. This is not perhaps as obvious as it should be, because the evolutionary narrative claims the support of plausible natural processes to account for the transformation of mud into a man, whereas *by definition* special creation can propose no such processes. But in *Who Made God?* I showed that the processes on which macroevolution relies are nowhere near as plausible as is claimed and, in the case of the origin of life itself, are actually nonexistent.

Doesn't this mean, however, that arguments in favor of special creation are intrinsically negative, being limited to rebutting the positive claims of evolution? My answer is no. What it means is that the plausibility of creation scenarios rest on a much broader foundation, namely, the totality of creative power that must be attributed to God if, indeed, he exists. For example, we shall see in Chapter 2 that the origin of the universe is only explicable logically in terms of the creative activity of a nonmaterial Creator. And if we take *that* concept onboard, then the special creation of Man with his "Godlike" attributes should present no difficulty to the rational mind, even though we can have no understanding of the miraculous processes involved. In

Chapter 12 we shall explore the whole question of special creation and the *imago dei* (the image of God in Man).[19]

Conclusion

Each of these four theories of human origin presents thinking people with significant difficulties, and it is the aim of this book to examine the evidence for and against each of them. But this will be no narrow enquiry consisting of a simple expansion of the points raised in this chapter. We shall, rather, find it necessary to range widely over science and philosophy, space and time, history and thought—but always I trust in a manner comprehensible to the lay reader. So fasten your seat belts and hold tight!

ENDNOTES:

1 Pope, Alexander; *An Essay on Man: Epistle II*

2 https://blogs.scientificamerican.com/guest-blog/
   the-fermi-paradox-is-not-fermi-s-and-it-is-not-a-paradox/

3 http://www.reelviews.net/reelviews/matrix-the

4 Tallis, Raymond; *Aping mankind* (Acumen Publishing Ltd., Durham, 2011) pp. 347–348.

5 *The Penguin Dictionary of Philosophy* (1996) p. 482.

6 Hawking, Stephen, and Mlodinow, Leonard; *The Grand Design*, (Bantam Press, Transworld Publishers, 2010) p. 34

7 The London *Times* newspaper, 22 January 2016, p. 1.

8 http://www.salk.edu/news-release/memory-capacity-of-brain-is-10-times-more-than-previously-thought/

9 Andrews, Edgar; *Who made God? Searching for a theory of everything* (EP Books, Darlington UK, 2009).

[10] Andrews, Edgar; *Who made God? Searching for a theory of everything* (EP Books, Darlington UK, 2009) pp. 198–199.

[11] http://www.the-scientist.com/?articles.view/articleNo/16649/title/Why-Do-We-Invoke-Darwin-/

[12] Tallis, Raymond; *Aping mankind* (Acumen Publishing Ltd., Durham, 2011).

[13] Fodor, J.; "Headaches have themselves," London Review of Books 29 (10) (24 May 2007) pp. 9–10.

[14] Lewis, C. S.; *The problem of pain* (Simon & Schuster, New York, 1966) p. 50.

[15] Genesis 1:26–27, ESV

[16] Genesis 2:7

[17] Hoyle, F. and Wickramasinghe, C.; *Evolution from Space* (J.M. Dent, London, 1981).

[18] https://en.wikipedia.org/wiki/Timeline_of_the_evolutionary_history_of_life

[19] https://en.wikipedia.org/wiki/Image_of_God

CHAPTER 2

If the universe is an accident of nature, then Man is also likely to be a meaningless accident. If, on the other hand, the universe was created by God, then humanity is also likely to be a purposeful creation. So the question "Where is Man?" will directly affect the way we resolve the basic issue, "What is Man?"

Until about 100 years ago, most scientists who studied the universe as a whole (cosmologists) believed the universe was eternal and had no beginning. But this began to change in 1916 when Albert Einstein published his general theory of relativity, which implied that the universe could not be static or unchanging. Subsequently in 1929, astronomer Edwin Hubble showed that the universe (or cosmos) is expanding, and this result was confirmed in 1963 by the discovery that the Earth is bathed in a background of weak microwave radiation—now interpreted as the remnants of a "hot big bang" origin of the universe. The Bible's opening verse declares that "in the beginning God created the heavens and the Earth," and the theological implications of these new discoveries greatly alarmed those who reject the ancient idea of divine creation.

In this chapter we trace the development of atheistic thinking about cosmic origins, and the successive ideas advanced to sidestep the conclusion that creation demands a Creator. The current atheistic claim is that the universe created itself from nothing without the involvement of any spiritual agency, alleging that the laws of nature must lead to the spontaneous creation of a material cosmos. Here we gently point out that even if this were the case, someone or something having a nonmaterial nature would have to create and host the laws of nature. Since these laws are essentially mathematical, only a nonmaterial intelligence could have composed them and put them to work. The atheists' theories therefore lead logically to the necessity of God.

THE CHESHIRE CAT COSMOS

Can a universe create itself from nothing?

Because there is a law like gravity, the universe can and will create itself from nothing.... Spontaneous creation is the reason there is something rather than nothing, why the universe exists, why we exist. It is not necessary to invoke God to light the blue touch paper and set the universe going.

STEPHEN HAWKING AND LEONARD MLODINOW. [1]

Before we proceed to consider "What is Man?" it will be helpful to ask a more down-to-earth question—*where* is Man? For if the universe (or cosmos) is a meaningless accident of nature containing billions of life-supporting planets, then everything in it, including Man, is also likely to be accidental. If on the other hand the cosmos was created by God, as the Bible claims, then Man is also likely to be special or even unique, brought into existence for a purpose. Our view of cosmic origins will inevitably affect the way we see human origins and the significance of Man.

So how did the universe come to exist? Why is there something rather than nothing? It is pleasing to report that atheists like cosmologists Stephen Hawking (cited above) and Lawrence Krauss (in his book *A Universe from Nothing*)[2] have come round to the idea that the universe did, after all, arise *ex nihilo* (out of nothing). Thus they endorse a view proposed by the Bible over 3000 years ago, while denying that God had anything to do with it. In this chapter we're going to see how they reached that opinion, but we shall do more. We shall also pursue their atheistic thinking to its logical endpoint, namely, the necessity of God! So let's retrace their collective steps as they stumble their way to this surprising conclusion. In order to do so, we need to review how atheistic thinking has evolved over the last 100 years or so.

WHO MADE GOD?

"Who made God?" is, of course, the title of the prequel to this book, but here we'll focus on the reason why this is the atheist's favorite ontological question. In full, the question reads, "If God made everything, who made God?" and is asked with an interesting purpose. To help explain this, I need to retell the story of the tower of turtles (or tortoises; a turtle is an aquatic tortoise). Anyone who has read *Who Made God?* or Stephen Hawking's book *A Brief History of Time*[3] will be familiar with the story but I need to repeat it here for newcomers. The apocryphal story relates how a little old lady challenged the speaker following a public lecture on astronomy and the solar system. "Your lecture is all wrong," she declared. "The Earth is not suspended in space but is supported on the back of a giant turtle." "So what is the turtle standing on?" asked the lecturer with a superior smile. "On the back of another turtle," she replied. "And what is *that* turtle standing on?" pressed the lecturer. It was the lady's turn to be scornful: "It's turtles all the way down!" she declared triumphantly.

Whether true or not, the story is surely a libel on little old ladies, but it does serve to introduce us to the fallacy of "infinite regress" (or "regression"). An infinite regress consists of an unending series of explanations in which each explanation needs, in turn, to be explained. Like the infinite tower of turtles, such explanations have zero explanatory power because they never make contact with the ground-level of reality. It is this kind of reasoning that lies at the heart of the "who-made-God?" question. Atheist standard-bearer Richard Dawkins seems to think it is a valid question. He writes, "A God capable of continuously monitoring and controlling the status of every particle in the universe *cannot* be simple. His existence is going to need a mammoth explanation in its own right."[4] Thus he argues that if God exists he is so complex that he must have evolved from (or been created by) some simpler preexisting entity. Anyone foolish enough to concede his point is then obliged to explain where this pretheistic entity came from, so launching irretrievably down the slippery slope of an infinite regress.

But of course, an intelligent atheist knows exactly how a theist will answer his question—no one made God because God is the uncreated ground of all existence. So why do atheists persist with it? They have a good reason for doing so. What they really want to establish is that by ascribing cosmic creation to God, theists have *already* committed themselves to an infinite regress without realizing it. Never mind the second turtle, God is the first turtle! Let's spell it out. We all agree that the universe exists but (say the atheists) those who claim it was created by God are replacing a real, visible and tangible cosmos by an invisible, immaterial and implausible spirit *as the fundamental existential reality*. And that, they maintain, makes no more sense than saying that the Earth hasn't dropped out of the Milky Way because it is supported by a turtle. The ball is surely in the theist's court? Well, yes, but it is returnable.

THE BRUTE-FACT UNIVERSE

The argument so far leaves atheists with a dilemma of their own, namely, an inexplicable universe. Firstly, any attempt to explain the origin of the universe in physical terms risks the danger of an infinite regress of material causes. Secondly, if the physical cosmos is itself the ultimate reality, then there is no point in trying to explain its existence—it must be accepted as an inexplicable "brute fact." Keith M. Parsons, professor of philosophy at the University of Houston, puts the matter clearly in a discussion with Ed Feser, associate professor of philosophy at Pasadena City College, California:

> "I think you and I agree that explanatory hierarchies will come to an end … with an uncaused cause—something that has no causal antecedents and is the original, fundamental, or primordial reality that possesses a set of distinctive properties which constitute the ultimate terms of every explanatory regress. I see no reason why that ultimate reality cannot be the original, fundamental, or primordial—and brutally factual—physical reality. Where is the incoherence? A brute fact would be a state of affairs that just is, with no cause or explanation of its existence or nature."[5]

Most older atheists like British philosopher Bertrand Russell (1872–1970) also embraced this worldview. To them the cosmos was the only accessible reality and must be taken as given. It would be delusional to seek to explain how it came to be. To quote the *Stanford Encyclopedia of Philosophy*:

> "Bertrand Russell denies that the universe needs an explanation; it just is. Russell, following Hume, contends that since we derive the concept of cause from our observation of particular things, we cannot ask about the cause of something like the universe [a cause] that we cannot experience. The universe is just there, and that's all."[6,7]

German philosopher Friedrich Nietzsche (1844–1900) held a quirky version of the brute-fact universe in which the cosmos recurs endlessly over infinite time and space, so that "all configurations that have previously existed on this Earth must yet meet [again]." This concept included a kind of personal reincarnation; "And thus it will happen one day that a man will be born again, just like me … only that it is hoped … that the head of this man may contain a little less foolishness…."[8] Although Nietzsche's theory strikes us as bizarre today, it lives on in those modern cosmological models in which the universe cycles endlessly between phases of expansion and contraction and in certain far-out multiverse hypotheses in which copies of ourselves exist in a myriad of parallel universes. (We'll meet the multiverse later. I should add that for various technical reasons, cyclic universe theories are currently out of fashion.)

Until scientists began to appreciate the implications of Einstein's general theory of relativity, published in 1915, the scientific consensus even among theists was that the universe was the eternal backcloth to our existence, an unchanging "stage" on which the drama of life and history was played out. In fact Einstein himself was troubled that his equations did not at first describe a static universe but only one that was either expanding or contracting. Believing that the fault lay in his theory, he therefore inserted a fudge-factor which he called the "cosmological constant" and which had the effect of allowing a static universe to exist. When twenty years later the cosmos was found to be expanding after all, he described the fudge as his "biggest blunder" (read the full story in Ch. 7 of *Who Made God?*).

WHATEVER HAPPENED TO THE BRUTE-FACT UNIVERSE?

As we saw in the previous section, some philosophers still cling to the brute-fact universe, but the great majority of scientists have moved on. There are two reasons for the near-demise of this attempt to circumvent the need to explain the origin of the cosmos. Firstly, it never did sit well with the incurable curiosity of the human mind. Tell scientists not to bother their heads about origins and they will redouble their efforts to find out where everything came from. A child's first sortie into philosophy is, "Mummy, where did I come from?" The child is not seeking a lesson in reproductive biology. Recognizing for the first time that it has a "self" which is distinct from the selves of its parents and siblings, it wants to know how that "self" came to exist. The curiosity only grows as we develop from childhood to maturity, and extends to every aspect of the world around us. Furthermore, it is this curiosity that drives the scientific enterprise. Why, for example, do we spend billions of dollars building atom-smashing machines like the Large Hadron Collider at Geneva, or radio telescopes seeking to tune in to alien versions of "family favorites"? Curiosity may be fatal to felines (curiosity killed the cat), but it is the lifeblood of pure science.

To be told that because the universe is the "ultimate reality" there is no point in asking where it came from simply does not satisfy our thirst for knowledge.

But there is a second and even greater problem for the brute-fact universe, namely that the overwhelming consensus among cosmologists today requires the cosmos to have *begun*. Once again I must refer the reader to *Who Made God?* for the full story, but the discovery that the universe is expanding leads most experts to believe that it had its origin in a "hot big bang" which itself emerged from an initial "singularity" (a theoretical condition where physical quantities like density and temperature are infinite and the laws of nature no longer apply). Although there is no shortage of speculations about how the singularity might be avoided, the evidence in favor of a singularity-origin of the cosmos is strong. One example is the mathematical proof by three leading cosmologists, Arvind Borde, Alan Guth, and Alexander Vilenkin (none of whom has any religious axe to grind). In the Tufts University newspaper *TuftsNow*, Jacqueline Mitchell writes:

> "By now, there's scientific consensus that our universe exploded into existence almost 14 billion years ago in an event known as the Big Bang. But that theory raises more questions about the universe's origins than it answers, including the most basic one: what happened *before* the Big Bang? Some cosmologists have argued that a universe could have no beginning but simply always was. In 2003, Tufts cosmologist Alexander Vilenkin and his colleagues, Arvind Borde … and Alan Guth … proved a mathematical theorem showing that, under very general assumptions, the universe must, in fact, have had a beginning."[9]

The article continues to explain that Vilenkin and his student Audrey Mithani have since examined three potential loopholes in the 2003 theorem, strengthening the original premise that the universe did, in fact, begin.

Vilenkin does not ignore the claim that as a singularity is approached with decreasing size, quantum physics may take over—making it doubtful that a singularity would ever actually occur and replacing it by a tiny quantum "egg." But he makes it clear that if this happened, some laws of nature would still need to operate (a point I shall develop shortly). He also argues that any such quantum egg would be unstable and unlikely to have existed eternally in the past. To summarize, Vilenkin himself is clear enough about the implications of his work:

> "It is said that an argument is what convinces reasonable men and a proof is what it takes to convince even an unreasonable man. With the proof now in place, cosmologists can no longer hide behind the possibility of a past-eternal universe. There is no escape, they have to face the problem of a cosmic beginning."[10]

The upshot of all this? Anything that begins to exist must have a cause, and if the universe had a beginning it must also have a cause. (This is fairly self-evident but is formalized in what is called the Kalam cosmological argument.[11]) It is such reasoning that has led atheists like Stephen Hawking and Lawrence Krauss to propose in recent books that the universe created itself, leaving God redundant. So let's consider their claims.

THE SELF-CREATING UNIVERSE

Allow me to repeat in part the Stephen Hawking quote that heads this chapter: "Because there is a law like gravity, the universe can and will create itself from nothing...." This, in a nutshell, is the latest atheist answer to the awkward *scientific* fact that the universe almost certainly began. Cosmologist Lawrence Krauss endorses and elaborates the idea in his own book, *A Universe from Nothing*, subtitled *Why there is something rather than nothing*. No one seems to have noticed that by proposing a DIY (do-it-yourself) universe, Hawking among others is quietly shelving earlier claims that the cosmos didn't have a beginning, and conceding that it did. So how exactly did something emerge from nothing? It all turns on the meaning of "nothing," of which there are two distinctly different definitions.

To the proponents of a DIY cosmos, "nothing" is simply a vacuum within the space-time continuum of the universe. Although such a vacuum is a space from which all matter and radiation has been removed, it is by no means empty. It contains its own energy and, according to latest ideas, is awash with an ocean of Higgs bosons (the misnamed "God particle" detected by the CERN Large Hadron Collider during 2011–2013). The Higgs particles hinder the movement of other particles and thus impart to them the property of mass. Think of this "Higgs field" as a kind of cosmic treacle or syrup. Open a tin of treacle, push a spoon into the viscous liquid and try to pull it out again. The spoon feels *much* heavier than it did when you picked it up from the table because you are now working against the viscous drag of the treacle. Thus, says the Standard Model of particle physics, the Higgs field bestows mass on any particle that interacts with it (though some, such as photons, don't interact and therefore have no mass).

But before we go any further, let me also point out that a Hawking/Krauss kind of "nothing" can only exist *within* the space-time continuum of an existing universe. It has physical attributes like dimensions and volume. It has an intrinsic energy that causes so-called "virtual particles" to pop into existence momentarily (in the form of particle/antiparticle pairs) and then vanish again by mutual annihilation. Also, crucially, the normal laws of physics operate within this vacuum. So their "nothing" can *only* be found inside an existing universe and has arrived far too late to create one.

A genuine *creatio ex nihilo* (creation from nothing) requires a completely different kind of "nothing," as I pointed out in *Who Made God?* in 2009, well before the Hawking and Mlodinow (2010) or Krauss (2013) books were published. There I called the Hawking/Krauss kind of nothing "void one" and the real nothing I labeled "void-zero." The latter is the only kind of nothing that can precede a true creation and it has *no physical properties at all*. This follows because Big Bang cosmology, if correct, is based on classical general relativity, and requires space, time, matter, energy and the laws of nature all to be brought into existence at the singularity with which it starts. Nothing of a physical nature can exist outside the singularity. Void-zero must therefore be nonphysical and nonmaterial and I identified it as the spiritual realm that the Bible calls "eternity"—quoting Isaiah 57:15, "For thus says the One [i.e. God] who is high and lifted up, *who inhabits eternity*, whose name is holy ..." (emphasis added).

LAWS OF NATURE ARE SCIENCE'S BEDROCK

As already mentioned, some cosmologists today argue that the singularity of Big Bang theory cannot actually happen. Instead, as we go back in time and the universe shrinks to a sufficiently small size, quantum effects take over from classical (nonquantum) behavior. At this point, we are left with an unbelievably small seed or egg in which time has no meaning but which has the potential to become the Big Bang of standard cosmology. I have also pointed out that Vilenkin believes that if it existed, this quantum egg would be unstable and could not therefore be eternal. He also agrees with the contention that some laws of nature would have to be in place already for such a quantum egg to come into (and remain in) existence. He says:

> "Quantum creation from 'nothing' … has a nice mathematical description, not just words. There's an interesting thing, though: the description of the creation of the universe from nothing is given in terms of the laws of physics. That makes you wonder, where are these laws? If the laws describe the creation of the universe, that suggests they existed prior to the universe. The question that nobody has any idea how to address is where these laws come from and why these laws in particular? So there are a lot of mysteries to keep us working." [12]

I must disagree with Vilenkin's claim that "nobody has any idea how to address … where these laws come from," as will appear presently, but he is the only cosmologist I've come across who faces up to the question. His hope that further work within a purely physical worldview might eventually provide an answer is forlorn, however, and that for an obvious reason—scientific explanations must always appeal to laws of nature; otherwise they are not scientific. This is an important point, so let me elaborate.

What do we mean when we talk about a scientific explanation? We mean that some observation or event can be traced back to the operation of one or more laws of nature. For example, planetary motion, the trajectory of an artillery shell, the weightlessness of astronauts in a space station, and the weight of those same astronauts when they return to Earth can all be explained in terms of the laws of gravity (either Newton's law or general relativity). By contrast, accounting for Earth's stability in space by invoking turtles fails as a scientific explanation—not only because we know there's no turtle there but also because turtles are not laws of nature. Suppose, however, we replace turtles by a strong cosmic magnetic field. Since Earth has a metallic core this could, in principle, suspend the Earth in space and would offer a *scientific* explanation because it appeals to known laws of nature. So we put the theory to the test and measure the magnetic field in space around the Earth—and find that it is far too weak to override or cancel out the gravitational pull of the sun.

So a scientific explanation can turn out to be false; what it cannot do is dispense with the laws of nature because they are the bedrock on which all science rests. Our perception of these laws may change, of course. We may find that certain laws can be refined or amalgamated into more general or more fundamental laws. We may discover new laws and perhaps one day physicists will find the holy grail of a "theory of everything." But such a theory will still be expressed in terms of laws of nature whose *origin* lies beyond the power of science to explain.

LOCATING THE LAWS OF NATURE

But let's get clear what we mean by "laws of nature." They are the rules that describe the way nature behaves. They are thus *descriptions* of the way the cosmos works and can have no natural existence apart from the cosmos. They are an integral part of the created order and are located *within* that order. How, then, could they have created the universe in the first place? Which came first, the cosmic chicken or the legal egg? Yet Stephen Hawking claims that "because there is a law like gravity, the universe can and will create itself from nothing." I call his reasoning "the Cheshire cat argument," after the iconic cat in Lewis Carroll's *Alice's Adventures in Wonderland*, which vanished leaving only its smile behind. Those who claim that the laws of nature created nature are observing the universe (the cat) with its face wreathed in smiles (the laws of nature) and then subtracting the cat, leaving only the smiles (the laws) behind, thus arriving at a starting point for their cosmologies. That's fine in children's fiction but hardly admissible in either science or logic.

However, for the sake of argument, let us suppose that the laws of nature did somehow preexist the universe and were thus available to create it. Two problems arise. Firstly, who or what created the laws of nature? Krauss addresses this problem in the final chapter of *A Universe from Nothing*, suggesting that universes can arise spontaneously *without* the help of *specific* laws of physics because at that stage the latter are "random." As a physicist I have no idea what he means by "random laws" and can offer no comment except that even random entities must *exist* if they are to produce effects.

But might the laws of nature (or some overarching precursor of these laws as we know them) constitute eternal truths having an eternal existence and thus no need to be created? If so we must ask in what form and medium did they exist? Where, exactly, might they be located? A helpful analogy is the purchase of a house "off-plan." This is when someone buys (or commits to buy) a house that doesn't yet exist, relying solely on the architect's plans. Although the house is not yet built, the plans and drawings specify exactly what will eventually be created. However, the plans must exist in some form or medium—on paper or a computer disc for example. But what if there are no such things as paper or computers, or any other storage medium where the plans can reside? This surely is the situation for laws that preexist the origin of the material universe—there would be no *material* medium or space in which to inscribe them, so where would they reside? There is, of course, one (and I think only one) answer: they could exist in conceptual space, in the mind of a cosmic architect! This makes a lot of sense because the laws of nature as we know them are fundamentally mathematical in character, and by its very nature mathematics requires a mind to conceive its concepts and perform its processes. One objector to this argument made the following claim: "The laws of nature don't have to reside anywhere—they can just be true in the same way that $2 + 2 = 4$ is true whether or not it is written down or thought about." But this objection fails, because to call something "true" requires us to define a realm (or logical space) called "truth" and distinguish it from the alternative realm of "falsehood." This separation is itself a logical process that can only be carried out by a mind.

Conclusion: the necessity of God

The only way that laws of nature could preexist nature, and thus be responsible for creating the universe, is that they existed in the mind of a nonmaterial being. This is the logical endpoint of current atheistic cosmology. The logic can be summarized as follows:

1. Science can only explain things (observations, events, processes, etc.) by relating them to laws of nature. This is the meaning of "scientific explanation." Explanations that do not

appeal to laws of nature are not scientific, though they may still be true.

2. This being the case, science cannot explain the *origin* of laws of nature since any attempt to do so must, by definition, appeal to deeper laws of nature, *ad infinitum.*

3. Since laws of nature are, again by definition, descriptions of the way nature (the cosmos) works, such laws cannot exist if there is no nature for them to describe. They are therefore internal, never external, to the cosmos and so cannot create a cosmos or universe.

4. There is only one possible exception to (3). The laws of nature could preexist creation in the mind of a nonmaterial being who is external to (not part of) any material cosmos.

5. In (4) the laws would have to reside in a mind because they are uniformly mathematical in character, and mathematics consists of mental concepts and processes.

6. True *creatio ex nihilo* thus requires the existence and activity of a spiritual (nonmaterial) mind.

7. This is as far as science can take us, not just now but for all time. To know more about this spiritual "architect," we need to look elsewhere.

ENDNOTES:

[1] Hawking, Stephen, and Mlodinow, Leonard: *The Grand Design* (Bantam Press, 2010) p. 180.

[2] Krauss, L., *A Universe from Nothing* (Atria books, 2013).

[3] Hawking, Stephen; *A Brief History of Time* (Bantam Press, 1988) p. 1.

[4] Dawkins, R., *The God Delusion* (Black Swan, 2007) p. 179.

[5] http://www.patheos.com/blogs/secularoutpost/2014/03/05/reply-to-prof-fesers-response-part-iv/#sthash.sxs2gfx2.dpuf

6   http://plato.stanford.edu/entries/cosmological-argument/

7   Russell, B. and Copleston, F; "Debate on the Existence of God" (1948), in John Hick (ed.), *The Existence of God*, (Macmillan, New York, 1964) pp. 167–190.

8   *Kaufmann; Friedrich Nietzsche. Transl., with comm. by Walter; The Gay Science with a Prelude in Rhymes and an Appendix of Songs 1st Ed. (Vintage Books New York, 1974) p. 16.*

9   http://now.tufts.edu/articles/beginning-was-beginning#sthash. sSwTAJQC.dpuf

10 Vilenkin, A., *Many Worlds in One* (Hill and Wang, New York, 2006) p. 176.

11 Kalam cosmological argument; http://www.reasonablefaith.org/ transcript-kalam-cosmological-argument

12 http://now.tufts.edu/articles/beginning-was-beginning#sthash. sSwTAJQC.dpuf

CHAPTER 3

It's easy to confuse SETI with YETI because both relate to creatures that probably don't exist. The Yeti is a proverbial beast that inhabits the Himalayas and walks upright like a human, but leaves huge footprints in the snow and strikes fear into the local populace. Related to America's Bigfoot, it is sometimes called the Abominable Snowman (apparently due to a mistranslation of its Nepalese name). SETI, on the other hand, stands for "the search for extraterrestrial intelligence"—the hunt for an intelligent alien who is so unlikely to show up that he might, with some justification, be called "the abominable no-man." Yet nations around the world are currently spending eye-watering sums of money looking for him in distant galaxies, and building bigger and better radio telescopes to further their quest. Why, I wonder, would they do that?

The answer is that SETI scientists and the governments and institutions that finance them believe that the discovery of alien intelligences would help answer our question, "What is Man?" For example, the European Space Agency claims that its new Extra Large Telescope "will answer fundamental questions regarding planet formation and evolution and will bring us one step closer to answering the question: are we alone? Apart from the obvious scientific interest, this would represent a major breakthrough for humanity."

So in this chapter we'll trace the history of SETI and its less ambitious (but no less expensive) sidekick, the search for any kind of life outside of Earth itself. Driving all this endeavor is the belief that finding extraterrestrial organisms would discredit the idea that God created life. It would do no such thing, of course; if God created life on one planet, he could do it on another.

Finally, we learn just how wonderfully planet Earth is suited to sustain life of all kinds, including our own intelligent selves. No other planet in the solar system can match its unique habitability, and the same is true of the thousands of extrasolar planets that have been detected to date. As far as we know, Earth is uniquely hospitable to life.

SMALL FLAT BUGS

Where is Man?

"Found, a planet like Earth but 5 billion years away—best chance yet of extraterrestrial life."

So ran a headline on page three of the London *Times* newspaper on 11 November 2009. Later the same day, a BBC TV news correspondent solemnly declared that the new planet was probably inhabited by "small flat bugs." The 5 billion years was a miscalculation by *The Times*—it should have been half a million *light* years. But what difference do a few zeros make to a gullible public? Furthermore, you must understand that the bugs in question have not actually been seen. Nor, come to that, has the planet, though its presence can be inferred with a fair measure of certainty. But small flat bugs? No chance. As Mark Twain once pointed out, "It's amazing how, for a small investment of fact, one can get such a large return in speculation." The slightest hint of life elsewhere in the universe, no matter how unlikely, sends the mass media into a frenzy (with NASA, which should know better, not far behind).

EXOPLANETS

Atheists like the idea that Earth is just one of a countless number of similar inhabited planets in the universe because if true (they argue), it would diminish the significance of life on Earth. This in turn would remove the need to think that Man is anything other than an accident of nature. So let's pursue our headline and consider the current excitement over what are called "exoplanets"—planets that exist outside the solar system. First, what are the facts? The search for planets orbiting stars in distant galaxies is a large and growing area of astronomical research. At the time of writing, the online *Extrasolar Planets Encyclopedia*[1] lists some 1000 cosmic planetary systems containing over two thousand planets which are known to be orbiting stars other than the sun. These numbers increase almost on a weekly basis.

How do they know? Most of these exoplanets have been detected using the "radial velocity" method which uses spectroscopy to measure the "wobble" of a star caused by an unseen planet's gravitational pull. The second most widely used method is the transit method which measures the tiny decrease in apparent brightness of a star as the planet passes in front of it. Both methods allow astronomers to work out the mass and orbital characteristics of the exoplanet, while the less reliable transit method also allows the planet size to be estimated.

The exoplanet featured in our headline is one of three believed to be orbiting a "red dwarf" star called Gliese 581 in the constellation *Libra*. The planet (graced with the catchy name Gliese 581c) was detected using the radial velocity method; that is, it has not actually been seen but its presence is inferred from small variations in the star's radial motion (deduced from effects in its light spectrum). Its discoverers claim that Gliese 581c is a rocky planet with a radius 50 percent greater than Earth and about five times Earth's mass. They estimate that its surface temperature lies between -3°C and 40°C, which places it within the "habitable zone" of its parent star because liquid water could exist there. And if a planet has liquid water (they argue), then life could have evolved on Gliese 581c "as it did on Earth." But why might it be inhabited by small flat bugs? Because with a mass five times that of Earth, the planet's gravity would also be five times greater—enough to flatten even a bug. Why small bugs? Perhaps because an uncritical public are more likely to swallow small bugs than little green men.

I should make it clear that the planet's discoverers said nothing about bugs—that was an invention by the BBC. But their claim that Gliese 581c is a rocky planet like Earth and has liquid water on its surface is itself based on a string of assumptions. An informed website respondent commented:

> "You must remember that neither the mass nor the radius of this planet are actually known. The mass is the *minimum* mass and since radial velocity cannot determine the angle of the system, the mass could actually be much larger. I would not be surprised if it turned out that these planets are all Jupiter-size. The quoted radius of 1.5 Earth radii is the size the planet *would be* if it were terrestrial [rocky] which is not known. We actually have no idea what the density of Gliese 581c is."

Another astronomer points out;

> "The habitable zone isn't a terribly robust definition. The inconsistencies in temperature [calculated by different

correspondents] are due to [assuming] different *albedos*, that is, how much of the incoming sunlight energy is absorbed.... I think a more important difference ... is the greenhouse effect, given that many of the most abundant molecules in the galaxy are greenhouse gases."

MARS AND THE SEARCH FOR EXTRATERRESTRIAL LIFE

But let's leave aside the ill-informed enthusiasm of the mass media and turn to serious science. The search for extraterrestrial life (SETI) goes back over a century. In August 1924 when Mars was at its closest approach to Earth, a 36-hour radio silence was observed in USA (for five minutes every hour) to listen for possible radio signals from Mars. The US Army's chief cryptographer was even assigned to translate any Martian messages that might be detected.[2] I imagine he was quite relieved when his services were not required.

This may all seem rather quaint to us but let's not forget that while we no longer expect to find *intelligent* life on Mars, the search for more humble life forms there (extant or extinct) continues unabated. As part of the aptly named ExoMars program, the European Space Agency and Roscosmos (the Russian space agency) launched a mission to the Red Planet in March 2016 to analyze the methane gas known to be present in the Martian atmosphere. In our own atmosphere, methane (the chief component of "natural gas") comes mainly from biological sources, either ancient (as in oil, shale, and coal deposits) or modern (produced by rotting vegetation, belching cows, and microorganisms). However, there are also geological sources of methane such as volcanoes and inorganic chemical processes. On Earth at least, biological methane contains more of a light carbon isotope than geological methane, allowing the two to be distinguished. The

ExoMars scientists thus hope their analysis might reveal the presence of life processes on Mars. However, interpretation of the evidence will be crucial. One commentator says:

> "Measurements of methane on Earth suggest that methane originating from geological processes as opposed to biological processes has a distinctive signature in hydrogen and oxygen isotopes ... [but] I've always wondered if we would be able to interpret what this would mean on Mars (for one thing, Mars is greatly depleted in light hydrogen versus deuterium)."[3]

Another correspondent points out that there is an abundance of methane in the atmospheres of Neptune and Uranus, neither of which are likely to harbor life. A follow-up ExoMars mission planned for 2018 will drill two meters [or metres] into the planet surface to seek evidence of subsoil life.[4] This is thought to be necessary since recent evidence suggests that the surface of Mars, irradiated as it is by UV light, is toxic to life on account of "oxidizing chemicals present there."[5]

The ExoMars scientists may be strongly tempted to "find" evidence of what they are looking for, sincerely interpreting their findings to fit their hopes. But even if they do find bacterial life on Mars, will it prove that life evolved there independently? Not at all. In 1996, there was great excitement when NASA claimed that a small rock found in the Antarctic had been ejected from Mars by a meteor impact and had finished up on Earth. The basis of this claim was that minerals and small gas occlusions in the rock had compositions characteristic of Mars.[6,7] Furthermore, examination of the rock (and two other meteorites from Mars) revealed chemicals associated with life on Earth and microscopic features that resembled fossilized bacteria. However, a 2006 article in *space.com* explains the reality:

"It was a science fiction fantasy come true: Ten years ago this
summer, NASA announced the discovery of life on Mars
… showing magnified pictures of a four-pound Martian
meteorite riddled with wormy blobs that looked like bacterial
colonies.… 'If the results are verified,' pronounced the late
Carl Sagan, 'it is a turning point in human history.' Ten years
later, the results have not been verified. Skeptics have found
nonbiological explanations for every piece of evidence that
was presented on Aug. 6, 1996."

The important point in this instance is not that NASA's claim lacks
credibility but that both they and their critics agree that the rock,
along with thirty-three other known meteorites, did indeed come
from Mars. If this is true, could not the return journey from Earth
to Mars also be made? Might not meteorite impacts on Earth have
ejected material which arrived on Mars carrying a complement of
Earth's bacteria? After all, Earth is a bigger target for cosmic bombardment than Mars. If rocks can reach Earth from Mars, they can surely
also reach Mars from Earth. Martian bugs, even if found, will have
to exhibit an alien *chemistry* of life to prove they are not immigrants.

SETI AND THE COSMOS

But let's return to the wider history of SETI.[8] In March 1955, John D.
Kraus published in *Scientific American* a proposal to scan the cosmos for natural radio signals using a radio telescope. Two years later,
and funded by US$71,000 from the National Science Foundation,
Ohio State University began constructing a radio observatory called
Big Ear—which later undertook the world's first continuous SETI
program. On 15 August 1977, Jerry Ehman, a project volunteer at
the observatory, observed a strong signal and wrote "Wow!" on the

recorded trace. Unsurprisingly known as the Wow! signal, some enthusiasts consider it the best candidate to date for a cosmic radio signal from an artificial source. However, additional searches have failed to reproduce the observation and recent investigations suggest that the signal was caused by a passing comet.[9,10]

One of the best known SETI programs began in 1960, when Cornell University astronomer Frank Drake launched Project Ozma (in honor of L. Frank Baum's fantasy *Queen of Oz*). Drake used a 26-meter radio telescope at Green Bank, West Virginia, to examine two stars (*Tau Ceti* and *Epsilon Eridani*) for radio transmissions. He chose to scan at frequencies close to those of hydrogen and hydroxyl spectral lines—frequencies an alien race might choose because these two chemical species are the most common in the universe. Result? He found nothing of interest.

Efforts to detect alien life were not limited to USA. Russian scientists also took a strong interest in SETI during the 1960s, using omnidirectional antennas to look for powerful radio signals from outer space. Space scientist Losif Shklovsky wrote a seminal book *Universe, Life, Intelligence* (1962) which was followed in 1966 by American astronomer Carl Sagan's best-selling book *Intelligent Life in the Universe*. In 1971, NASA funded a SETI study that involved Drake, Bernard Oliver of Hewlett-Packard Corporation, and others. They recommended the construction of a radio telescope array with 1,500 dishes at a cost of US$10 billion. Known as Project Cyclops, the proposal never saw the light of day, but the report was a major influence in much SETI work that followed.

THE COST OF SETI

It may come as a shock to learn just how much money is currently being spent on the search for extraterrestrial life. The ExoMars program referred to earlier, for example, has a cost-cap of one billion euros. The European Union is also building the world's largest optical telescope in Chile, with the search for extraterrestrial life as a primary objective. The construction cost is estimated to be €1.055 billion and the operations are planned to start in 2024. The European Space Organization official publicity states:

> "The E-ELT [European Extra Large Telescope] will answer fundamental questions regarding planet formation and evolution and will bring us one step closer to answering the question: are we alone? Apart from the obvious scientific interest, this would represent a major breakthrough for humanity."[11]

For many years the US government provided funds for SETI projects but this ceased in 2011. However, in July 2015 a new initiative was launched under the title *"Breakthrough Listen"*— a ten-year project with $100 million funding, to search for intelligent extraterrestrial communications.[12] In a substantial expansion of earlier efforts, and deploying methods not previously used for the purpose, *Breakthrough Listen* has been described as the most comprehensive search for alien communications to date. The project will use thousands of hours every year on two major radio telescopes, the Green Bank Observatory in West Virginia, and the Parkes Observatory in Australia. The Automated Planet Finder of Lick Observatory will also search for optical signals such as laser transmissions.

In yet another SETI development, ABC News announced in March 2016 that the world's largest radio telescope was nearing completion in the southwestern province of Guizhou in China and, in fact, it began to operate on 25th September 2016. The 500-metre Aperture Spherical Radio Telescope (FAST) will apparently be used to search for signs of alien life. According to the authorities, more than 9,000 people have been forced to move from the area to create a quiet "electromagnetic wave environment." FAST, built at a cost of 0.2 billion US dollars, dwarfs the currently largest radio telescope, the 300-meter instrument at the Arecibo Observatory in Puerto Rico.[13]

SO WHERE IS EVERYBODY?

The failure of SETI to produce any return on investment naturally raises questions. If there are billions of Earthlike planets out there in the universe as many claim, and if intelligent life arises whenever the conditions are just right, where are all these advanced civilizations hiding? Those concerned are ready with answers. In an interview posted in *TechCrunch* in February 2016,[14] journalist Emily Calandrelli asked SETI astronomer Jill Tarter why we haven't found intelligent life yet. (In case you're interested, Jill Tarter was the real-life model for Dr. Ellie Arroway in Carl Sagan's science-fiction novel *Contact* and the corresponding 1997 film in which Arroway was played by Jodie Foster.)

In reply, Tarter offered two explanations. Firstly, "the universe is vast and we haven't been able to look everywhere yet. With our current technologies and the time we've dedicated to SETI, we've only searched an incredibly small portion of the universe for intelligent life." Secondly, "we may not have found intelligent life yet because we're stuck with the physics and the technology that we have in the twenty-first century. We may not have invented the right way to do this yet." In brief, then, we're stuck with a big universe and rusty technology. There's not much we can do about the first problem, but Tarter is more hopeful about the second. She suggests that "in the near future, SETI scientists will be able to search for intelligent life in pools and lakes" on exoplanets. That would surely be the biggest fishing expedition ever undertaken, but catching fish may prove difficult.

However, SETI supporters are born optimists—witness how Jill Tarter thinks the meetup would go if intelligent aliens (not just their radio signals) ever arrived on Earth. Citing Harvard University psychologist Steven Pinker, she claims, "Pinker's work suggests that humankind is getting kinder and gentler as we evolve. He has noted that "today we may be living in the most peaceable era in our species' existence."

You will be forgiven if you hadn't noticed that. Stephen Hawking was probably nearer the truth when he said; "If aliens visit us, the outcome would be much as when Columbus landed in America, which didn't turn out well for the Native Americans." [15]

So why bother?

Whether or not these expanded SETI efforts will yield any results is doubtful, whatever amount of money is spent in the attempt. So why does anyone bother? Clearly, there must be strong motivations behind the search for extraterrestrial life to justify so huge a cost in time, money, expertise, and nervous energy. Let me respond by matching Jill Tarter's two answers by two of my own.

I suggest firstly that we persist in seeking this tiny needle in the cosmic haystack because the human race is incurably curious about the universe in which we live. It is this curiosity that drives exploration of all kinds—whether geographic, oceanographic, scientific, psychological, or any other kind. Asked, "Why did you want to climb Mount Everest?" George Mallory who died attempting to scale the mountain in 1924 famously replied, "Because it's there"—adding, "Everest is the highest mountain in the world, and no man has reached its summit. Its existence is a challenge. The answer is instinctive, a part, I suppose, of man's desire to conquer the universe."[16]

Mallory's insight regarding Man's "desire to conquer the universe" fits uncannily well with modern preoccupations like SETI. We appear to be hardwired with a need-to-know mentality that goes far beyond the curiosity that, proverbially, causes feline fatalities. This in itself tells us something important about the nature of mankind and reflects the biblical command to Man (sometimes called "the cultural mandate") to "have dominion" over the created order.[17]

But I believe there is a more focused reason for the insatiable search for "life out there," namely, the need to understand ourselves. We *need* an answer to the Psalmist's question, "What is man?" and many believe that the discovery of intelligent extraterrestrial life would give us one. Of course, finding bugs on Mars (small, flat, or otherwise) is quite a different matter from getting an e-mail from an extraterrestrial. But atheists argue that either discovery would tend to favor the claim that humanity is an uncreated accident of nature that could occur anywhere in the universe given the right conditions. But if SETI continues to prove unfruitful in spite of all our efforts, we may well have to conclude instead that *as far as we know* humanity is unique on a cosmic scale.

In any case, of course, the atheist's logic is flawed. If God created Man on Earth there is nothing to stop him creating life elsewhere in the universe, and nothing to prove that he hasn't already done so. If life were to be found elsewhere in the universe, it would prove nothing concerning human origins. But as long as skeptics *think* that such discovery would be a nail in the coffin of creation, they will pursue it with vigor. Equally, a failure to find extraterrestrial life (intelligent or not) proves nothing in itself. Mankind could be both accidental and still apparently unique. But given the arguments considered earlier about the supposed abundance of Earthlike planets, a unique humanity would imply something more like a miracle than an accident.

BACKLASH

So much for SETI; let's return to Earth. A proverb that doesn't yet exist in the English language (but probably ought to) runs as follows: "Where there's a lash, there will also be a backlash." If we assume that hordes of rocky exoplanets do indeed exist throughout the universe, a new question arises—what exactly does it take for a planet to nurture and sustain life? What is needed to allow the development and survival of a teeming biosphere such as we find on Earth?

An increasing number of authors and scientific commentators are fuelling a backlash against the idea that life must be common in the universe—pointing out that stringent conditions must be satisfied for planetary life to exist. I am not here referring to the "fine-tuning" of the laws of nature, without which a life-sustaining *universe* could not exist. We'll consider that in the next chapter. I'm thinking rather of the physical environment that makes Earth "just right" as a home for living creatures, while Mars and Venus, for example, are "just wrong" in this regard.

The backlash actually takes two forms. Firstly, many who are metaphysically committed to the existence of alien civilizations have offered reasons why they remain undetected. Secondly, there are others who believe that Earth is such an unusual (even unique) planet that the likelihood of life arising elsewhere is remote. An absorbing example of the first is a book by the respected and well-qualified writer, Paul Davies, published in 2010 and dedicated to SETI pioneer Frank Drake. It is entitled *The Eerie Silence: Are We Alone in the Universe?*[18] In chapter 2 he asks the question, "Life: freak sideshow or cosmic imperative?" Ignoring other possibilities such as divine creation or even alien invasion, he plumps for a "cosmic imperative"—the belief that in the course of time, life will inevitably appear on myriads of Earthlike planets throughout the universe. He does, however, sound a cautionary note: "The fact that a planet is habitable is not the same as saying it is inhabited" (p.24). He also recognizes that to justify the cosmic imperative requires a plausible scenario to explain the fortuitous undesigned origin of life from nonbiological chemicals— acknowledging that no such scenario yet exists. If the probability of such an origin is zero, then no matter how many zillions of biofriendly planets there may be, the cosmos will be barren of life. So far so good. But, sadly, Davies then commits the common fallacy expressed by the syllogism:

1. Life exists on Earth;
2. Life on Earth arose by spontaneous chemical reactions;
3. Therefore life must exist on Earthlike planets throughout the cosmos;
4. Therefore life is a cosmic imperative.

But the only justification Davies can offer for (2) is that perhaps there exist as-yet-unknown "higher" laws of nature that might explain the chance origin of the complex information and organization on which life depends. This isn't science, of course, but rather a metaphysical scheme in which creative powers are attributed to nature itself (pantheism) or to an unknown suprascientific agency (deism), but never to a personal God who created Man in his own image (theism).

ALIEN MAGIC

Returning to the title of his book, Paul Davies (having embraced the cosmic imperative) must explain, in wholly natural terms, why there is an eerie silence. If we are not alone in the universe, why do we seem to be? His curiously titled chapter "Evidence for a Galactic Diaspora" (Ch. 6, p. 116 *et seq.*) actually offers no evidence whatever for the existence of alien civilizations. What it does do is speculate for twenty-four pages on *why we have no evidence.* Possible reasons offered include the idea that advanced galactic civilizations are already in active communication with one another using a kind of GWW (galactic worldwide web) but we just haven't noticed it yet. Alternatively, the problem could be that aliens were in the communication business long before the solar system was formed, so we weren't around when it was in fashion. Or, yet again, mankind is ahead of the game and will have to wait for extraterrestrial civilizations to catch up with us (it could be a long wait). Put less flippantly, these ideas boil down to the possible existence of a limited cosmic window-of-opportunity during which communication between (or space exploration by) alien races might have occurred in the past or might yet occur in the future. Only if we happen to live within a certain time window will we be able to gatecrash the party.

In a further chapter titled "Alien Magic," Davies examines yet another possibility. Alien technology may be so advanced that we wouldn't recognize it if we saw it. We see here another unintentional echo of biblical wisdom in the arguments offered by skeptics, for writing to the Romans another Paul accuses the ancient world of just such a failure—in this case their reluctance to recognize the handiwork of God in the created order. He writes:

> "For [God's] invisible attributes, namely his eternal power and divine nature, have been clearly perceived ever since the creation of the world in the things that have been made, so they are without excuse."[19]

The awesome "divine technology" revealed by modern science in the world around us, from the genetic code to cosmic "fine tuning" and the laws of nature, today go unrecognized as such, and are attributed instead to chance and accident.

However, to be fair, Paul Davies is wise enough to acknowledge the possibility that we don't hear from our cosmic next-door neighbors because, in spite of the multitude of exoplanets, the aliens simply aren't there. For example, he examines a theory proposed by Brandon Carter[20] that the time required for intelligent life to arise by chance, even on a hospitable planet, may exceed the duration of the habitable zone around its star. This duration is estimated at around five or six billion years, which is far short of the 200 billion years it allegedly took for intelligent life to appear on Earth. Carter concluded that life on Earth must be a statistical fluke and Davies adds, "If Carter is right, then Earth is a *very rare* exception and the emergence of intelligent beings like humans is a freak event" (p. 89). Having embraced the cosmic imperative, of course, Davies must conclude that Carter is somehow wrong, but at least he gives him a fair hearing.

THE PRIVILEGED PLANET

The second kind of backlash is less common but held with equal fervor. In a book entitled *Lucky Planet: Why Earth Is Exceptional and What That Means for Life in the Universe*, geologist David Waltham presents an interesting thesis—that the Earth has enjoyed a rare and possibly unique stability of climate, allowing life and the whole biosphere to evolve at a safe and leisurely pace. The back-cover blurb puts it thus: "The Earth may have had four billion years of good weather purely by chance: we are on a rare planet where all the bad things that could have happened to the climate have fortunately cancelled each other out."[21] For example, Waltham argues that a growing intensity in the sun's energy output over billions of years has been offset by a progressive decrease in Earth's atmospheric carbon dioxide (a "greenhouse" gas that retains heat on Earth's surface). The net result is a thermostatic balance that kept Earth's temperature within the limits needed to sustain life. The book is an ingenious and well-argued narrative but depends heavily on speculation and the occasional circular argument (as when oxygen produced by flourishing organisms is said to stabilize the climate to allow organisms to flourish).

Dissenting from this "lucky planet" approach, Guillermo Gonzales and Jay Richards, in their magisterial work *The Privileged Planet*, argue that Earth is special not only because it is habitable but also because it is ideally suited for scientific observation and enquiry. They conclude:

> "Even more mysterious than the fact that our location [in the cosmos] is so congenial to diverse measurement and discovery, is that these same conditions appear to correlate with habitability. This is strange because there's no obvious reason to assume that the very same rare properties that allow

for our existence would also provide the best overall setting to make discoveries about the world around us.... It cries out for another explanation...."[22]

WATER, WATER EVERYWHERE

But let me approach the privileged nature of planet Earth in a more amusing way. Everyone seems to agree that without water there could be no life on Earth or anywhere else. In searching for extraterrestrial life, the first thing astronomers look for is water; few people outside the cast of *Star Trek* expect to find living lithospheres or vital signs in vapors. (A lithosphere is the outer solid shell of a rocky planet.) But water, though not itself alive, is a potential host for all manner of life forms, even though (as I explained in *Who made God?*) it presents serious problems for the *origin* of life since water disrupts the chemical linkages needed to build DNA or protein molecules. Water has some unique properties such as the *decrease* in density that occurs as the temperature drops from 4°C to its freezing point. This means that water freezes from the top downwards, generally leaving liquid water below the ice where marine life can survive (as long as oxygen is not depleted there). It is also a solvent for a huge range of other substances, many of which are partly ionized in water into positive and negative ions—facilitating all manner of chemical reactions and processes including those involved in living organisms. Water vapor is also important, acting as a powerful greenhouse gas and creating the hydrological cycle of evaporation and rainfall. As far as we know, there can be no life on a planet devoid of liquid water. You can find an extended discussion of water and its benefits to planetary life in Michael Denton's book, *The Wonder of Water*.[23]

But (in English; my apologies to translators) "water" is also an acronym for some of the other key requirements for planetary life, namely the right kinds of Weather, Atmosphere, Temperature, Environment, and Repulsion.

- Firstly, consider *weather*. Although life is maintained by the hydrological cycle, it is easily destroyed by seriously bad *weather* such as catastrophic floods and the effects on weather of Earthquakes, volcanic eruptions, and meteorite impacts.
- Secondly, the right kind of *atmosphere* is also vital for planetary life to survive. This includes a "just right" level of oxygen—too much is poisonous, too little is fatal (unless you're an anaerobic microbe); the presence of carbon dioxide to support plant life and stimulate breathing in animals; the absence of poisonous gases such as sulfuric acid (found on Venus); excessive levels of carbon dioxide (Mars and Venus); and hydrogen, helium, methane, and ammonium (Jupiter, Saturn, Uranus, Neptune).
- Thirdly, *temperature* is what defines the so-called "habitable zone" around a star. If the planet surface is too hot or too cold, life will be respectively fried or frozen out of existence. An even narrower range of life-supporting temperatures is mandated by the need for liquid water. We have already considered the need for a planet to be in some sense thermostatically controlled if life is to survive over long periods of time.
- Fourthly, living things are dependent upon their *environment* for survival. This obviously includes temperature and water supply, but also involves ecological factors such as the presence of nutrients in soil, the existence of food chains, and protection from the elements.
- Fifthly and finally, life requires the *repulsion* of destructive influences such as ultraviolet light (Earth is shielded by the

ozone layer); cosmic radiation (largely deflected and trapped by the Van Allen belts created by Earth's magnetic field); and meteorite bombardment (our massive sister planet Jupiter attracts much of the space debris that might otherwise fall on Earth with dire consequences for our biosphere). Yes, Earth does appear to be a rather special planet. It could also be unique in its ability to support life.

Conclusion

So where does this search for extraterrestrial life leave us? How does it help us answer the question "What is Man?" While much remains obscure, several things are clear.

1. For whatever reason, the likelihood of our discovering extraterrestrial life is slim at best. If evidence for life (past or present) is found on Mars, we shall need to keep a careful watch on the way this evidence is interpreted—given the strong motivation the researchers will have for finding what they are looking for. But even if life on Mars were proven beyond reasonable doubt, it is far more likely to have arrived there from Earth (or arrived on Earth from Mars) than to have originated separately on each planet.

2. Again for whatever reason, the likelihood of our detecting *intelligent* extraterrestrial life is remote. But even if this were to happen, it would actually prove nothing about Man's origin. The atheist might argue that the rise of multiple alien civilizations would suggest that each arose by the same

accident of nature, but is it really logical to believe in multiple accidental coincidences? Would the data not fit better with multiple and *intentional* acts of creation by a single spiritual Being? Occam's razor would surely favor a single cause.

3. Optimists and pessimists appear to join forces in agreeing to ignore or dismiss any possibility of divine creation. It is an article of faith for them that life, whether on Earth or elsewhere, is a lucky fluke having no intrinsic meaning. Purpose or teleology is excluded from their considerations *ab initio*, in spite of the arguments advanced in Chapter 2 (and in theological discourse generally) that all our knowledge of the universe points to creation and the necessity of God, rather than the imperatives of chance and accident.

4. However, there is one area of agreement to which almost everyone subscribes: the study of the cosmos and the role of life within it should help us to answer the question, "What is Man?" The reason for this is clear: the search is not ultimately for small flat bugs or even superintelligent aliens. It is for our own roots as human beings—an extension of the search for human identity that we discussed in Chapter 2. Paul Davies confirms this assertion:

"Can SETI be justified, given the poor prospects of success? I believe it can, for several reasons. First, it forces us to confront those great questions of existence that we should be thinking about anyway. What is life? What is intelligence? What is the destiny of mankind? As Frank Drake has remarked, SETI is in many ways a search for ourselves—who we are and where we fit into the universe."[24]

Yes, indeed, though Davies' logical slip is showing. It is not SETI that forces us to confront these questions but rather the questions themselves that fuel and drive the SETI project, as the quote from Frank Drake correctly implies. If this were not the case, it would make much more sense to sit back and wait for advanced aliens to adopt a don't-call-us-we'll-call-you approach. The totality of the efforts described in this chapter, with all the dedication, expectation, frustration and costs they involve, can be traced back to Man's need to know who and what he is. It might be unkind to compare this frenetic activity to the biblical tower of Babel but there is a certain resemblance. The Babylonian builders declared, "Come, let us build ourselves a city, and a tower whose top is in the heavens; let us make a name for ourselves lest we be scattered abroad over the face of the whole Earth."[25] They wanted to make a name *for themselves*. They felt the need to establish their own identity independent of any relationship to God. And so, unwisely, many do today.

ENDNOTES:

1 *Extrasolar Planets Encyclopedia,* http://exoplanet.eu/catalog/

2 *Dick, Steven; The Biological Universe: The Twentieth Century Extraterrestrial Life Debate (1999). ISBN 0-521-34326-7.]*

3 http://www.planetary.org/blogs/guest-blogs/2014/1216-like-a-bad-penny-methane-on-mars.html

4 https://exomars.cnes.fr/en/EXOMARS/index.htm

5 https://www.theguardian.com/science/2017/jul/06/mars-covered-in-toxic-chemicals-that-can-wipe-out-living-organisms-tests-reveal?CMP=share_btn_fb

6 Crenson, Matt; *"After 10 years, few believe life on Mars". Space.com. Associated Press. Archived from the original on 2006-08-09.*

7 McKay, David S. et. al. *"Search for Past Life on Mars: Possible Relic*

Biogenic Activity in Martian Meteorite ALH84001." Science (1996) **273** *(5277): 924–30.*

8   Information in this section derived from https://en.wikipedia.org/wiki/Search_for_extraterrestrial_intelligence

9   https://en.wikipedia.org/wiki/Ohio_State_University_Radio_Observatory. It is now believed that the 'Wow' signal was caused by a passing comet.

10 It is now believed that the 'Wow' signal was caused by a passing comet. https://phys.org/news/2017-06-wow-mystery-space.htm but not everyone agrees.

11 http://www.eso.org/public/teles-instr/e-elt/e-elt_exo/

12 https://en.wikipedia.org/wiki/Search_for_extraterrestrial_intelligence#cite_note-washingtonp1-44

13 http://www.abc.net.au/news/2016-03-14/china's-alien-hunting-telescope-before-and-after/7245690

14 http://techcrunch.com/2016/02/04/seti-scientist-explains-why-we-havent-found-aliens-yet/

15 http://news.bbc.co.uk/1/hi/8642558.stm

16 https://en.wikipedia.org/wiki/George_Mallory.

17 Genesis 1:28.

18 Davies, Paul; *The Eerie Silence*, (Penguin, 2010).

19 Romans 1:20.

20 Carter, Brandon; *'The anthropic principle and its implications for biological evolution,' Philosophical Transactions of the Royal Society of London*, A310 (1983) p. 347.

21 Waltham, D; *Lucky Planet* (Icon books Ltd, London, 2014).

22 Gonzalez. Guillermo, and Richards, Jay W; *The Privileged Planet: How Our Place in the Cosmos Is Designed for Discovery* (Regnery Publishing Inc., 2004) p. xv

23 Denton, Michael; *The Wonder of Water: Water's Profound Fitness for Life on Earth and Mankind* (Discovery Institute 2017).

24 Davies, Paul; loc. cit. p. 205.

25 Genesis 11:5.

CHAPTER 4

We have all heard musicians tuning their instruments before an orchestral performance. If they neglected to do so, there would be disharmony when they began to play. Scientists who study the cosmos have enlisted the idea of precise tuning to help describe a remarkable fact, namely that the laws of nature are just right ("fine-tuned") to allow us to live harmoniously in what would otherwise be a lifeless universe. Cosmologist Luke Barnes has made a special study of the subject and concludes that "the universe is fine-tuned for the existence of life. Of all the ways that the laws of nature, constants of physics, and initial conditions of the universe could have been, only a very small subset permits the existence of intelligent life."

Almost all cosmologists agree that fine-tuning is real and needs to be explained. The explanations offered, however, differ dramatically. By far the simplest explanation is that the universe was deliberately designed to permit the existence of life—which necessitates a nonmaterial Creator. Atheists, however, must seek alternative explanations, of which there are really only two on offer—sheer chance and the multiverse. We'll learn about the multiverse in Chapter 5, but here we use Martin Rees' popular book *Just Six Numbers* and some homely analogies to help us understand what it is about the cosmos that is fine-tuned to support life.

THE COSMIC COOKBOOK

A fine-tuned universe

"A common-sense interpretation of the facts suggests that a super-intellect has monkeyed with physics."

SIR FRED HOYLE, 1982.[1]

"Six numbers constitute a 'recipe' for a universe. Moreover, the outcome is sensitive to their values. If any one of them were to be "untuned," there would be no stars and no life."

SIR MARTIN REES, 2000.[2]

In the previous two chapters, we have already seen that the question *"Where* is Man?" has a strong and direct bearing on the primary issue of "What is Man?" but there is still much more to say about the cosmic environment in which we find ourselves. So we're going to pursue the matter further by exploring the so-called "fine tuning" of the universe—the fact that its physical properties are just right to permit the existence of planets and life.

JUST SIX NUMBERS

I should explain at the outset that there is an enormous literature on the subject, much of it highly complicated and mathematical. I shall mention some of this specialized material and provide references for those who want to go deeper, but the treatment here will only skim the surface—though hopefully in an accurate, interesting, and informative way.

In his book *Just Six Numbers*, Sir Martin Rees (Britain's Astronomer Royal) describes how the physical laws and constants of our universe appear to be "fine-tuned" to support life. In doing so, he asks the following question:

> "Is this tuning just a brute fact, a coincidence? Or is it the providence of a benign Creator? I take the view that it is neither. An infinity of other universes may well exist where the numbers are different."[3]

Martin Rees was being honest. He was writing a book which celebrates the fact that our physical universe appears to be amazingly well suited to provide for our existence. That is, the laws of nature (and specifically the values of the constants that appear in these laws) are exactly what they need to be. If some of them were different, even by very small amounts, life would be impossible anywhere in the universe. Rees wanted to avoid the "brute fact" explanation that we considered at some length in Chapter 2 because he recognized that it actually explains nothing. But on the other hand, he wasn't keen to give credit for this fine tuning to a nonmaterial Creator (*aka* God). So he sought and found an escape route, claiming that among an infinity of possible universes, ours is a lucky one where the laws and constants just happen to be hospitable to intelligent life. This, of course, is no more than an extension of the "lucky planet" narrative we studied in Chapter 3. We shall examine the validity of multiverse scenarios later, but first we need to know more about the fine-tuning that Martin Rees highlights and is seeking to explain (or rather, explain *away*).

Rees limits himself to "just six" fine-tuned physical quantities for two reasons. Firstly, he was writing a popular-level book and wanted to keep it simple. Secondly, he believed that the selected "numbers" really are the most important. Some writers go much further, identifying as many as ninety-three instances of finely tuned physical quantities. Here, for simplicity, I shall follow Martin Rees' example and limit myself to his six case studies. They will be quite sufficient to make the point.

MONKEYING WITH PHYSICS

The fact that our universe (or cosmos) appears to be fine-tuned to permit the existence of life, and specially intelligent life, is called the "anthropic principle" (from the Greek *anthropos* meaning "man"). Most scientists working in relevant fields agree that certain of the physical constants that define the behavior of matter and energy *need* to have the values that they do for the universe to be habitable. Even slight variations from the observed values would render life impossible. Remarking on this fact, the British astrophysicist Sir Fred Hoyle (1915–2001) declared, "It looks like a put-up job" and later wrote, "A common-sense interpretation of the facts suggests that a superintellect has monkeyed with physics."[4] What prompted his suspicions? He had realized that the basic building block of living things (the element carbon) could only be formed in stars from hydrogen and helium if the carbon atom had a special "resonance" at a particular energy. (A resonance is the ability of a system to absorb energy when conditions are just right. A wine glass may shatter when a singer hits *exactly* the resonant frequency of the glass, and a bridge may begin to sway dangerously if soldiers march across it in step at a *particular* speed.) Hoyle predicted that carbon must possess the precise resonance needed for its formation in stars and this was later shown to be correct.[5]

The famous Princeton physicist Freeman Dyson also recognized the reality of fine-tuning, saying: "The more I examine the universe and the details of its architecture, the more evidence I find that the Universe in some sense must have known we were coming."[6] Likewise, cosmologist Stephen Hawking, in his book *A Brief History of Time*, declares:

"The laws of science ... contain many fundamental numbers, like the size of the electric charge of the electron and the ratio of the masses of the proton and the electron. We cannot, at the moment at least, predict the values of these numbers from theory—we have to find them by observation.... The remarkable fact is that the values of these numbers seem to have been very finely adjusted to make possible the development of life."[7]

Physics professor and writer Paul Davies calls fine-tuning "the goldilocks enigma"[8] because (like Little Bear's porridge, chair, and bed in *Goldilocks and the Three Bears*) the physics of our cosmos are to a remarkable degree "just right" to support life. He also confesses, "Through my scientific work I have come to believe more and more strongly that the physical universe is put together with an ingenuity so astonishing that I cannot accept it merely as a brute fact."[9]

Finally, in a foreword to a recent book by Geraint Lewis and Luke Barnes entitled *A Fortunate Universe; Life in a Finely Tuned Cosmos*, the 2011 Nobel Physics Laureate Brian Schmidt says the authors ...

> "take you on a tour of the Cosmos in all of its glory and all of its mystery. You will see that humanity appears to be part of a remarkable set of circumstances involving a special time on a special planet, which orbits a special star, all within a specially constructed Universe. It is these ... conditions that have allowed humans to ponder our place in space and time. I have no idea why we are here, but I do know the Universe is beautiful. *A Fortunate Universe* captures the mysterious beauty of the Cosmos in a way that all can share."[10]

EXPLAINING FINE-TUNING AWAY

Although the degree (or even existence) of fine-tuning is disputed by some scientists, notably the late Victor Stenger,[11] most experts agree that it is a genuine and quite remarkable phenomenon that cries out for an explanation. Of course, a simple explanation is that the universe was deliberately made this way by an intelligent and nonmaterial Creator who knew what he was doing—in short, by God. But those who reject the concept of divine creation often invoke the idea of a "multiverse" (or MV) to escape the theological implications of fine-tuning. They argue that our universe is simply one of a potentially infinite number of possible universes, each having its own different physical constants and/or laws of nature. Among such an infinitude of possible worlds, they say, there must, by pure chance, be one that has just the right combination of physical attributes to give rise to intelligent life. We just happen to live in that favored but fortuitous universe (if we were anywhere else we wouldn't exist).

So can we dismiss fine-tuning as a happy accident? I don't think so. You've heard the saying "divide and conquer" but it is sometimes more effective in ideological warfare to "multiply (universes) and conquer." During the Vietnam war, the British *Evening News*[12] carried the following report:

> "The Pentagon is buying huge quantities of tinsel-like chaff to throw a blizzard of confusing images into radars guiding North Vietnam's antiaircraft guns.... The chaff, made up of thread-sized strips of aluminum-coated fiberglass, is fired in puffs by American pilots approaching bombing target areas. The puffs reflect enemy radar signals and create blips on radar screens just like planes, confusing antiaircraft crews."

So might the multiverse be just a diversionary tactic—an escape mechanism crafted from conceptual tinsel to prevent atheistic cosmologies being shot down by the evidence? It's a serious question and one we must explore.

Those who propose the existence of a multiverse claim that it provides a naturalistic (though hardly scientific) explanation of why our universe seems designed to support life. Cosmologist Luke Barnes sums up the debate in his exhaustive technical review of fine-tuning (FT) and offers us two options:

> "(1) This universe is one of a large number of variegated universes, produced by physical processes that randomly scan through ... the set of possible physics. Eventually, a universe will be created that is a member of the life-permitting set. Only such universes can be observed, since only such universes contain

observers. [Alternatively] (2) There exists a transcendent, personal ... entity [who] desires to create a universe in which other minds will be able to form. Thus, the entity chooses from the set of possibilities a universe which is foreseen to evolve intelligent life." [13]

Of course, the divine "entity" could also have dispensed with evolution, but either way we clearly have a choice! Barnes goes on to affirm the reality of fine-tuning, concluding that "the universe is fine-tuned for the existence of life. Of all the ways that the laws of nature, constants of physics, and initial conditions of the universe could have been, only a very small subset permits the existence of intelligent life."

FINE-TUNING NEEDS TO BE EXPLAINED

Let's pause to summarize what we've seen so far. Most cosmologists agree that the laws of nature in our universe are, for no obvious *scientific* reason, "just right" to support life. However, many people dismiss this observation by saying that if this were not the case, we wouldn't be here to tell the tale. That is no doubt true, but it doesn't alter the fact that fine-tuning needs an explanation. Why not? Here are two reasons.

Firstly, the universe would still be fine-tuned for life even if we weren't here—and indeed *had to be* fine-tuned before life could begin or survive on planet Earth. This is what Freeman Dyson meant by suggesting that the universe knew "we were coming," as quoted earlier. When I was commuting regularly to London by train, I once fell asleep on the evening return journey. A fellow traveller who knew where I always got off the train kindly woke me up. But suppose he hadn't done so and I had slept on until the train reached its final destination. If, on arriving there, I saw a banner saying "Welcome, Edgar Andrews," I would have been immensely surprised, since no one could have known I was coming. An explanation would have been needed. Any such anticipation of the future (or "teleology") implies purpose, and purpose requires the activity of mind. Creation by God explains both fine-tuning and purpose, but chance can provide neither.

Secondly, it is a complete fallacy to argue that the existence of an infinite number of universes would guarantee the presence of some that are life-supporting. You could have an infinite number of universes composed entirely of Higgs bosons or hydrogen molecules that would be completely sterile. It's not just weight of numbers that is needed but a combination of physical processes that provide:

1. A *mechanism* for making universes that scans systematically through all possible variations of physical laws and constants, making universes as it goes.
2. A *database* containing all possible laws and constants from which the mechanism can select ingredients. In other words, there has to be a "cosmic cookbook" from which the recipe for each new universe can be selected.
3. A *guarantee* that at least one such recipe contains the ingredients necessary to support life.

This, I suggest, is quite a tall order for a process completely unknown to science. But let's suppose that such a cosmic scan was indeed completed. Since every possible combination of laws and constants had been tried, wasn't the creation of our own universe inevitable? Not at all. Who is to say which combinations are "possible" and which are not? Some rules would need to be imposed to exclude, say, self-contradictory combinations, but establishing such a filter would require a rational process. Then again, why should the cosmic cookbook referred to in [2] above include any life-sustaining recipes? You may reply that the database must include such options because we live in a life-sustaining universe. But this is a circular argument, since it *assumes* the existence and contents of the database—the very things that (according to multiverse supporters) fine-tuning is supposed to demonstrate.

The existence of one life-friendly universe actually tells us nothing about the existence or nonexistence of a cosmic cookbook that contains the ingredients needed to create it. Our universe could be a completely stand-alone phenomenon. Even if a cosmic database does exist, who is to say that the fine-tuned cosmos we know is derived from that database and is not an independent phenomenon that owes nothing to the hypothetical database?

Suppose, for example, that police are using a DNA database to identify the perpetrator of a crime, but that the database contains only records of offenders over twenty. Then a complete scan of the database would produce no match with the DNA of a teenage suspect, but that wouldn't mean that the teenager was innocent of the crime. In the same way, there is no guarantee that a cosmic database would include the combination of factors necessary for the support of life—unless of course it had been designed to do so. And if a cosmic cookbook does exist, who or what compiled it? As with the authorship of the laws of nature we considered in Chapter 2, the only candidate I can see for the role of master-chef is God.

We'll consider multiverses at length in the next chapter, but let's now look in more detail at Martin Rees' six necessary ingredients for a life-supporting cosmos.

RELIANCE ON BIG BANG COSMOLOGY

Before we go any further, I should make one thing clear. The science-based fine-tuning argument, whether advanced by Rees, Barnes, or anyone else, relies heavily upon Big Bang cosmology—the idea that the universe originated in a tiny volume that *contained* all space, time, energy and matter, and then expanded to its present size over vast periods of time (and continues to do so). The experimental evidence supporting this so-called "Standard Model" of the cosmos has persuaded all but a few cosmologists of its basic truth, though they still argue over important details. The fine-tuning scenarios advanced by the scientists quoted above (and many others like them) are based largely on a single idea—the universe evolved from a Big Bang origin in such a way that, for no obvious reason, certain effects balanced out (to a remarkable degree) to provide a habitable universe.

I am conscious that some readers will reject this view on theological grounds. For example, it is logically possible to maintain that the Big Bang never happened—that the universe is fine-tuned simply because God made it that way *de novo*, so there is nothing further to discuss. For any who take this view, the remainder of this chapter and the next may, perhaps, seem pointless. But I hope not. Many who, like myself, do believe in divine creation, see value in the discussion we've embarked upon. Why? Because working on the evidence provided by *secular* science, it allows us to build a case for creation that cannot be dismissed out of hand even by skeptics. We have in fact already trodden some way down this path in Chapter 2, where we saw that purely secular thinking can lead unexpectedly to "the necessity of God."

What exactly is fine-tuned?

So let's now consider what exactly has been fine-tuned. It depends on who you ask. For example, while Martin Rees talks about "just six numbers," Christian apologist Hugh Ross[14,15] recognizes ninety-three fine-tuned life-supporting quantities in the cosmos, while others offer intermediate estimates. In this chapter I shall adopt Rees' parsimonious option, if only to be brief (for my benefit) and avoid boredom (for yours). Luke Barnes points out that Rees himself could easily have included other constants in his fine-tuning argument.[16] So please accept my apologies now if I don't say anything about your own favorite example of fine-tuning.

The "six numbers" that Martin Rees says are fine-tuned are "constants" that turn up in certain laws of nature. Notice that Rees refers to "the physical laws and constants of our universe," making a distinction between "laws" and "constants." By "laws" he means the way relevant *variable* quantities relate to one another. By "constants" he means nonvarying terms that are included when laws are expressed mathematically. So let me unpack the difference between "constants" and "variables." Suppose you go to a particular cinema (theatre, concert hall; take your pick) on a regular basis. The building doesn't change. It's always in the same place; it always has the same size and seating arrangements; you may not like the acoustics or the décor, but you have to put up with them because they don't change from month to month. These "always-the-same" things are "constants" of your experience as a cinemagoer. But each time you go, there are some things that do change, specifically the film you watch and the people who attend. These "things-that-change" are "variables" in your experience. In the same way, laws of nature, when they are written down as equations, usually contain both constants and variables. For example, Newton's law of gravity is written,

$$F = Gm_1m_2/d^2$$

where F is the gravitational force between two masses m_1 and m_2, d is the distance between them, and G is the "gravitational constant." Obviously, the two masses and their separation can change from case to case, which also causes a change in the force. These things are therefore variables. But the gravitational constant G never changes. It is a fixed constant of nature, and its value can be measured but not predicted by any theory. It is a brute fact that we have to put up with. A second well-known example is Einstein's famous equation linking mass and energy;

$$E = mc^2$$

where E is the energy content of a mass m, and c is the speed of light. Again, E and m are obviously variable and can have any value, depending on the mass selected. But the speed of light is a constant—whose never-changing value can be measured but not *predicted*. It too is a brute fact of nature.

In discussing fine-tuning, it is the constants of nature that are important. Most fine-tuning claims concern the specific values of these constants which, it is argued, are just right (within narrow ranges) to permit the existence of biological life in the universe. Since we have no idea why a constant of nature takes the value it does, these values are (from our perspective at least) arbitrary—they could have been different. But if they were different, the universe as we know it, and life in particular, could not exist. This cries out for an explanation. (To avoid misunderstanding, it is possible to make theoretical predictions of some constants-of-nature but only by introducing further arbitrary constants in the predictive theories. The problem is thus simply shifted rather than removed.)

THE COSMIC COOKBOOK

Suggesting that there are "just six" constants that must be fine-tuned to allow life to exist, Martin Rees writes:

> "These six numbers constitute a 'recipe' for a universe. Moreover, the outcome [the kind of universe that results] is sensitive to their values. If any one of them were to be 'untuned,' there would be no stars and no life.... It is astonishing that an expanding universe, whose starting point is so 'simple' that it can be specified by just a few numbers, can evolve (if these numbers are suitably 'tuned') into our intricately structured cosmos."[17]

This statement actually undermines the idea that the laws and constants of nature might vary so promiscuously across a vast multiplicity of universes that the happy accident of life has to occur in at least one of them. According to Rees, you don't *need* an infinity of universes to create a life-supporting cosmos. You only need a subset of universes which possess laws like our own and include six constants that are tunable within certain ranges. Why stock your kitchen with an infinite range of commodities when six ingredients (which you can use in different amounts) are all you need to create a mouth-watering menu of acceptable meals? If Rees is right, just six ingredients are sufficient to provide a cookbook full of life-supporting universes—a fact that suggests design rather than random chance. He is surely right to be astonished. And in case anyone thinks my analogy is spurious, let me point out one incontrovertible fact. It is infinitely more *probable* that only universes containing these six constants exist (whatever values they take) than that an infinite number of universes exist which lack this constraint and where anything goes.

So what are Rees' six numbers, and why are they so important?

THE FIRST NUMBER: THE ELEPHANT AND THE MOUSE

Imagine a tug-of-war between an elephant and a mouse. There's no prize for guessing which would win. Like the elephant and the mouse, there are two kinds of force in nature that have large effects on the cosmos, and one is very much stronger than the other. They are respectively electrical forces (the elephant) and gravitational forces (the mouse). The two forces can be directly compared because they both get weaker in the same way as the distance between interacting objects increases—both forces vary as the inverse square $(1/d^2)$ of the distance. The ratio of electrical force to gravitational force is Rees' first "number." Denoted "N," this ratio is a huge number which can be written as 10^{36} (that stands for one followed by thirty-six zeros; this is the only civilized way to write down huge numbers and we'll use it throughout this discussion). Since this means that the electrical force is N times larger than the gravitational force, we would expect electrical forces to dominate the universe and gravitational forces to be negligible. But this doesn't happen, and that for an interesting reason.

Gravitational forces always attract while electrical forces can both attract and repel. Electrical charges can be positive or negative, and opposite charges attract each other while similar charges repel. So now try setting up the tug-of-war between an elephant on one side and a mouse-plus-elephant team on the other. Now who wins? Feeble as it is, the mouse triumphs because the two elephants cancel each other out. So while electrical forces hold atoms together, the positive charge on an atomic nucleus exactly balances the total negative charge on its surrounding electrons, so that whole atoms are electrically neutral—along with anything made of atoms like pennies, people, and planets. It would, of course, be difficult to find two elephants with exactly the same strength, but the electrical forces in an atom achieve this balance with effortless precision. This means that gravitational forces, weak though they are (like the mouse), dominate the interaction between large scale objects because these forces can only attract. Among other things, this leads to a really neat separation between the microscopic world, dominated by electrical forces, and the macroscopic world, dominated by gravitational forces. This could itself be considered a fine-tuning effect.

According to Rees, if N were significantly smaller, the larger gravitational forces would make galaxies form quickly and pack stars together more closely. Stellar "traffic accidents" would be frequent, and collisions between stars would make planets too hazardous to nurture life. Stars would also be smaller and would burn out more quickly, while gravity would be so strong that not only bugs would be "small and flat;" a creature the size of a human being would be crushed to death by its own weight.

THE SECOND NUMBER: STICKING TOGETHER

You may not know what is meant by "the strong force" in physics, but I'm sure you are familiar with plastic wrap (*aka* cling film or food wrap). I'll use the British term "cling film," because "cling" is the property I want to talk about. When cling film was first introduced, it was a good idea that didn't always work. As you were trying to cover the leftovers from lunch to stop them drying out in the fridge, the thin plastic film would often fold and stick to itself, defying all efforts to smooth it out again. Its "cling" was just too high. The manufacturers tried to correct the problem but the modified product didn't stick very well to anything—its "cling" was now too low. Finally they got it sorted out and produced a film with a cling that was "just right." Perhaps this will help explain the importance of Rees' second number, which is governed by the "cling" force that holds particles together in atomic nuclei.

Every atom consists of a positively charged nucleus orbited[18] by enough negatively charged electrons to balance its electrical charge, so that the atom as a whole is electrically neutral. But here we are only interested in atomic nuclei, which consist of one or more positively charged "protons" (a single particle that is the nucleus of a hydrogen atom), accompanied by a roughly similar but not always equal number of "neutrons" (think of a neutron as the uncharged twin of a proton). But what keeps these particles together in a stable nucleus? The positive charges of the protons ought to repel one another and make the nucleus fly apart, but that doesn't happen. Within the confines of the nucleus there exists a "strong force" that opposes the electrical repulsion between protons and makes all the nuclear particles cling together. Its effects are highly localized and felt only inside the nucleus, but without the strong force nothing could exist except hydrogen.

The strong force is a tad difficult to study, being tucked away inside atomic nuclei, but there is a simple indirect way of measuring its effect. I'll explain this using an example. When two protons and two neutrons combine to form a helium nucleus, the mass of the new nucleus is a little lower than the combined masses of the separate particles that make it up. So some mass disappears when a helium nucleus is formed. Since the masses of the proton, neutron, and helium nucleus are accurately known, this mass reduction or "deficit" is also precisely known and provides an indirect measure of the strength of the strong force. For hydrogen-to-helium conversion, the deficit (expressed as a fraction of the original masses) turns out to be 0.7 percent. This deficit is Rees' second number and is denoted ε.

So what's that got to do with cling film? Simply this: the original over-sticky cling film represents what would happen if the strong force between nuclear particles were too large. Rees claims that if the strong force had been larger by just 15 percent, the protons in the early universe would all have stuck to one another—leaving no free atomic hydrogen to provide fuel for stars, combine with oxygen to make water, or initiate the formation of heavier atoms like carbon and oxygen. The universe would then be lifeless and probably featureless. The version of cling film that didn't stick to anything pictures the opposite case. If the strong force was weaker by 15 percent, the protons and neutrons couldn't cling together at all and the universe would consist entirely of hydrogen gas. So just like cling film, the nuclear strong force needed to be fine-tuned to lie within a narrow range of values. Otherwise the universe could not be hospitable to life.

THE THIRD NUMBER: SHAPING THE COSMOS

I imagine that everyone outside the Flat-Earth Society knows that the Earth is a sphere, so you would be mightily surprised if you overheard a scientist asserting that the whole *universe* is flat. Of course, it does rather depend on what you mean by "flat." Cosmologists talk about the "shape" of the universe and picture it by representing the real three-dimensional cosmos by a two-dimensional analogue. For example, if the universe were analogous to the two-dimensional *surface* of a sphere, it would mean that a ray of light emitted in the real world could in theory return to its starting point, just as a "straight" line drawn on the surface of a sphere would do. Such a universe is described as having a "closed" shape. A saddle-shaped 2D surface, which curves in two opposite directions at the same time, like a "pringles" potato chip, would correspond to an "open" universe. Finally, a flat 2D surface would represent a "flat" 3D universe in which parallel lines always remain parallel, however long they are.

So what determines whether the real universe is closed, open, or flat? The answer lies in another tug of war—the balance between (1) the mutual gravitational attraction of matter in the universe (which tends to make it collapse), and (2) the momentum of the Big Bang (that keeps it expanding). Assuming that (2) is fixed, our attention focuses on (1), the strength of which depends on the total amount of matter in the universe. We don't know what this is, of course, but we can estimate the next best thing, namely, the *average density* of matter in the *visible* cosmos. This can be expressed as atoms per cubic meter.

If (and only if) this average density has a certain critical value, the universe will be flat—and the ratio of actual to critical density (denoted by Rees' third number, Ω) will be unity. This appears to be the case with the cosmos we inhabit. The NASA website states, "We now know (as of 2013) that the universe is flat with only a 0.4 percent margin of error."[19] This result has fine-tuning implications, since only a "flat" universe has long-term stability, neither collapsing on itself due to high gravity nor flying catastrophically apart due to low gravity (leaving insufficient time for galaxies to form). This "somewhat surprising" result greatly enhances the life-friendly character of the cosmos.

But is this really a case of fine-tuning? After all, flatness is a common feature of our everyday world. That's true, but complete flatness is actually extremely rare in nature and is almost always due to human contrivance! We have flat tables, flat mirrors, flat floors, flat roofs, flat sidewalks and so on, but total flatness is never present in nature. I can think of only one apparent exception—the surface of a lake or pond. But even that flatness can be disturbed by frogs, fish, wind, reeds, and raindrops. And no matter how flat it looks, the pond surface isn't flat at all, since it actually follows the curvature of the Earth. In the same way, a universe that is flat in the cosmological sense is a rarity of an extreme kind, because it could have had an infinite number of possible curvatures. This is fine-tuning at its best.

THE FOURTH NUMBER: AN ACCELERATING UNIVERSE

Rees' fourth number relates to the speed with which the universe is expanding and is called "the cosmological constant" (denoted λ). It was originally introduced by Einstein, whose general relativity theory predicted that the universe could be expanding or contracting but could not be static. Since Einstein and his contemporaries believed that the universe *was* static, he added λ as a constant to balance the inward pull of gravity and make his equations compatible with his expectations. When fifteen years later Edwin Hubble showed that the universe was, after all, expanding, the cosmological constant became an embarrassment and was relegated to the trash can (or, more delicately, set equal to zero). It is indeed very close to zero and that is the significant point—it is close to zero but apparently not equal to zero.

This means that the expansion of the universe, far from slowing down as might be expected, appears to be speeding up. Only slightly, mind you, but according to the latest measurements it is a real effect.

Something is still pushing the universe apart long after the Big Bang explosion has dissipated its power. This mysterious force is now called "dark energy" and cosmologists suggest that it represents the intrinsic energy of space itself. However, the fact that the cosmological constant is very close to zero, when it could in principle have any value, is a further example of fine-tuning.

THE FIFTH NUMBER; GRAVY GRANULES

Maybe I'm just unlucky, but when I make gravy by pouring hot water on to instant gravy granules there's an even chance that it will have lumps in it, which defy every effort to smooth away. If I stirred the mixture vigorously enough while pouring the water I would, no doubt, get the rich smooth product promised on the packet, but once the granules begin to clump together all is lost. What is going on? When the dry granules come into contact with water they become sticky and tend to clump together, but if the water is sufficiently agitated it will tend to sweep the individual granules apart before they can clump, allowing them to dissolve and produce a smooth result. Success, therefore, depends on getting the balance right between the stickiness of wet granules and the speed with which they dissolve. I'm sure that wasn't easy for the manufacturer, since both stickiness and dissolution are caused by the same agency, namely water.

In the initial fireball theorized in "hot Big Bang" cosmology, all the contents of the infant universe were so close together that they shared their thermal energy; the temperature was uniform throughout and the mix had no lumps—like the dry gravy granules before water is added. But as the fireball expanded and cooled (like adding water to the granules), tiny fluctuations in density could respond in one of two ways. The denser regions could either clump together under the influence of gravity or disperse uniformly under the influence of expansion. Which happened in the infant cosmos? Apparently, the result was a finely tuned balance between the two options. It seems the manufacturer got it just right.

The point is this: while gravy is best when completely smooth, that isn't true of universes. A completely smooth universe would have no galaxies, no stars, no planets, and no life. On the other hand, a really lumpy universe would also be uncongenial to life, because although stars and planets could form, they would be too close for comfort, allowing no habitable zones or goldilocks planets. So what determines whether or not the lumpiness of a universe is "just right"? Well, like the shape of the universe considered earlier, the players are gravitational attraction, making things clump together, and the expansion energy making them fly apart. But there is a crucial third factor, namely, the initial graininess of the early universe. So to get a "just right" amount of cosmic lumpiness, we need just the right degree of granularity in the early universe.

That such granularity did exist can be deduced from the tiny temperature variations observed in what is called the "cosmic microwave background" (CMB). The CMB is highly uniform but it isn't *perfectly* uniform; some spots and patches are very slightly hotter than others and this indicates that some regions of the fireball were denser than others. In other words, the fireball was slightly lumpy. This brings us to Martin Rees' fifth number denoted Q. This quantity measures the amplitude of these primordial density fluctuations—that is, the amount by which the hottest and coldest spots differ from the average.

According to Big Bang cosmology, these denser lumps were the seeds of all the cosmic structures we observe today. The "seeds" eventually became clouds of hydrogen, leading to the formation of galaxies and stars—while the regions between the lumps lost out and became dark empty space. If this scenario is correct, as most cosmologists think it is, our modern universe with galaxies, stars, planets and the potential to support life depended on two things. Firstly, there must have been an *appropriate* level of granularity (lumpiness) in the Big Bang fireball to begin with, and secondly, the gravitational attraction must have been just right—large enough to stop the lumps being broken up by the expansion of space but not so great as to clump all the matter together and suffocate the formation of planetary systems. So is the value of Q fine-tuned? Yes, replies Rees, for:

> "If Q were smaller than 10^{-6}, gas would never condense into gravitationally bound structures at all, and such a universe would remain forever dark and featureless.... On the other hand, a universe where Q were substantially larger than 10^{-5} ... would be a turbulent and violent place."[20]

[**Note:** just as 10^6 means one followed by six zeros (that is one million), so 10^{-6} means one divided by one million, or one millionth].

THE SIXTH NUMBER: NO PLACE FOR HOGWARTS

In one sense, the sixth number is the easiest to grasp—but at the same time it could be the most mysterious. It is the number of dimensions in space. Imagine for a moment that you are a two-dimensional inhabitant of a two-dimensional world. Your alimentary tract (food in, waste out) would divide your body into two parts joined only by the top of your head, which would at best be inconvenient and at worst fatal. No nerve or blood vessel could cross another without a set of traffic lights, and there would be so many of those that gridlock would ensue. You couldn't see sideways and there would be nothing straight ahead to look at because it would exist only in a third dimension. (Homework: design a two-dimensional living creature in which these problems are overcome. Take your time.) No, clearly, you wouldn't want to live in a 2D world.

How about a world with four space dimensions? At first sight, that would provide a lot more scope for designer organisms. Think of all the extra storage space it would afford and the traffic congestion it would avoid. When driving in heavy city traffic, I have found there is only one rule of the road you need to remember—never occupy the same road space at the same time as another vehicle. This simple but effective precept actually helps us to envisage how a 4D world might work, because we can imagine time, relieved of its one-directional limitations, as a fourth space dimension. Think it through: it might even allow me to be in two different places at the same (fifth-dimensional) time.

This thought-experiment creates a *spatial* 4D world that we can at least imagine. So let us now ask what is meant by an "orbit" in such a world. The answer? There can be no such thing! Why not? Because the timelines of star and planet, which are necessarily identical in a 3D universe, would be decoupled in our 4D simulation. What was formerly a one-dimensional, one-way timeline in 3D now has the same properties as the three original dimensions of space—allowing an object to move to any position it likes in that dimension. As a result, the sun can go anywhere it chooses in the fourth dimension, as also can the planet; there is nothing to make them move in concert. The planet's path relative to the star might, for example, be a spiral. Gravitational attraction would still exist, but the planet no longer has to follow an orbit in a plane that passes through the sun—its position relative to the star in the new fourth dimension would depend on its velocity along the new dimension. It seems to me, therefore, that the concept of an orbit, and all that goes with it in terms of habitable zones and goldilocks conditions, vanishes in a 4D universe, along with the possibility of planetary life.

One last thought. Why should there be a whole number of dimensions? The fictional wizard Harry Potter caught the train to Hogwarts on platform nine-and-three-quarters, as the "Historic UK" travel guide explains:

> "For those of you that have ever read a Harry Potter book or seen one of the films, Platform 9¾ needs no introduction. For those of you who haven't, this pseudofictional location at Kings Cross train station is where the Hogwarts Express begins its long journey to Hogwarts School."[21]

But even in string theory, which needs at least ten dimensions of space[22], there's no such thing as nine-and-a-half dimensions. You can have as many dimensions as you like in physics but there can only be a whole number of them. This fact in itself could be seen as an exotic example of fine-tuning.

(**Caveat:** in mathematical topology as distinct from physics, there are things called Hausdorff dimensions which *can* take noninteger values and are useful in describing fractals and similar "sets." You can look it up on the internet but unless you're a topologist I don't recommend it.)

Conclusion

This chapter has put flesh on the bones of fine-tuning. We have only considered the six fine-tuned quantities that Martin Rees chose to illustrate the wider picture of a universe that is surprisingly suited to play host to life. Some will say that the majority of our cosmos is horrendously inhospitable to life, and this is no doubt true. But that doesn't alter the fact that we live in a universe having the fundamental properties necessary for our existence, and that is what demands an explanation. So can it be explained by invoking a multiverse, as Martin Rees suggests? We'll try to answer that question in the next chapter.

ENDNOTES:

[1] Hoyle, Fred; "The Universe: Past and Present Reflections," in *The Annual Review of Astronomy and Astrophysics,* 20 (1982) p. 16

[2] Rees, Martin; *Just Six Numbers* (Basic Books, 2000) p. 4.

[3] Rees, Martin; *Just Six Numbers, loc. cit.*

[4] Hoyle, Fred, *loc. cit.*

[5] Gribbin, John; *In Search of the Multiverse* (Penguin, London, 2010) p. 39.

[6] Dyson, Freeman; *Disturbing the Universe* (Harper and Row, New York, 1979).

[7] Hawking, Stephen; *A Brief History of Time* (Bantam Books, 1988) p. 125.

[8] Davies, Paul; *The Goldilocks Enigma,* (Penguin, London, 2007).

[9] Davies, Paul; *The Mind of God* (Simon & Shuster, New York, 1992) p. 169.

[10] https://www.facebook.com/afortuneuniverse/?notif_t=fbpage_fan_invite&notif_id=1463963309639596

[11] Stenger, Victor; *The fallacy of fine-tuning* (Prometheus Books, 2011).

[12] *The Evening News*, London, 4 December 1967

[13] Barnes, Luke; Cornell University Library arXiv:1112.4647v2 [physics. hist-ph].

[14] http://www.allaboutphilosophy.org/teleological-argument.htm

[15] Most of the source references to these quantities may be found in Ross, Hugh; *The Creator and the Cosmos, 3rd edition* (NavPress, Colorado Springs, 2001) pp. 145–157, 245–248.

[16] Barnes, Luke; *loc. cit.* p. 33.

[17] Rees, Martin; *loc.cit.* p. 4.

[18] This 'solar-system' picture of the atom is not strictly correct; the electrons don't occupy orbits in the planetary sense but occupy 'energy-levels' which can change but only by whole quanta of energy. An electron can be 'excited' to a higher level (by heating, for example) and then drop back to its original level by emitting light.

[19] For more detailed information see http://map.gsfc.nasa.gov/universe/ uni_shape.html

[20] Rees, Martin; *loc. cit.* p. 128

[21] http://www.historic-uk.com/HistoryMagazine/DestinationsUK/ Harry-Potter-Platform-9-Three-Quarters

[22] String theory is explained in a layperson-friendly in Chapter 3 of my book *Who made God?* (EP Books, Darlington, 2009).

CHAPTER 5

It's strange how many serious scientists are willing to embrace pseudoscience, but the current enthusiasm of leading cosmologists like Sir Martin Rees and Stephen Hawking for the multiverse is a striking example. They propose that the cosmos in which we live is just one of many universes, perhaps even an infinite number. However, I label it pseudoscience because there is no experimental evidence for such a "multiverse." But might a belief in the multiverse be justified in the absence of such evidence by appealing to theoretical models? So let's be fair and take a close look at the most popular multiverse theories. We shall consider several conflicting versions of the multiverse to which I'll give the following homely names; the "home-alone multiverse"; the "patchwork quilt multiverse"; "the eternal inflation multiverse"; and "the quantum cat universe." In the process we'll uncover both their admitted ingenuity and the inherent failings and fallacies that each of them displays. Why do intelligent people indulge in such speculations? Because they offer an escape route from things that science cannot, or does not want to, explain—such as the implications of quantum strangeness and cosmic fine-tuning. It's a shame that that the problems they create are bigger than the ones they claim to solve.

DEUTSCH'S DAUNTLESS DINOSAURS

Exploring the mega-multiverse

"The true multiverse idea strikes at the heart of our understanding of science, addressing puzzles such as the reason why the laws of physics are the way they are, and why the universe is a comfortable home for life…. Universes in which dinosaurs have developed cities, space-probes and computers using silicon-based microchips undoubtedly exist."

JOHN GRIBBIN, *IN SEARCH OF THE MULTIVERSE*, 2010.[1]

W e'll get to the dinosaurs later but let's begin with Alexander the Great, who is said to have wept when he realized there were no more lands he could conquer. In his essay *On Contentment of the Mind*, the Greek historian Plutarch (46–120 AD) wrote, "Alexander cried when he heard Anaxarchus talk about the infinite number of worlds in the universe. One of Alexander's friends asked him what was the matter and he replied: 'There are so many worlds, and I have not yet conquered even one.'" In the light of our present discussion, his words sound eerily prophetic.[2] Fortunately, some modern scientists are made of sterner stuff than Alexander. Tired of exploring our own universe, they have invented a huge number of alternative universes and set out to conquer them—at least in terms of speculative thought. But they don't stop there: there are at least five different versions of the multiverse and they are by no means mutually compatible. If the collective noun for universes is "multiverse," what, I wonder, is the collective noun for multiverses? Megamultiverse? Ultraverse? Polymultiverse? I'll settle for the first of these, but whatever label we adopt, there appears to be a supermarket where we can take our pick and select whichever multiverse (MV for short) we prefer.

Professor David Deutsch is a physicist and author of a book entitled *The Fabric of Reality*.[3] Popular science writer John Gribbin declares:

> "Deutsch is completely convinced of the reality of the multiverse, and takes the Many Worlds Interpretation [see later] entirely at face value. He accepts that there is, for example, a vast array of universes with different versions of himself in them, so that in some he is (not 'might be' but really is) a professor in Cambridge instead of working in Oxford, while in others he is not a scientist at all."[4]

Gribbin isn't being funny; he is himself quite convinced about the reality of some kind of multiverse.

Admittedly, neither Deutsch nor Gribbin can see, hear, or otherwise communicate with their multiversal cousins. Indeed, these *doppelgängers* are utterly undetectable and unknowable. But the current enthusiasm for MVs among leading scientists, like Sir Martin Rees and Stephen Hawking, must surely mean that the MV is *there*— its constituent universes perhaps only millimeters away from one another in multidimensional space like so many superimposed snap-shots? Well, actually, no. What we shall see in this chapter is that the MV concept is a bit like a get-out-of-jail-free card in the game of Monopoly—an escape route or bolt hole from various unwelcome difficulties and implications thrown up by modern physics and cosmology. Instead of struggling with the intransigent realities of the one universe we actually know, we can explain away these difficulties by invoking the MV. It intrigues me that some of the MV's greatest enthusiasts accuse theists of appealing to a "God of the gaps" to account for things that science cannot explain, while they themselves claim that one or more inaccessible multiverses can explain otherwise inexplicable scientific observations. But as Luke Barnes says:

> "The main selling point for multiverse theory—all those other universes with different fundamental constants—will forever remain beyond observational confirmation. And even if we postulate a multiverse, we would still need a more fundamental theory to explain how all these universes are generated, which could raise all ... kinds of fine-tuning problems."[5]

In reality, the MV is the ultimate speculation-of-the-gaps, being (almost by definition) that which lies beyond the reach of science. This statement will be challenged, so let me elaborate. One attraction of the MV is that the laws of nature could be different in different universes. There are exceptions, but the MV loses much of its appeal (and indeed purpose) if all those other universes work, scientifically speaking, in the same way as our own. Yet the only science known to man is that which explores and describes the universe in which we actually live. Our own "local" science cannot (again by definition) be used to investigate, or even recognize, alleged universes which may operate on different principles and according to different laws of nature. Any such exouniverse remains firmly beyond the reach of science as we know it.

So let's see how the various MV scenarios stand up to the *real* realities of life and logic. I'll give them names now and then look at some of them more closely in the following pages. Brian Greene helpfully lists most of them in his book *The Hidden Reality*[6] and where his names differ from my own I'll put his titles in square brackets. They are, respectively: the "home-alone [anthropic or landscape] multiverse"; the "patchwork quilt [quilted] multiverse"; "the eternal inflation multiverse"; "the quantum cat universe" [the quantum multiverse, otherwise known as "the Many Worlds hypothesis"]. This list is not exhaustive and, for example, I won't cover the "brane multiverse" or the ultraspeculative "holographic multiverse" that even Brian Greene struggles to describe in his book. Don't get nervous; all will become clear.

THE HOME-ALONE MULTIVERSE

The "home alone," "anthropic," or "landscape" MV is the bargain-basement article discussed earlier and which Martin Rees favors in his book *Just Six Numbers*. It claims that our own universe is indeed rare or even unique in its ability to sustain life but that this is just a lucky accident. There exist such a vast number of universes with different laws and constants of nature that, by sheer luck, one of them had to be just right for life. However, lurking in the shadow of the anthropic MV is the unavoidable idea that the laws and constants of nature are arbitrary and fortuitous. They can take on any character or value they care to, and *must do so* in an infinite[7] array of universes. If this is so, there can be no rationality in the laws we observe in our own cosmos—and thus no rationality in the science that depends on their existence. There is, of course, the proviso that the laws and constants in any one universe must not be mutually contradictory, but even then they might change arbitrarily from place to place or time to time. The chaotic state of affairs I have just described should be deeply troubling to any thoughtful person because it implies that the holy grail of physical science—the "theory of everything" diligently sought by scientists since Albert Einstein set us on its trail—is an illusion. If an MV exists in which the laws of nature vary arbitrarily from one universe to the next there can be nothing fundamental or even meaningful about these laws (and the constants that go with them) in *any universe including our own*. The dilemma is well summarized by MIT physicist Alan P. Lightman, writing in *Harper's Magazine* in 2011:[8]

"Dramatic developments in cosmological findings and thought have led some of the world's premier physicists to propose that our universe is only one of an enormous number of universes with wildly varying properties, and that … features of our particular universe are … a random throw of the cosmic dice. In which case, there is no hope of ever explaining our universe … in terms of fundamental causes and principles…. [cosmologist] Alan Guth … says the multiple-universe idea severely limits our hopes of understanding the world from fundamental principles. And the philosophical ethos of science is torn from its roots."

You may not personally be overly concerned about the philosophical ethos of science but, surprisingly perhaps, it does affect the outlook of society generally. During the past two centuries, modern science has transformed both our way of life and our understanding of the cosmos—and thus of ourselves. Most of the pioneers of modern science were not only men and women of science but also of faith, believing that their research was, in some way, uncovering "the mind of God" evidenced by an orderly cosmos. Even Stephen Hawking seemed to accept this concept in his 1988 book *A Brief History of Time*.[9] But that ethos has been swept away, and science is today commonly recruited to promote agnosticism, atheism or mere indifference to anything of a spiritual nature. At a popular level at least, science is being used (wrongfully and aggressively) to convert Western society to materialism. That is its current ethos and we need to recognize and beware of it. When Lightman says "the philosophical ethos of science is torn from its roots" he is simply pointing out that the MV hypothesis undermines the age-old concept of an orderly and rational creation on which modern science has hitherto been grounded. It's a classic case of sawing off a tree branch while sitting on the wrong side of the saw-cut. Lightman continues by quoting Nobel Prize-winning physicist Steven Weinberg;

> "If the multiverse idea is correct, the style of fundamental physics
> will be radically changed ... [and] the historic mission
> of physics to explain all the properties of our universe in
> terms of fundamental principles ... is futile, a beautiful
> philosophical dream that simply isn't true. Theoretical physics
> is the deepest and purest branch of science. It is the outpost of
> science closest to philosophy and religion.... The underlying
> hope and belief of this enterprise has always been that these

basic principles are so restrictive that only one, self-consistent universe is possible, like a crossword puzzle with only one solution."

Verdict: The "home-alone MV" fails because it makes the constants and/ or laws of nature arbitrary and liable to random variation from one supposed universe to another. It thus undermines the age-old concept of an orderly and rational creation on which modern science has hitherto been grounded. It requires us to abandon the idea that the physical cosmos is governed by *unique and necessary* laws of nature which Man can seek out using the methods and techniques of science.

THE PATCHWORK MULTIVERSE

Our next version of the MV is described in some detail by Brian Greene in his book *The Hidden Reality* and pictures the universe as a three-dimensional analogue of a two-dimensional patchwork quilt. The patchwork MV has the advantage that it does not require the laws of nature to vary from one universe to another, which is a decided improvement on the home-alone multiverse. Instead, it majors on the idea that our "patch" of the overall universe is reproduced many times in regions of space that we cannot observe. The two-dimensional patchwork quilt is just a model that helps us visualize a 3D reality in which our observations of the cosmos are restricted to a spherical volume of space centered on ourselves as observers.

This theory is based on the fact that no observer within the universe can ever see the whole universe; there is always a "cosmic horizon" beyond which nothing is visible. To explain why, imagine that you, the observer, are standing on a sea cliff watching a ship sail off into the distance. Eventually the ship will disappear from sight, but why should it do so? There are several possible reasons but the one that concerns us here is that the ship has passed beyond the horizon. That is, your line of sight has been cut off by the curvature of the Earth and light rays from the ship simply cannot reach your eyes.

To apply this illustration, we need to realize that when we look out into space we are also looking back in time. This is because light from distant stars takes time to reach the observer. Even when we look at our own sun, we are seeing it as it was eight minutes earlier, since that is the time it takes for light to travel the 93 million miles that separate the sun from Earth. More remote stars and galaxies are so far away that their distance is measured not in miles but in "light years"—the number of years it takes for light to travel across the intervening space. The nearest-neighbor star to the sun, *Proxima Centauri*, is 4.24 light years away, while the most distant galaxy so far observed lies about 13.3 billion light years from Earth.[10]

We next have to factor in the expansion of the universe, where the speed at which a galaxy is receding from us is proportional to its distance from us. So what happens when a galaxy is so far away that its speed of recession reaches the speed of light itself? Answer: it passes beyond our cosmic "horizon" and we can no longer see it. The "horizon" in this case is nothing to do with cosmic curvature but is caused by the expansion of space and the finite speed of light. (Note that although nothing can travel *through* space faster than the speed of light, *space itself* can expand faster than light.)

The practical effect? Beyond the cosmic horizon lie regions of space that we can neither see nor communicate with. We live in a *visible* universe that is restricted to a sphere centered on ourselves as observers. Beyond our horizon there could be other observers living in their own cosmic bubbles, who are just as ignorant of our existence as we are of theirs. Pictured in two dimensions for simplicity, this array of bubbles can be likened to a patchwork quilt in which each patch is isolated from those around it by its own cosmic horizon and can have no influence upon them. This in itself wouldn't constitute a multiverse, since there is no reason to think that regions of space outside our own patch are any different in essence from our own. To construct a credible multiverse, we would need some *additional* factor, and this is where the patchwork MV comes in—and also runs into trouble.

The additional ingredient is the idea that there are only a limited number of ways in which matter and energy can be arranged within a given patch. If the universe is infinite in extent, it contains an infinite number of patches—and sooner or later there will be a patch that has to duplicate our own. This twin universe reproduces the precise arrangement of atoms, molecules, force fields, and energy concentrations that make up our own visible cosmos. In other words, somewhere "over the rainbow" of our cosmic horizon there's a land *exactly* like our own, and this is repeated *ad infinitum*. So precise must this reproduction be that you have an infinite number of twins, in an infinitude of other patches, doing just what you are doing in yours. It gets even more exciting, of course, if you allow some minor rearrangements of matter and energy rather than a precise duplication. Then the "you" in another patch might be eating a pizza while you are enjoying a hamburger. The possibilities are endless.

The whole argument is, of course, highly suspect. As Brian Greene confesses, it is based on the materialistic assumption that everything that exists and happens in our universe arises exclusively from the arrangement and rearrangement of matter and energy. He writes:

> "I believe that a physical system is completely determined by the arrangement of its particles…. The position that makes most

> sense to me is that one's physical and mental characteristics
> are nothing but a manifestation of how the particles in one's
> body are arranged. Specify the particle arrangement and
> you've specified everything."[11]

To say this "begs the question" is the understatement of the year. Even if it were true, we have to ask what determines the arrangement of particles. Do they arrange themselves, and if so, what rules do they follow in the process? Are we not personally involved moment by moment in deciding how these particles are arranged? For example, I just reworded the previous sentence; so does this mean that my ghost in another universe had no option but to do *exactly* the same? To validate his argument, Greene must adopt the position of absolute determinism and assume that we actually have no choice or free will. Yet to do so he would have to reject quantum mechanics, especially Heisenberg's uncertainty principle, though in fact he frequently appeals to it. And is he not aware that life is based primarily on *information* which is nonmaterial, rather than simply on chemistry and physics? It is the information stored in the DNA of living things that guide the chemistry of life, not the other way about. And those are just objections from science, without beginning to think about philosophy, spirituality, and God.

Verdict: The patchwork MV fails on three counts. Firstly, it assumes without justification that the universe is so large that the "patches" of which it consists outnumber the possible arrangements of particles in any patch. Secondly, it requires that everything in the physical cosmos is reducible to arrangements of particles. Such absolute determinism is incompatible with quantum mechanics. Thirdly, it assumes that all *nonphysical* entities (from mathematics to morals, faith to feelings, philosophy to God) can *also* be reduced to arrangements of particles—a view that self-destructs by undermining the validity of the very mental processes that gave it birth.

THE ETERNAL INFLATION MULTIVERSE

We all know that inflation is a problem in advanced economies, but that's nothing compared to the problem it causes in cosmology (where, of course, it means something completely different). Most experts subscribe to the idea that the universe, as we know it, began its existence in a so-called "big bang," but there's a special difficulty with this theory. The Earth is bathed in a "cosmic microwave background (CMB)" which consists of low-frequency radiation coming from space in all directions. It is believed to represent the dying embers of the big bang. The interesting thing is that this radiation is amazingly uniform, having the same wavelength (and thus temperature) regardless of the direction from which it comes. This implies that the temperature of the whole cosmos was also the same everywhere during the big bang. But that wouldn't have been possible in a simple model of the expanding universe.[12] Cosmologists therefore introduced a modification known as "Inflationary Theory" (see later), which solves the problem by invoking the idea that the universe expanded faster than light during a brief early phase of its existence. (Reminder: nothing can travel faster than light *through* space, but theory allows *space itself* to expand faster than light.) But while inflation solved one problem, it created new ones. Writing in *Discovery Magazine* on 20th February 2015, physicist Max Tegmark, a keen protagonist of multiverses, nevertheless comments as follows:

"Physics is all about predicting the future from the past, but
inflation seems to sabotage this: when we try to predict the

probability that something particular will happen, inflation always gives the same useless answer: infinity divided by infinity. The problem is that whatever experiment you make, inflation predicts that there will be infinitely many copies of you far away in our infinite space, obtaining each physically possible outcome, and despite years of tooth-grinding in the cosmology community, no consensus has emerged on how to extract sensible answers from these infinities. So strictly speaking, we physicists are no longer able to predict anything at all!"[13]

So be warned: the "eternal inflation" MV is built on cosmological quicksand. The theory of inflation was introduced to explain some puzzling features of the universe as we observe it today—specifically (1) its overall uniformity, as mentioned above; (2) its "flatness" as discussed in Ch. 4; and (3) the low entropy (high orderliness) the universe must have had at its inception (which also gives rise to the arrow of time as discussed in Ch. 8 of my book *Who made God?*). Briefly, the theory runs as follows. Having started in some unknown way, the universe sat quietly as a tiny "seed" long enough to attain thermal equilibrium, that is, to have the same temperature everywhere. The space within the seed was suffused by a mysterious and hypothetical "inflaton field." ("Inflaton" is not a misprint but an invented word; a "field" is something that permeates space invisibly but has the power to make things happen—like the electromagnetic fields that brings messages to your TV or cell phone.) Because of this inflaton field, the tiny cosmic seed had the potential to become one or more universes like our own, just as an acorn has the potential to grow into a mighty oak. How did this happen? According to inflation theory, the inflaton field acted like a negative pressure causing the seed to expand

and encompass more space. But because the field was *a property of space itself*, the more space it created the greater became the energy it contained. As a result, the total energy of the field built up exponentially, driving the expansion of space faster and faster until the speed of expansion was orders of magnitude greater than the speed of light. This inflationary phase of the early universe lasted only seconds but caused the tiny seed to grow to the immeasurable size of our present universe.

MOLEHILLS AND VOLCANOES

That's just the beginning of the story, but let's pause for breath and try to visualize all this by thinking of the birth of a volcano. The volcano begins life no larger than a molehill but as molten rock (magma) is forced up from below and flows out from the volcanic pipe, it solidifies and begins to build a volcanic cone. The magma in this illustration represents the inflaton field and the growing mountain represents the expanding universe. But we now have to imagine something that doesn't happen with volcanoes, namely, that the amount of magma it produces increases in proportion to the size of the mountain. This represents the idea that the total energy of the inflaton field rises in proportion to the amount of space in the universe. The effect is obvious. The growth of our volcano becomes exponential because the bigger it gets the more magma it produces. This mirrors the exponential growth of space under the influence of the inflaton field.

However, sooner or later the pressure forcing the magma to the surface will be relieved and although the volcano may still remain active, any further mountain building will be slow. This represents the end of the inflationary phase of the universe. A further point: the growing volcano not only pictures the expanding universe but also involves solidification of the liquid magma into rock. By analogy, as the growing universe cools, the energy of the inflaton field "solidifies" into a host of subatomic particles—which constitute the matter and radiation that populate our familiar universe.

But doesn't that still leave us with just one universe? Not necessarily, says the "eternal inflation" scenario. Let's revisit our volcano. Suppose the underground reservoir of magma is, in fact, unlimited. Suppose also that instead of forcing its way to the surface as one volcano, it erupts through a large number of fissures to create a landscape dotted with volcanoes. And further imagine that this doesn't happen all at once but that new volcanoes are constantly popping up throughout the unlimited future. Each volcano goes through the sequence I described earlier (molehill, eruption, inflation, cooling and solidification) and each volcano represents a brand-new universe separated from past and present universes by as-yet unbroken ground. Hey, presto! We have created the "eternal inflation multiverse"—composed of past, present, and future universes (each of which is unaware that the others exist, for reasons I won't go into here).

You may complain that I've forgotten to tell you exactly what the inflaton field is. I haven't forgotten; it's just that no one has the slightest idea what it is, where it came from, and even whether it actually exists. It might be related in some way to "dark energy" but since this is an equally mysterious field (inferred indirectly from its effects), this doesn't really help. Confronted with the shifting sands of "eternal inflation" theory, I feel like someone invited to climb to a higher level of cosmic comprehension on a ladder of mathematical theory. When the climber points out that most of the rungs are missing, his protests are met with an assurance, "Don't worry, the rungs really are there; it's just that they are hypothetical, so up you go!"

Verdict: The eternal inflation multiverse fails on account of these "missing rungs." What are they? Firstly, there's inflation theory itself. Remember Max Tegmark"s statement which began this section, "When we try to predict the probability that something particular will happen, inflation always gives the same useless answer." Secondly, the inflaton field which (along with its hypothesized properties) remains completely unknown as to its physical nature or source. Thirdly, the idea, based on mathematics rather than physics, that an inflationary scenario must be repeated over and over again to provide a multiverse. I advise you to avoid that ladder until some solid rungs are installed.

The quantum cat multiverse

Otherwise known as the quantum MV or Many Worlds Hypothesis, this was one of the earliest multiverse proposals, advanced by Hugh Everett in 1955. But before we get to that, let me explain how a cat got into the act.

Erwin Schrödinger, one of the founding fathers of quantum mechanics, proposed an experiment involving a cat. Fortunately for the cat it was a "thought experiment"—no real cat was involved and there's no need to report the matter to the RSPCA.[14] In the experiment, a cat is placed in a box along with a radioactive atom, a Geiger counter, and a poison capsule that breaks if the Geiger counter records the arrival of an electron or photon. As long as the radioactive atom remains unobserved, quantum theory deems it to be in a "superposition" of states in which, during a given interval of time, it has *both* (1) remained undecayed *and* (2) has decayed (releasing an electron or photon). In case (1) of course, the cat comes to no harm, but in case (2) the Geiger counter is activated, the poison released, and the cat is dead. Until the box is opened, Schrödinger maintained, the *unobserved* cat is also in a superposition of states, being both dead and alive at the same time. Only when an observer opens the box does the cat's "wave function" (which describes superposed quantum states) collapse to reveal either a live cat or a dead one (but not both). His aim was to show that such a ridiculous outcome must signify that quantum mechanics was, at that time, an incomplete theory. However, it was quickly pointed out that the activation of the Geiger counter is itself an act of observation; wave functions don't necessarily need a *conscious* observer to make them collapse into a single reality. Nevertheless, Schrödinger's cat lives on (so to speak) and the cat paradox is still debated today.

The reason I tell the story is this. It is the nature of atomic and subatomic quantum systems to exist in superimposed states until something happens to make their wave functions "collapse" into one or other of the states. When collapse occurs, there is no longer any uncertainty about the state of the system, which behaves in a classical manner (meaning it is no longer subject to quantum effects). Wave function collapse can be caused by an experimental observation of a quantum system or by interaction with other particles (this is called "decoherence," which routinely happens when the quantum system is just part of some larger object). However, the cause of wavefunction collapse is still a mystery and the subject of much debate.

Everett's solution to the problem was radical. He suggested that wave functions never actually collapse into one or other of their superimposed states but that *both* states live on in *different* worlds. Thus, in one world the cat is alive and in the other world the cat is dead. Every time any quantum system seems to suffer wave function collapse, he claimed, a split occurs and two new worlds are created—in each of which, one of the originally superimposed states survives. If Everett was right, you have probably created a zillion new worlds as your quantum-controlled brain cells puzzle over the last few paragraphs.

You will never know, of course, since the many different worlds so created are beyond our reach and we cannot communicate with them as they go their separate ways in an ever-growing multiverse. However, in David Deutsch's version of the "many worlds hypothesis," there is some weak interaction between adjacent universes—"interferences" that might explain some of the strange effects of quantum mechanics[15] in any one universe.

So, apart from offering a highly exotic explanation of wave function collapse and certain other mysteries of quantum theory (including quantum computing), what's the point of the quantum multiverse, seeing that there are alternative explanations of these things? Deutsch argues that he is seeking ultimate truth[16] and that his MV really does represent "the fabric of reality." But here are some of the problems with his claim.

Firstly, it leads us down the "yellow brick road"[17] of science fiction rather than truth. According to John Gribbin,[18] Deutsch believes that "universes in which dinosaurs have developed cities, spaceprobes, and computers using silicon-based microchips 'undoubtedly' exist, because *that's what the laws of physics tell us*." I have italicized the last statement for two reasons. (1) It isn't true, and (2) it exemplifies a faulty argument that frequently lies hidden in multiverse scenarios. This argument can be loosely summarized as follows. "If I can devise an elegant mathematical formula that describes some unobservable entity, then that entity must exist, even if no possible experiment could prove it." As physicist Lee Smolin warns, "Lots of beautiful [scientific] theories have turned out to have nothing to do with nature."[19]

Secondly, it dehumanizes Man. If you visit a hall of mirrors you may find two full-length mirrors facing each other and set strictly parallel. If you stand between the mirrors you will see in each mirror an apparently infinite series of your own reflections. However, there is only one real you; all the other images are truly "imaginary." But in Deutsch's multiverse, his innumerable *alter egos* are as real as himself. It's no use asking, "Please, will the real David Deutsch stand up" because there is no real person (that is, someone with a definable identity) to respond. He claims that in another universe he might not be a scientist. Presumably he could be a taxi driver or a fishmonger, and might ridicule the very idea of the multiverse. Alternatively, he could be a rapist or murderer. Or even a computer-literate dinosaur. Why not? In the quantum MV, anything goes. So who or what exactly is David Deutsch? In his multiverse he exists only as an option, not a person. I would prefer to think more highly of him (and everyone else) than that.

Verdict: The quantum multiverse fails firstly because although it offers an explanation of certain observed quantum effects (albeit an extravagant one), its predictions also embrace nonsensical science-fiction scenarios. Secondly, it dehumanizes Man by confusing and ultimately destroying the identity of individual persons.

AN OVERALL FAILURE

Exponents of multiverse theories give their books grandiose titles like *The Fabric of Reality* (Deutsch), *The Hidden Reality* (Greene), and *The Grand Design* (Hawking) but they rapidly get lost in a jungle of unreality. It has been said that neurotics build castles in the air, psychotics lives in them, and psychiatrists collect the rent. Scientists who urge upon us the "reality" of their mathematical castles-in-the-air are neither neurotics nor psychotics (though they might, of course, be psychiatrists). They are among the most intelligent of people. But their supposed "realities," when examined in the cold light of day, turn out to be mirages masquerading as science. They certainly do nothing to advance our understanding of ourselves but serve only to dehumanize Man—with the added unintended consequences of casting doubt on the rationality of science and on the validity of their own thought processes. So why do they do it? The one common factor is a determination to exclude from their worldviews any trace of "God, who made the world and all that is in it" and in whom "we live and move and have our being" (Acts 17:24, 28). We won't find the answer to the question "What is Man?" in the multiversal supermarket, so we had better look elsewhere.

ENDNOTES:

[1] Gribbin, John; *In Search of the Multiverse* (Penguin, London, 2009) p. 62 and p. 8.

[2] See http://www.pothos.org/content/indexa410.html?page=quotes

[3] Deutsch, David; *The Fabric of Reality: The Science of Parallel Universes and Its Implications* (Allen Lane/The Penguin Press, New York, 1997).

[4] Gribbin, John; *loc.cit.* p. 62.

[5] Barnes, Luke; "Human Uniqueness in the Cosmos," *The New Atlantis*, http://www.thenewatlantis.com/publications/the-fine-tuning-of-natures-laws

[6] Greene, Brian; *The Hidden Reality* (Allen Lane, Penguin Books, London, 2011).

[7] Proponents of this view are not actually obliged to invoke an "infinite" number of alternative universes but use figures like 10^{500} (one followed by 500 zeros) as the number of universes required by their theory. This, of course, remains an unimaginably huge number.

[8] Lightman, Alan; *Harper's Magazine*, December 2011.

[9] Hawking, Stephen; *A Brief History of* Time (Bantam Press, 1988) p. 175.

[10] See more at: http://www.space.com/18502-farthest-galaxy-discovery-hubble-photos.html#sthash.s5n1YKM7.dpuf

[11] Greene, Brian; *loc. cit.* pp. 33–34.

[12] Greene, Brian; *loc. cit.* pp. 41–44.

[13] Tegmark, Max; in *Discover Magazine*, http://blogs.discovermagazine.com/.../infinity-ruining-phys.../...

[14] RSPCA stands for the British animal rescue charity "The Royal Society for the Prevention of Cruelty to Animals."

[15] Quantum mechanics leads to some strange effects as discussed at length in Ch. 2 of "Who made God?"

[16] Johnson, George; www.nytimes.com/1997/10/05/books/shadow-worlds.html. In his review of *The Fabric of Reality*, writes: "The [book] is full of refreshingly oblique, provocative insights. But I came away from it with only the mushiest sense of how the strands in Deutsch's tapestry hang together. Early on he entertains the notion that, as he writes *The Fabric of Reality*, other David Deutsches in other universes are also writing books: many of those Davids are at this moment writing these very words. Some are putting it better. Others have gone for a cup of tea. I wish I could reach into one of those worlds and grab a clearer version of this perplexing book."

[17] The "Yellow Brick Road" was the magical road that led to the fictional land of Oz. It was first introduced in L. Frank Baum's book *The Wonderful Wizard of Oz*, published in 1900.

[18] Gribbin John; *loc. cit.* p. 62.

[19] Smolin, Lee; *The Trouble with Physics* (Penguin/Allen Lane, London, 2007) p. 194.

CHAPTER 6

"Plenty of animals can express the fact that they are hungry," wrote Julian Huxley in 1947, "but none except man can ask for an egg or a banana." You probably didn't need Huxley to tell you that. The differences between humans and even the most intelligent of other living creatures are not exactly subtle. We open this chapter by pointing out that human beings are, for example, the only life form known to worry about such things as death and taxes (the two things that Benjamin Franklin said were inevitable). But although everyone knows that Man is indeed unique, we are constantly assured by experts and media that we are, after all, nothing but clever apes. Evolution simply dealt us a good hand and gave us a lucky break. In this chapter we shall question that claim and find it cannot begin to explain what evolutionist Theodosius Dobzhansky called "the biological uniqueness of Man." We focus on the huge differences between ourselves and our alleged closest relative, the chimpanzee, and go in search of the "last common ancestor" (LCA) from which both species are said to have diverged some seven to thirteen million years ago. We are not alone in failing to identify any likely candidate. It turns out that common ancestors are decidedly uncommon, and the LCA we're looking for either never existed or else bore a surprising resemblance to a chimpanzee. And that leaves us with no materialistic explanation whatever for the amazing uniqueness of Man.

CHAPTER 6

DEATH AND TAXES

Human uniqueness

"The most pressing problems of evolutionary biology seem, at present, to belong to two groups—those concerned with the mechanics of evolution and those dealing with the biological uniqueness of man."

Theodosius Dobzhansky, 1958[1]

"Plenty of animals can express the fact that they are hungry, but none except man can ask for an egg or a banana."

Julian Huxley, 1947[2]

Writing to the French scientist Jean-Baptiste Leroy in 1789, Benjamin Franklin (1706–1790) declared, "Nothing is certain except death and taxes." Franklin was actually referring to the USA's Constitution which had been adopted in Philadelphia two years earlier, but the generality of his *bon mot* was quickly appreciated and widely quoted—and still is today.

What is seldom recognized, however, is the curious fact that among the millions of living species that inhabit planet Earth, the only one that actually cares about death and taxes is *Homo sapiens*—which neatly flags up the uniqueness of mankind among living organisms.

Man's uniqueness is something people take for granted. Yet at the same time we unthinkingly buy into the idea that we are just highly evolved animals who differ from our animal precursors only in degree and not in essence. This, at least, is the narrative that has come to dominate Western thought in recent decades—but is it true? In this chapter we'll begin to examine what Theodosius Dobzhansky called "the biological uniqueness of Man." (Dobzhansky was one of the founding fathers of the modern Darwinian evolutionary "synthesis.")

But let's start with taxes. They are by no means a recent innovation as some might think, but an almost inevitable consequence of the way human society works. Many other creatures form societies—from ants to elephants and bees to basking sharks—but they are blissfully ignorant of taxation. It is a phenomenon both unique to and universal among humans. Even the most primitive societies pay taxes in some form or other. They may consist of tribute to chiefs and rulers, or to witch doctors and shamans for protecting them from real or imagined evil. Material and monetary offerings to God or gods were (and still are) commonly used to support priestly castes. These may not be taxes as we know them, but a tax by any other name is still a tax. As far as I am aware, all developed civilizations, no matter how ancient, have had systems of taxation. I would be very surprised to learn of any human social structure that didn't tax its members in some way or another. Yet even the most highly organized animal societies, where every individual knows its place and function, are wholly innocent of the concept. This illustrates Raymond Tallis' argument (cited in Chapter 1) that "the human world is materially rooted in the natural world but is quite different from it. It is populated by individuals who are not just organisms ... [but] inhabit an acknowledged, shared public sphere, structured and underpinned by an infinity of abstractions, generalizations, customs, practices, norms, laws, institutions, facts and artifacts unknown to even the most social of animals."[3]

ATTITUDES TO DEATH

So much for taxes; what about death? This surely is common to all organisms? Yes, indeed, but the *attitude* to death adopted by human beings is decidedly different from that of every other sentient species. Most of us perceive death as a serious misfortune. It is something we don't like to talk about, yet it holds a strange and undeniable fascination for us. Pick up any daily newspaper and count how many column inches are devoted to death, whether through illness, accident, murder or war. My newspaper today has twenty-two pages of general and world news of which the equivalent of four pages are devoted to death in one form or another, plus a further three pages of formal obituaries (that's a total of 27 percent of relevant content). Bookshop shelves are loaded with "whodunnit" novels and murder mysteries, and most of us enjoy reading such material (as long as the culprit is suitably punished, of course). No TV drama or detective series is complete without multiple deaths. Our fear and fascination over death appears to be deeply ingrained.

Animals don't bury or cremate their dead but humans have always done so, usually with a degree of ceremony. There are some apparent exceptions. For example, a BBC website states, "Elephants are known to bury their own dead under foliage and often stay with the body, apparently in mourning. A cow whose calf has died will often stay with the dead baby for days, according to the Kenya Wildlife Service."[4] However, it is all too easy to attribute human thoughts to animals and such actions could be explained more simply. The mothers in question may simply be shielding from the elements what they think is a sick calf and waiting in the hope that it will recover. There have also been accounts of whales and dolphins gathering around a dead offspring and even carrying it for days on end. For example:

> "Scientists in the Red Sea observed … [a] bottlenose dolphin push a smaller, deceased dolphin through the water on its fin. The dolphin was badly decayed, and had probably been dead a while. A killer whale, called L72, which had recently given birth, was seen carrying a dead newborn in her mouth. 'She was trying to keep the [dead] calf up at the surface the entire time…,' says study coauthor Robin Baird…. 'The animals go through a period where they're experiencing the same kind of emotions you or I would when a loved one dies.'"[5]

However, such observations are rare (the report is based on just fourteen events) and the article sensibly warns, "When we hear news like this, we have to be careful to get all the facts and not anthropomorphize the situations…." As with the elephants, the behavior of these ocean mammals could arise from a belief that the offspring concerned are sick and might recover if protected and cared for. Why else would the air-breathing dolphin try to keep the dead calf above the surface? There really are no grounds for concluding that the animals concerned are mourning their dead as humans do.

Preparing for the afterlife

No animal provides its dead with equipment for the afterlife, but such practices abounded among ancient civilizations. For example, the "anthropology-world" website[6] cites a *National Geographic* article as follows:

> "*National Geographic* (2009) explored and discussed ancient Egyptians beliefs about life after death. According to Dr. Zahi Hawass, ancient Egyptians treated the afterlife as the beginning of a fascinating journey … [and] engaged in unprecedented preparations for death to … minimize the dangers on their way to the highest levels of resurrection and spirit. In Ancient Greece, [they] believed that to cross [the river] Styx and to enter the afterlife, the deceased had to pay several coins to the ferryman; for this reason, Greeks buried their dead with several coins in their mouths."

Many further examples can be given. The terracotta army buried with the first Chinese Emperor Qin Shihuangdi is a notable case:

> "Today the mausoleum complex is enormous, containing thousands of clay warriors as well as other artifacts. Uncovering all of that takes time, and the dig continues to this day. Each discovery within Qin's lavish mausoleum offers more proof that the emperor was determined to have every Earthly comfort, even in the afterlife."[7]

Anglo-Saxon kings were buried with boats, weapons, and other accoutrements deemed necessary for an afterlife befitting such august personages. A particularly fine example is the ship burial at Sutton Hoo in England, where:

> "The most significant artifacts from the ship burial, displayed in the British Museum, are those found in the burial chamber, including a suite of metalwork dress fittings in gold and gems, a ceremonial helmet, shield and sword, a lyre, and many pieces of silver plate from Byzantium. The ship burial has ... prompted comparisons with the world described in the heroic poem *Beowulf,* which is set in southern Sweden. It is in that region ... that close archaeological parallels to the ship burial are found, both in its general form and in details of the military equipment contained in the burial."[8]

These are just a few examples of a huge number of practices worldwide in which burial ceremonies and rituals demonstrate a belief in life after death. As the "anthropology-world" article concludes:

> "The results of the current analysis show that most societies treat death not as a transition into nothingness but to some other, unknown state (Parkes, Laungani and Young, 1997[9]). To ensure that this transition is smooth and nonproblematic, living people must engage in a predetermined set of rituals, in accordance with all cultural norms and expectations."

Whether or not any particular beliefs and practices are justified or mere superstitions is not the point at this juncture. Either way, they demonstrate that Man is unique in *perceiving* death as a transition rather than obliteration. This is true historically and remains true today.

BEHAVIOR, BIOLOGY AND BRAINS

So far in this chapter we've looked at just two example of the unique *behavior* of Man but, of course, behavior is far from being the whole story. Dobzhansky wrote of the *biological* uniqueness of Man in his 1958 article cited above. This might have been a Freudian slip, because his later writings on human uniqueness refer only to Man's *evolutionary* uniqueness (for example, "The evolutionary uniqueness of Man"[10] in *Evolutionary Biology Vol. 6*, 1995). *Biological* uniqueness is, of course, compatible with a nonevolutionary origin for Man. Either way, however, the uniqueness of Man among sentient creatures is incontestable.

Biological uniqueness can be roughly subdivided into bodily (anatomical or physiological) features and cognitive (mind-related) ones. Although body, behavior, and cognition are strongly interrelated, I'll put them into separate categories for convenience. And to keep this discussion within some kind of bounds, we'll concentrate on a single animal/human comparison, namely, the differences between Man and our allegedly closest animal relative, the chimpanzee. An article in *Genome Research in* 2005[11] addresses the differences between Man and chimpanzee as follows [note: the words "phenome" and "phenotype" refer to the sum of an organism's visible characteristics, including both appearance and behavior]:

> "We have many characteristics that are uniquely human. Table 1 lists some of the definite and possible phenotypic traits that appear to differentiate us from chimpanzees.... For the most part, we do not know which genetic features interact with the environment to generate these differences between the phenomes of our two species. The chimpanzee has also long

been seen as a model for human diseases because of its close
evolutionary relationship.... Nevertheless, it is a striking
paradox that chimpanzees are in fact not good models for
many major human diseases/conditions."[12]

A table[13] in the paper lists some 200 "phenotypic traits" of humans for
comparison with those of great apes under various headings. The list is
headed by cultural and behavioral differences with fifty-eight entries,
and cognitive (mind-related) and social differences with twenty-three
entries. But many other differences are listed in fields such as life
history, anatomy, physiology, reproductive biology, embryology, bio-
mechanics, cell biology, biochemistry, endocrinology, pharmacology,
pathology (diseases), dental biology, skin biology, nutrition, neuro-
anatomy, neurobiology, and neurochemistry. You don't have to know
what all these words mean to recognize the huge differences between
apes and Man that evolution, if true, must explain. It is at best a struggle and at worst a lost cause.

Putting aside for a moment the cognitive, social and behavioral
differences, here are some of the actual biological (anatomical and
physiological) features that distinguish humans from chimpanzees.
Prolonged helplessness of young; long childhood; adolescence; age
at first reproduction; longevity; bipedal gait; absence of skull crest
and brow ridge; inner ear canal orientation; bone cortex thickness;
laryngeal position; pharyngeal air sacs; earlobes; tear gland structure;
visible whites of the eyes; thumb movement; skeletal muscle strength;
fine motor coordination; hand-eye coordination; sustained running;
voluntary control of breathing; ability to swim; ability to swim underwater; and emotion-prompted tears.

But what is the point of such comparisons? Aren't many of these
differences obvious anyway? Perhaps so, but apparently not obvious

enough. Evolutionists have long claimed that humans and chimpanzees diverged from a common ancestor some five to seven million years ago, though recent studies have revised this upwards to 13 million years (see later). How do they know this? Because examination of chimp and human genomes (the totality of their respective DNAs[14]) suggest that Man shares with chimpanzees over 98 percent of his genes (DNA regions that contain the code to make proteins). They therefore conclude that chimps and humans must be separated by only a tiny step in evolutionary terms.

But this is simplistic. As we shall see in the next chapter, the difference between the genes is actually more like 4 percent—involving about 35 million single nucleotide differences in the DNA and 90 megabases ("Mb") of insertions and deletions ("indels"). One Mb is a million single "letters" in the DNA code, while indels are DNA sequences present in or missing from one or other of the two genomes in comparable regions. Moreover, genes constitute only about 3 percent of Man's genome, and the difference between the *complete genomes* of chimp and human may be as high as 30 percent.[15] To put this in perspective, while 96 percent of human genes are also found in chimps, we also share some 88 percent of our genes with mice, 73 percent with zebra fish, 47 percent with fruit flies, 38 percent with roundworms, and 18 percent with baker's yeast.[16] An even higher figure for fruit flies is given by the National Human Genome Research Institute (a division of USA's National Institutes of Health) which states:

> "A study discovered that about 60 percent of genes are conserved between fruit flies and humans, meaning that the two organisms appear to share a core set of genes. Two-thirds of human genes known to be involved in cancer have counterparts in the fruit fly."[17]

The lesson? Chimps are no more 96 percent human than fruit flies are 60 percent human. Evolution attributes these similarities to common descent, but all they really tell us is that to be alive on planet Earth, an organism needs certain indispensible proteins—to capture energy, ensure its structural integrity, and provide a basic cellular tool kit.

UNCOMMON ANCESTORS

The strange thing about evolution's common ancestors is that they are amazingly uncommon ("elusive" might be a better word). The problem is a general one which was highlighted in my 1978 book *From Nothing to Nature*.[18] You can draw a Darwinian "tree of life" that purports to show how all life forms have arisen from a single root via a trunk, separating into main side branches, then into smaller branches and so on—terminating in a vast number of twigs on the periphery of the tree's canopy. But where on this "tree of life" do we find all the life forms known to us today, whether living species or fossil remains?

Answer: as specialized organisms fully adapted to their environments, they are all located at the extreme ends of the outermost twigs. The multitude of alleged intermediate forms that in theory populate the inner regions of the canopy (and should be found sitting at every branch point) are simply not there. Every organism present in the modern biosphere or in the fossil record is a fully adapted life form showing no signs of wanting to become something else. The alleged common ancestors are at best hypothesized and at worst unknown. To repeat: common ancestors are uncommon, to say the least.

Let me illustrate this in relation to the alleged common ancestor of chimps and humans. A recent study published online in the *Proceedings of the National Academy of Sciences* is entitled *Fossil hominin shoulders support an African ape-like last common ancestor of humans and chimpanzees*. The research, it says, "suggests that the simplest explanation—that the [common] ancestor looked a lot like a chimpanzee or gorilla—is the right one, at least in the [shape of its] shoulder."[19] An identity parade featuring nothing more than "suggested shoulder shapes" is, I submit, unlikely to produce a convincing candidate. So let's try again. A 2013 article in the respected online journal *Phys.org*[20] offers a contrary theory;

> "The last common ancestor of Man and Ape was not a knuckle-walking, tree-swinging hominid resembling today's chimpanzee, said a study ... challenging some long-held theories of human evolution. Rather than a prototype chimp as commonly believed, our common forefather was an ape unlike any that exists today...."

The researchers themselves write:

> "Our ... reconstruction reveals that some Miocene apes represent a more appropriate model for the ancestral morphology from which hominins (humans and their ancestors) evolved than do (living) great apes.... The last common ancestor, whose identity remains uncertain, most likely walked around on all fours like today's apes, but leaning on its palms instead of front knuckles."

Notice that the common ancestor is "unidentified," its "identity remains uncertain," and it "most likely" walked on the palms of its hands. An online article from the University of California at Berkeley sums the matter up:[21]

"The narratives of human evolution are oft-told and highly
contentious. There are major disagreements.... Interpretations
of almost every new find will be sure to find opposition
among other experts. Disputes often center on diet and
habitat, and whether a given animal could walk bipedally
or was fully upright. What can we really tell about human
evolution from our current understanding of the phylogenetic
relations of hominids and the sequence of evolution of their
traits?... Hominid evolution should not be read as a march to
human-ness (even if it often appears that way from narratives
of human evolution)."

The article goes on at some length to remind the reader that Man
really is just another ape, and implies that looking for a specific common ancestor is rather pointless. Certainly, it offers no candidate
for this attractive but unoccupied post. "Where is the last common
ancestor of humans and chimps? "I would love to know" says Sergio
Almécija of the George Washington University in Washington, DC.
"That question is keeping me awake at night."[22]

HALDANE'S DILEMMA

In the next chapter we shall dig more deeply into the genetic similarities between chimps and humans, but there is one last matter that we
must examine here. In 1957, evolutionary biologist J. B. S. Haldane
published a calculation of the rate at which evolution by classical neo-
Darwinian processes should take place. Based on his assumptions, he
concluded that it takes on average 300 generations of an organism for
a novel version of a single gene (a new allele) to spread to all members
of a colony (and thus to become irreversibly "fixed" in the population). He wrote:

"The number of loci [genes] in a vertebrate species has been estimated at about 40,000. 'Good' species, even when closely related, may differ at several thousand loci.... If two species differ at 1000 loci and the mean rate of gene substitution as has been suggested is one per 300 generations, it will take 300,000 generations to generate an interspecific difference. It may take a good deal more...."[23]

This refers to a single interspecific difference (that is, a difference between species). If we take the 200 differences between chimps and humans discussed earlier and assume that phenotypic changes occur sequentially, this would mean 60 million generations—30 million between the last common ancestor (LCA) and chimps and 30 million between the LCA and Man. Of course, if several different genetic mutations were being introduced at the same time this number would be reduced accordingly, but it is widely recognized that such parallel changes in different genes rapidly reduce species viability as the number of such changes increases.[24]

Female chimpanzees usually give birth to their first offspring between the ages of eleven and twenty-three years,[25] but let's be generous and assume that a generation among primates represents as little as ten years. This gives 300 million years for the antiquity of the common ancestor—at least twenty times any conceivable evolutionary scenario. Simultaneous or parallel changes, if they occurred consistently, might reduce this by a factor of three or so. However, in this simple calculation we are attributing each of the 200 differences between chimps and humans to only a single protein difference, which is obviously not true. For example, how many genetic mutations would be required to produce the upright stance and bipedal gait that is unique to Man? Surely dozens, if not hundreds.

THE GENETIC WAITING ROOM

If you went into a surgery and found all the seats occupied by skeletons, you would conclude that the doctor had a waiting time problem. If Haldane is right, macroevolution is no more viable than the doctor's practice. Understandably, therefore, some biologists argue that evolution by random mutation and natural selection actually occurs far more rapidly than Haldane's calculation allows. One article even claims that "no more than 238 fixed beneficial mutations is what separates us from the last common ancestor of chimps and humans."[26] Others, however, disagree profoundly. In a detailed research paper entitled *The waiting time problem in a model hominin population*,[27] John Sanford and coauthors used an established modeling computer program, and generous assumptions for beneficial mutation rates, to estimate the time required for genes to evolve by neo-Darwinian mechanisms. [note: hominins are a group consisting of humans and their alleged apelike ancestors]. They write:

> "We have focused on the waiting time problem as it would apply
> to an evolving hominin population of 10,000–100,000....
> Our numerical simulations consistently reveal that in such
> a population the waiting time problem is profound. Even
> waiting for the fixation of a single point mutation ... is
> problematic. The waiting time for the establishment of such a
> simple event requires on average over 1.5 million years.... This
> is a very long time to wait for such a tiny genetic modification
> of a prehuman genome. It causes us to ask: 'Is such a long
> waiting time credible?'"

Needless to say, even if there were only 238 mutations separating us from the alleged common ancestor (and allowing for a limited degree of parallel evolution), the timescale on Sanford's calculation would still be far too long (of the order of 100 million years) to allow a credible evolutionary scenario.

A CURIOUS FACT

We shall have to leave the various protagonists fighting it out in their attempts to date the unknown common ancestor. Such a technical debate isn't going to be resolved in a popular-style book like this one. I really only want the reader to grasp one thing—the question of Man's biological ancestry remains unresolved, in spite of the confident assertions of the evolution-friendly mass media. But there is one final curious fact. If humans and chimpanzees did both arise from a common ancestor over a comparable timescale (however long that time might be) and given that mutation rates in modern chimps and Man are known to be the same, why is Man so much more highly "evolved" than his alleged cousin? In fact, if evolutionist Ian Musgrave is correct, the situation is even worse. He claims:

> "While we are around 240 genes away from the LCA [last common
> ancestor], we are around 594 genes away from the chimp,
> [so that] they have fixed about 50 percent more genes since
> the LCA than we have. Most of the genes substituted are for
> immune and reproductive system genes, and only a handful
> seem to have anything to do directly with brain function."[28]

This can only mean that chimps have actually evolved from the alleged common ancestor 50 percent faster than humans. How can it be, then, that the LCA was *itself* a great ape and (according to some anthropologists) uncommonly like a chimpanzee? There are only two possible answers. Either there was no common ancestor, or else chimps wasted their beneficial mutations on keeping fit and having kids. By contrast Man, while not neglecting his "immune and reproductive system genes," also used his smaller set of mutations to master fire, invent language, do cave-painting, write music, learn mathematics, discover DNA, and build zoos to accommodate chimpanzees. Certainly we can't blame this vast difference in mutational productivity on natural selection, since both chimps and humans "grew up" in broadly similar environments. Evolution is an endless source of wonder.

ENDNOTES:

[1] Dobzhansky, Theodosius; *Evolution at work*, Science, 127, 1958, p. 1092

[2] Huxley, Julian; "The Uniqueness of Man" in *Man in the Modern World* (Mentor, New York, 1947) p. 2.

[3] Tallis, Raymond; *The Aping of Mankind* (Acumen Publishing Ltd., UK, 2011) p.11. Now published by Routledge with the title *Aping Mankind*.

[4] http://news.bbc.co.uk/1/hi/world/africa/3818833.stm

[5] http://www.sciencealert.com/ scientists-find-whales-and-dolphins-mourn-their-dead-too

[6] http://anthropology-world.blogspot.co.uk/2013/11/life-after-death.html The author is not named and the article appears to be a translation from Russian, but it gives every appearance of a scholarly piece of work.

[7] Bailey, Diane; Emperor Qin's Terracotta army; (Abdo Publishing, Minneapolis, 2015) p. 28. (https://books.google.co.uk/books?id=SzxFB AAAQBAJ&pg=PA45&dq=terracotta+army&hl=en&sa=X&ved=0ahUK EwjW5-zxrtjOAhWGtBoKHTUXDFAQ6AEITTAH#v=onepage&q=terraco tta%20army&f=false

[8] https://en.wikipedia.org/wiki/Sutton_Hoo

[9] Parkes, Colin, *et al* (editors), *Death and Bereavement across Cultures* (Routledge, London & New York,1997)

[10] In *Evolutionary Biology Vol. 6* (Springer Verlag, 1995).

11 *Genome Res. 2005. 15: 1746–1758*

12 Varki, Ajit, and Altheide, Tasha K.; *Genome Res. 2005. 15: 1746-1758* (Cold Spring Harbor Laboratory Press). http://genome.cshlp.org/content/15/12/1746.full.pdf+html

13 http://genome.cshlp.org/content/15/12/1746/T1.expansion.html

14 There are various definitions of the word "genome" which is sometimes used to describe the whole set of chromosomes (which include proteins as well as DNA) and is sometimes deemed to include epigenetic structures as well as the DNA itself. In this book we shall restrict the meaning of "genome" to the totality of an organism's DNA.

15 Bergman, Gerald, and Tomkins, Jeffrey; *Proceedings of the Seventh International Conference on Creationism. Pittsburgh, PA: Creation Science Fellowship*; www.icr.org

16 https://www.statsmonkey.com/hbar/13236-human-genes-compared-with-other-animals-and-plants.php OR http://imgur.com/gallery/Sdz10eh

17 National Human Genome Research Institute; https://www.genome.gov/11509542/

18 Andrews, Edgar; *From Nothing to Nature* (Evangelical Press, Darlington, 1978).

19 Young, Nathan M. *et al.* Fossil hominin shoulders support an African ape-like last common ancestor of humans and chimpanzees. *PNAS*, published online September 8, 2015; doi: 10.1073/pnas.1511220112

20 http://phys.org/news/2013-12-human-ancestor-less-chimp-like-thought.html

21 http://evolution.berkeley.edu/evolibrary/article/evograms_07

22 https://www.newscientist.com/article/2081012-just-how-are-we-related-to-our-chimp-cousins/

23 Haldane, J. B. S., The cost of natural selection; *Journal of Genetics* 55 (1957) pp. 511-524. Also at https://link.springer.com/article/10.1007/BF02984069

24 https://en.wikipedia.org/wiki/Haldane%27s_dilemma

25 http://cimps.weebly.com/reproduction---mating-systems.html

26 http://www.pandasthumb.org/archives/2007/07/haldanes-nondil.html

27 Sanford, John; Brewer, Wesley; Smith, Franzine; and Baumgardner,
    John; Theoretical Biology and Medical Modeling; 2015; 12: 18.
    Published online 17/09/2015 doi: 10.1186/s12976-015-0016-z
28 Musgrave, Ian; http://www.pandasthumb.org/archives/2007/07/
    haldanes-nondil.html

CHAPTER 7

In 1986 I debated head-to-head with Richard Dawkins at the Oxford Huxley Memorial Debate. During a coffee break, and after we had both made our speeches, he and a colleague (both biologists) explained to me that the genes of humans and chimpanzees were 98 percent identical—proof, they claimed, that both had descended from a common ancestor. Fortunately I had enough biological knowledge to reply that however similar the genes might be, they are clearly *expressed* very differently in the two species. They had to agree, and herein lies a profound mystery. We now know that a single gene can code for hundreds of different proteins, so that the characteristics of any species depend primarily not on its genes but on the marvelous control mechanisms that dictates how those genes are expressed. We take a close look at one of the major mechanisms called "alternative splicing" in which complex molecular machines decide what sections of the gene are required to make a given protein, remove the unwanted portions, and link the needed bits back together. Books on beekeeping and a Christmas cake help us understand the technical issues covered in this chapter.

THE DEVIL IN THE DETAILS

Digging deeper into genes and genomes

"By selecting a subset of descriptive details from a larger body of options, we can frame our descriptions in such a way that we cue the reader's imagination in a desired direction."

CRAIG CLEVENGER, *THE DEVIL IN THE DETAILS*[1]

"We must concede that there are presently no detailed Darwinian accounts of the evolution of any biochemical or cellular system, only a variety of wishful speculations."

FRANKLIN M. HAROLD, PROFESSOR EMERITUS OF BIOCHEMISTRY, COLORADO STATE UNIVERSITY.[2]

The first of these two quotes comes from an article on creative writing, but it has a far wider significance than the author perhaps intended. It can readily be applied, for example, to political pronouncements, where the use of selective information is better known as "spin." Sadly, it also turns up in scientific claims and publications—not least in the contention that humans and chimps both owe their existence to a common ancestor (and ultimately to some primeval microbe). So we are going to take a close look at the use of selective data and related issues and ask whether or not the biological facts actually support the evolutionary paradigm (biochemist Franklin Harold, who provides our second chapter head quote, clearly has his doubts). But before we can proceed, we need to understand a bit more about the molecular basis of life. This won't take long and you can skip the opening section if you already know it all.

MOLECULAR GENETICS FOR BEGINNERS

The information needed to build a living organism (the genetic "blueprint" for its construction) is stored on the DNA molecules found in its cells. DNA molecules are long strings of chemical groups called "nucleotides," and each nucleotide contains a smaller group of atoms (called a "base") that sticks out sideways from the string. If it helps, think of a daisy chain in which each daisy is a nucleotide and the end of its stalk is a base. Under most conditions, two such strings (or strands) of DNA combine to form a "double helix." This can be pictured as a spiral staircase in which the two nucleotide strands form the support rails and the bases protrude inwards to form the steps. Each step therefore consists of two bases (one protruding from each support rail) which join together in the center of the spiral to form a complete step (a "base pair"). The two base "half steps" are linked together by so-called "hydrogen bonds" which can be easily broken and remade without affecting the integrity of the DNA strands themselves. This allows the two strands of the double helix to be pulled apart temporarily (or permanently in cell division) to expose unpaired bases—which then collectively provide a template that can be copied (or "transcribed") on to another kind of long-chain nucleic acid called RNA. These RNA molecules then carry the information copied from the DNA to various regions of the cell to facilitate or promote processes such as protein manufacture. That's why this particular kind of RNA is called "messenger RNA" or mRNA.

So how is the information stored? In the arrangement of bases along the DNA molecule. DNA contains four different bases (abbreviated[3] C, G, A, and T) which can be lined up along the DNA molecule in any order. However, their different sizes mean that C can only fit together with G to form a base pair, while A can only fit together with T. This means that only four different kinds of step exist in the double helix, namely, C-G, G-C, A-T and T-A. These four steps constitute a kind of four-letter alphabet which allows information and instructions to be stored—in exactly the same way that a human language uses sequences of letters to form words which, in turn, are organized into sentences that store and convey information and instructions.

The DNA molecules are packaged, along with special proteins, into the "chromosomes" which become visible under a microscope just before a living cell divides into two new cells. As mentioned in the previous chapter, the totality of an organism's DNA is called its "genome," while "genes" are those stretches of a DNA molecule which contain the information needed to make proteins (they "code for" proteins).

MISLEADING COMPARISONS

That's enough molecular genetics for the moment. Let's now return to our main concern, namely, the similarities between the chimp and human genomes—similarities that undergird the evolutionary claim that the two species have descended from a common ancestor which lived between six and thirteen million years ago. In the previous chapter we saw that chimpanzees and humans share 96 percent of their genes and perhaps as little as 70 percent of their entire genomes—though a higher figure of around 81 percent is more widely accepted. We also noticed that gene-sharing between species is virtually universal, and that humans share 88 percent of their genes with mice and even 18 percent with baker's yeast. In evolutionary theory this is held to be strong evidence for common descent, but all it really proves is that certain genes and gene-types are essential for life of any kind, with greater similarity existing between organisms with similar needs (birds need to fly and fishes need to swim).

However, in addition to this general conclusion, we must now look more closely at the similarities reported between genes in different organisms, especially chimps and humans. These reports can be misleading for several reasons, and we'll explore some of them in this chapter, considering in turn (1) selective bias, (2) incongruent genealogies, (3) epigenetics, and (4) alternative splicing. Don't worry: all will be explained in due course.

SELECTIVE BIAS

If you wanted to compare what kind of transport people prefer in London and New York respectively, you wouldn't limit your survey to pedal cyclists. Yet the methods used to compare genes and genomes involve highly selective procedures in which only those DNA segments that are broadly similar in the two organisms are taken into account. Sections of DNA that bear no resemblance to each other are simply ignored and dismissed as "junk" DNA—the supposed detritus of eons of evolutionary trial and error. However, the idea of junk DNA has itself been junked following closer study of the human genome—particularly a worldwide cooperative project known as ENCODE (the *Encyclopedia of DNA elements*). This project was launched in 2003 with the purpose of identifying all the functional elements in the human genome[4] and provides strong evidence that much of the so-called junk DNA does have a biological function. I'll have more to say about it later.

Geneticist Jeffrey Tomkins explains the problem of selective methods of gene comparison as follows:[5]

> "Scientists just published a study describing chimp DNA mutation rates and compared a number of cherry-picked genomic regions to human—and this research doubled their evolutionary timeline…. The researchers then compared selected DNA segments between chimpanzee and human that were highly similar, omitting the many nonsimilar regions … the scientists only used the regions that were about 98 percent similar and essentially threw out everything else. These are the regions that the researchers stated 'can be aligned with high confidence.' It appears that all the dissimilar DNA regions got tossed out because they didn't fit the evolutionary paradigm…."

To be fair, the work cited was only concerned with the speed at which genetic changes would have occurred *assuming that chimps and humans both descended from a common ancestor*. If that assumption were correct, it should not matter which DNA regions are compared, so that "cherry picking" for convenience becomes permissible. However, it is a very different matter if selective comparisons are used to *support the assumption* that common descent has occurred.

Elsewhere[6], Tomkins and Bergman provide a detailed technical review of the common claim that the human and chimpanzee genomes are nearly identical. They found these claims to be "highly questionable [based on] an analysis of the methodology and data outlined in an assortment of key research publications." The analytical methods in question are technical and I won't attempt to explain them here, but full details are given in the Tomkins and Bergman paper.

How is it done?

Geneticist Richard Buggs explains the procedure simply:[7]

"To compare the two genomes, the first thing we must do is to line up the parts of each genome that are similar. When we do this alignment, we discover that only 2,400 million of the human genome's 3,164.7 million 'letters' align with the chimpanzee genome—that is, 76 percent of the human genome. Some scientists have argued that the 24 percent of the human genome that does not line up with the chimpanzee genome is useless 'junk DNA.' However, it now seems that this DNA could contain over 600 protein-coding genes, and also code for functional RNA molecules."

Dr. Buggs goes on to explain that this is just the start. Artificial gaps have to be inserted into one or other of the genomes in order to properly align the "matching" regions, which introduce a further 3 percent difference. Other effects of a smaller kind are also found, as when two sections of one genome align with only one section of the other, creating a further 2.7 percent difference. Added together, these considerations reduce the overall similarity between the chimp and human genomes to around 70 percent.

The common assertion that the human and chimp genomes are over 98 percent similar clearly needs to be treated with skepticism. The truth is, of course, that regions *selected because they are similar* are, in fact, 96 percent similar. True, but tautological. To enlist this observation in support of common descent comes close to circular reasoning. Of course, evolutionists can claim that these similar regions, being rich in genes, are the only ones that matter, but this requires them dismiss as redundant the 24 percent of each genome that is unique to its species (leaving us wondering why humans are so bad at climbing trees). To say that this 24 percent can be safely ignored because it is only "junk DNA," denies the results of ENCODE—which tell us that noncoding DNA plays a vital role in controlling the way genes are expressed (see below).

BEEBOOKS

As noted at the beginning of the chapter, selective comparisons have persuasive power—they can "cue the reader's imagination in a desired direction." Selective comparison of genomes greatly increases the apparent similarities between two organisms and thus gives traction to the theory of common descent. So let's try to illustrate the dangers of drawing conclusions from this kind of comparison.

Suppose you are comparing two modern books by different authors on, say, beekeeping. Let's call the books "Perfect Pollinators" (PP) and "Busy Bees" (BB) respectively. You notice that there are certain similarities between the two books and conceive the idea that both books were plagiarized from an earlier untraceable tome. You want to prove your point by carefully comparing the words and sentences in the two modern books. Starting with words, you find that 70 percent are common to the two books, whereas they share only 50 percent of their words with Margaret Mitchell's 1936 novel *Gone with the Wind*. You attribute this to the existence of a common source of PP and BB, ignoring the fact that the two authors are dealing with a common subject and are thus likely to use similar vocabularies. You then get to work on sentences, but this proves more difficult. For example, BB has a chapter on beehive construction whereas PP doesn't cover this subject at all—so there are no comparable sentences dealing with this matter. So you decide to compare only the 5 percent of those sentences in the two books that, while differing in detail, nevertheless do closely resemble each other.

You conclude that both modern authors have lifted these sentences from an unknown common source, and submit an article to the *Journal of Beekeeping* accusing both authors of plagiarism. Not surprisingly, the journal rejects your conclusions, pointing out that all your data can be better explained by the similarity of the subject and the identical desire of two independent and original authors to document their passion for bees.

The illustration applies to genomes because triplet sequences of letters in the DNA four-character "alphabet" can be regarded as three-letter "words," each of which codes for one of the twenty different amino acids used to assemble proteins. Then, just as in human language, the *sequence* of these DNA "words" spells out a "sentence" which specifies which of the thousands of proteins found in living cells will be made by copying that particular gene. While no illustration is perfect, our beekeeping parable should warn us that the observed similarities between chimp and human genomes are far from proving the existence of a common ancestor.

MIXED-UP (INCONGRUENT) GENEALOGIES

A second problem emerges when the genome comparison is widened to include other great apes besides chimpanzees. Evolutionary geneticist Ingo Ebersberger and coworkers sum the matter up thus:[8]

"In two-thirds of the cases [of gene comparison among great apes],
a genealogy results in which humans and chimpanzees are
not each other's closest genetic relatives. The corresponding
genealogies are incongruent with the species tree. In
accordance with the experimental evidences, this implies
that there is no such thing as a unique evolutionary history of
the human genome. Rather, [the human genome] resembles
a patchwork of individual regions following their own
genealogy."

Note well the phrase "no such thing as a unique evolutionary history
of the human genome." As far as I can see, the conclusion would be
equally well stated by leaving out the word "unique." For since different parts of the human genome appear to have different evolutionary
histories, there seem to be only two options. Either Man was somehow
created by stitching together genetic material from a variety of apelike
creatures, known and unknown, or else his "evolutionary history" is a
figment of evolutionary imagination.

Our beekeeping analogy can be extended to illustrate this.
Suppose you are comparing not just two modern books but, say, five
(call them PP, BB, XX, YY, and ZZ). You continue to believe that they
are all plagiarized from the early unknown work because of similarities between the word counts and sentences. However, as you examine
the details, you realize that one chapter of PP might actually have been
plagiarized from XX and another from ZZ. In fact, PP seems to be
a patchwork of plagiarized passages from the other four books and
even from more than one unknown source. Contrary to your original belief, PP might therefore have little or no connection with the
first hypothesized unknown source. Your head begins to ache and you
decide to abandon beekeeping and take up stamp collecting instead.

As Franklin Harold concedes, there are no "detailed Darwinian accounts of the evolution of any biochemical or cellular system, only a variety of wishful speculations."

EPIGENETICS (OR THE ICING ON THE CAKE)

A third issue stems from the fact that large phenotypic (visible) differences between species can be produced by processes that involve no change at all in their genomes. I'm sure you will agree that a caterpillar and a butterfly are two very different things. Anyone unfamiliar with their life cycle would immediately conclude that they are two completely different species, having entirely different appearances, lifestyles, appendages, means of locomotion, diets, and so on. Yet when the genomes of a caterpillar and its corresponding butterfly are compared, they turn out to be identical.[9] Obviously, DNA differences cannot be the whole story when comparing organisms with different appearances, so what is going on? The answer is "epigenetic processes"—in which living cells control the way their genes are used (or "expressed").

Potentially, this offers a further reason why comparing chimp and human genes doesn't prove common descent, so how do epigenetics work? Genes occupy less than 2 percent of the total human genome[10], so most of our DNA is called "noncoding" and was once considered to be "junk DNA." However, ENCODE research has shown that perhaps as much as 80 percent of the human genome is transcribed (copied) into RNA on a regular basis—suggesting that most so-called noncoding regions of the genome are actually *used* for some purpose. At present no function has been identified for much of this material, but since *useless* transcription wastes precious energy, it shouldn't happen (it should have been eliminated by natural selection). This strongly suggests that all such transcription of DNA into RNA does have a function, even though at present we may not know what it is. What we do know, however, is that a lot of noncoding RNAs contribute to the "epigenetic" processes that regulate the way in which genes are expressed or employed (for example, by switching genes on or off as required by the cell).

"Epi" is the Greek word for "upon," and epigenetic processes are those that affect or regulate the way genes are expressed *without altering the genes themselves*. Let's illustrate it in a simple way. Suppose you are making a Christmas cake. You first bake the cake itself, but it's not yet a *Christmas* cake. You still need to cover the cake with marzipan (almond paste), sugar icing, and decorations. Adding these extras doesn't *change* the original cake. The layers of icing are superimposed on the basic cake without altering it in any way, and could therefore be called "epicake layers." What they do achieve, however, is to transform the appearance and taste of the cake—they change the way the cake is "expressed." And just as there may be several layers of icing and decoration superimposed on a cake, so there are also several layers of epigenetic control affecting the way genes are expressed in a living organism.

This means that two organisms with closely similar genes may exhibit large differences in development, appearance and behavior, as different epigenetic effects come into play. The implications of this are still being actively researched, but already some experts (both evolutionists and nonevolutionists) claim that epigenetic effects play a far greater role in biology than do random mutations in the genes themselves. For example, as long ago as 1975, King and Wilson wrote:

> "We suggest that evolutionary changes in anatomy and way-of-
> life are more often based on changes in the mechanisms
> controlling the expression of genes than on sequence changes
> [mutations] in proteins. We therefore propose that regulatory

mutations account for the major biological differences
between humans and chimpanzees."[11]

Again, Danish researchers reported in 2013 that cloned pigs (which
have identical genomes) vary just as much as naturally propagated
pigs due to epigenetic factors[12], while in 2016 Oxford University
scientists "found that different levels of nitrogen in a parasite's diet
contributed to changes in its DNA."[13] The fact that, to adjust for external factors, the cell as a system can change the way its DNA is used,
throws entirely new light on the nature and function of genes. It has
been suggested that an organism's genome is more like a read/write
CD than an unchanging library of genetic information. This means
that anyone trying to explain why humans and chimps are so different could be wasting their time by simply comparing genes. Could the
differences be largely due to epigenetic factors? Could chimpanzeelike
ancestors be the "caterpillars" that turned into human "butterflies"?

Probably not. While epigenetic processes warn us that comparing the genes of two species won't necessarily explain the differences
between them, these processes themselves create major problems
for macroevolution theory. Remember that the theory of common
descent demands that enormous amounts of *new* genetic information must have been created in the proposed evolutionary journey
from microbes to Man. Traditional neo-Darwinism claims that this
came about by trial and error, as random mutations in the DNA of
lowly organisms produced accidental improvements in their viability,
leading to a superior version of that organism. These improvements
then became fixed in populations of the creature by natural selection.
By contrast, while epigenetic effects can influence (and sometimes
improve) the way information is *extracted* from a genome, they are
incapable of *creating* information that is not already present. Why not?

Because by definition, epigenetic processes do not change the DNA's information storehouse—only the way that information is used.

ALTERNATIVE SPLICING

There are many "layers" of epigenetic processes but one is of special significance to this discussion, namely, something called "alternative splicing." Picture it this way. Suppose the top of your Christmas cake is populated by numerous small figurines of snowmen and polar bears, arranged randomly around the circumference of the cake. And suppose you have an aversion to polar bears but like snowmen, and want to choose only segments of cake that feature your favorite figurines. You can easily do this by selectively slicing the cake, leaving behind the unwanted parts. You could then, if you chose, join all your snowman slices together on your plate, forming a snowman segment to enjoy at your leisure.

Something rather like this happens in living cells after a gene is copied on to the RNA molecule that will carry that gene's information to other parts of the cell. In higher life forms, the RNA is "edited" by removing unwanted segments of the raw transcript and splicing together the remaining segments. The spliced product is then used to make a particular protein elsewhere in the cell. The segments cut out and discarded are called "introns" (think polar bears) and those retained and joined together are called "exons" (think snowmen). The original genetic information is thus carefully edited, and only when this editing process is complete is the RNA molecule (now a mature "messenger RNA" or mRNA) unleashed to do its work.

But here comes the bombshell. The same stretch of raw transcribed RNA, containing *all* the information from the gene, can be edited in different ways by "alternative splicing" to produce a variety of *different* proteins from the same DNA gene. In the Christmas cake analogy, instead of choosing just snowmen you could select 75 percent snowman slices and 25 percent polar bear slices (or *vice versa*). But even this is an oversimplification. You could, for example, cut your slice through a snowman, keeping some of it on your slice but leaving the rest of it behind. The possibilities are endless. Where does this leave us? The US National Cancer Institute explains:[14]

> "One gene can encode more than one protein (even up to 1,000). The human genome contains about 21,000 protein-encoding genes, but the total number of proteins in human cells is estimated to be between 250,000 to one million."

On average, then, a single gene can code for ten to fifty *different* proteins through the mechanism of alternative splicing. But who or what wields the cake knife? What decides which slices to use and which to reject? The cutting and splicing is carried out by large molecular "machines" called spliceosomes (think cake knife), but it remains a matter of speculation as to what *tells* these machines to produce one mRNA (and thus one protein) rather than another. Even when the mechanism involved is finally worked out (as it surely will be), it will only demonstrate that alternative splicing is a masterpiece of editorial art rather than an accident of nature.

CAN EPIGENETIC EFFECTS BE INHERITED?

Whether or not epigenetic effects can contribute to permanent differences between genomes, and thus to the creation of new species, turns on a further question: can epigenetic changes in parents be inherited by their offspring?

Most evolutionists today would probably argue for a combination of traditional gene mutations that directly affect protein production, and mutations in the "noncoding" DNA responsible for epigenetic control. But epigenetic control mechanisms must function with extreme precision (and usually cooperatively) to achieve their purpose—such as switching genes on or off, or "reading" the same gene sequences in different ways. It is difficult to see, therefore, how random mutations in the molecular assemblies (such as spliceosomes) responsible for epigenetic effects could ever be beneficial (and thus selectable) in a macroevolutionary sense.

It is true that epigenetic changes arising from "selective pressures" (such as changes in climate or food supply) can be inherited. A recent study of lizards, for example, describes adaptation to a new environment that was far too quick to be due to the fixation of random mutations. The abstract of the paper reads as follows:[15]

> "Here we show how lizards have rapidly evolved differences in head
> morphology, bite strength, and digestive tract structure after
> experimental introduction into a novel environment. Despite
> the short time scale (≈36 years) since this introduction, these
> changes in morphology and performance parallel those
> typically documented *among species and even families* of
> lizards in both the type and extent of their specialization"
> (emphasis added).

Since these changes happened too quickly to be explained by neo-Darwinian mutations and natural selection, they must be due to epigenetic processes. This kind of adaptive effect is probably quite common, and might, for example, help to explain the famous cases of Darwin's finches and the peppered moth, where changing environments seem to produce marked phenotypic adaptations (which are, however, reversible[16,17]).

Again, a Swedish study[18] reported that:

> "Death related to diabetes increased for children if food was plentiful
> during [a] critical period for the paternal grandfather, but it
> decreased when excess food was available to the father. These
> findings suggest that diet can cause changes to genes that are
> passed down through generations by the males in a family,
> and that these alterations can affect susceptibility to certain
> diseases."

The changes, however, were clearly not "fixed" in the population, since the same factor (well-fed progenitors) caused opposite effects in children and grandchildren respectively. No permanent "evolution" took place. What is well-established, however, is that epigenetic mutations commonly result in disease. Dr. Danielle Simmons writes:

> "While epigenetic changes are required for normal development
> and health, they can also be responsible for some disease
> states. Disrupting any of the three systems that contribute
> to epigenetic alterations can cause abnormal activation or
> silencing of genes. Such disruptions have been associated with
> cancer, syndromes involving chromosomal instabilities, and
> mental retardation."[19]

The bottom line? While epigenetic effects may alter the way genes are expressed, and can even in principle create new proteins in an organism, their effects are usually reversible and often deleterious. They cannot create new genes and cannot therefore account for macroevolution or common descent. Nor, by the same token, can they circumvent the "waiting time" problem that we discussed in the previous chapter.

GETTING BACK TO CHIMPS

So how about chimps? Not surprisingly, closely similar genes in humans and chimpanzees are commonly expressed very differently, and this is often the result of alternative splicing in the two species. Reporting the work of Professor Blencowe at the Banting and Best Department of Medical Research and Molecular Genetics, the online journal *Science Daily* explains:[20]

> "It's clear that 'humans are very different from chimpanzees on several levels, but we wanted to find out if it could be the splicing process that accounts for some of these fundamental differences,' says Blencowe. 'The surprising thing we found was that six to eight per cent of the alternative splicing events we looked at were showing differences, which is quite significant. And those genes that showed differences in splicing are associated with a range of important processes, including susceptibility to certain diseases....' The new findings reveal that the alternative splicing process differs significantly between humans and chimpanzees."

How did these splicing differences arise? We do not know. Evolution would no doubt argue that random mutations in the noncoding regions of the common ancestor and its descendants became fixed by natural selection. But remember that genetic changes become fixed in populations, not in individuals, and that happens only after hundreds of generations. It is very difficult to see how random mutations could give rise to significant splicing differences between two groups within the same population. Put another way, Darwinian mechanisms would require the splicing differences between chimps and humans to arise only *after* the two species had already divided into separate populations. Why is that? Because interbreeding within a single population would randomize the effects of alternative splicing and frustrate the emergence of two distinct species. They cannot therefore be responsible for *causing* a subspecies separation event in the first place. Yet they constitute an important element in the distinction between chimps and humans.

Let's go over that again, because it is important.

1. A mutation in the noncoding regions of one species but not another could arguably change a spliceosome structure and lead to alternative splicing in the first species that doesn't occur in the second.

2. But to fix this mutation in a population takes many generations of that species and cannot happen as long as those possessing the mutation interbreed freely with those who lack it. Fixation requires an isolated breeding stock.

3. So for a particular epigenetic control mechanism to arise in one species and not in a closely related one requires that the two species first form distinct and separate populations.

4. The said control mechanism cannot therefore be the *cause* of speciation. That is, it cannot cause a single breeding stock to split into two noninterbreeding populations.

But what if a geographical or similar isolation event triggers speciation? Two populations that are at first genetically identical could become separated geographically or ecologically and then go their separate ways genetically speaking. Well, yes, that could theoretically happen. But it would have to occur over and over again, in a serial manner, for the hypothetical common ancestor to give rise to *all* the great ape species—and there is not the slightest reason why the various forest-dwelling apes should have suffered such isolation from one another.

However, there is an even stronger reason to reject this scenario. It is difficult, and perhaps impossible, to see how random mutations in one branch of an evolutionary tree eventually produced a highly advanced species (Man), while all the other branches starting from the same common ancestor (an ape) only produced other apes barely distinguishable from the ancestor. If a horse race starts with twenty horses but only one proceeds to the finish, while nineteen contentedly nibble grass around the starting gates, we would suspect a put-up job.

BEYOND EPIGENETICS

Are there other processes besides epigenetic ones that could cause evolution? Some geneticists believe there are. This is not a subject we can explore here, but I include this note for the sake of completeness. A growing number of evolutionists believe that the simple neo-Darwinian mechanism of random mutation and natural selection cannot account for the world of living things we know today. They argue that other processes, which go beyond epigenetics, have played a major role in shaping the genomes of modern organisms. These processes include "hybridization," "transposition," "symbiogenesis" and "horizontal gene transfer" and are explained briefly in an endnote to this chapter.[21] The interested reader can learn more about them from recent books such as *The Paradigm Shifters*[22] and *Evolution 2*.[23] Even more recently, some geneticists have proposed an "omnigenic" model in which phenotypic traits are determined, not by one or a handful of genes, but by the coordinated action of hundreds of different genes working in concert.[24] I guess we'll need to "watch this space," but one thing is clear. Comparing genomes provides no support for the common belief that Man descended from an ape. The chimpanzees in your local zoo are not your closest relatives, and you don't need to send them birthday cards.

ENDNOTES:

1   Clevenger, Craig, Essay, "The Devil in the Details," 7 October 2011; https://litreactor.com/essays/craig-clevenger/the-devil-in-the-details

2   Harold, Franklin M., *The Way of the Cell: Molecules, Organisms and the Order Of Life*, Oxford University Press, New York, 2001, p. 205.

3   These abbreviations stand for cytosine, guanine, adenine, and thymine.

4   www.genome.gov/10005107

5   http://www.icr.org/article/8196/ by Jeffrey Tomkins

6   Tomkins, Jeffrey, and Bergman, Jerry, Genomic monkey business; estimates of nearly identical human-chimp DNA similarity re-evaluated using omitted data, Journal of Creation, 26(1) 2012. p. 94.

7   Buggs, R. 2008. Chimpanzee? *Reformatorisch Dagblad*. Retrieved from http://www.refdag.nl/.chimpanzee_1_ 282611.

8   Ebersberger, Ingo, et al *Mapping human genetic ancestry*, Molec. Biol. Evol. 24:2266-2276, 2007. https://www.researchgate.net/profile/Arndt_Von_Haeseler/publication/6177609_Mapping_Human_Genetic_Ancestry/links/00b4953c7a64573e5d000000.pdf?origin=publication_detail

9   http://www.isciencemag.co.uk/blog/butterflies-brains-dna-games/

10   Other estimates put this figure at around 5 percent rather than 2 percent. It depends in part on whether the coding genes are considered *in toto* or whether only exons are counted, but there are other uncertainties that make these figures subject to variability. For example, the figure differs in different chromosomes.

[11] King, M. C. and Wilson, A. C., Evolution at two levels in humans and chimpanzees, *Science*, 188: 107–116, 1975.

[12] http://sciencenordic.com/does-perfect-clone-exist

[13] Emily A. Seward, Steven Kelly. Dietary nitrogen alters codon bias and genome composition in parasitic microorganisms. *Genome Biology*, 2016; 17 (1) DOI: 10.1186/s13059-016-1087-9.

[14] National Cancer Institute (part of the National Institute of Health). http://proteomics.cancer.gov/whatisproteomics

[15] Herrel, Anthony, *et. al.* Rapid large-scale evolutionary divergence in morphology and performance associated with exploitation of a different dietary resource; *Proc. Nat. Acad. Sci. USA*; 105 no. 12, 4792–4795; http://www.pnas.org/content/105/12/4792.full

[16] Wells, Jonathan; *Icons of Evolution* (Regnery Publishing Inc., Washington DC, 2000) pp. 146, 168.

[17] http://science.sciencemag.org/content/305/5689/1462

[18] Simmons, Danielle; Epigenetic influences and disease; http://www.nature.com/scitable/topicpage/Epigenetic-Influences-and-Disease-895

[19] See reference 14. http://www.nature.com/scitable/topicpage/Epigenetic-Influences-and-Disease-895

[20] https://www.sciencedaily.com/releases/2007/11/071114151513.htm

[21] Hybridization occurs when two different species mate. A well-known example is when a male donkey mates with a female horse to produce a mule—a new 'species' which is, however, almost always sterile. This is because horses have 64 chromosomes while donkeys have 62, which leaves the mule with 63. Hybridization among plants (and a few animals) is usually more productive, producing so-called "diploid" offspring that possess a full set of chromosomes from each parent species. This double-sized genome then adjusts itself using epigenetic on-off switches to silence unwanted genes and the hybrid species can then propagate in the normal way. Although hybridization can produce new viable species, it is unlikely to have contributed significantly to the multiplication of life forms.

Transposition occurs when sections of DNA are cut from one part of a genome and reinserted in different location. This often occurs as a repair process after a genome has been damaged, but (in lower life forms at least) can also be a response to high environmental stresses like starvation. The term "natural genetic engineering" has been introduced to describe situations where a cell's genome is apparently changed by internal processes to compensate for damage or external stress.

Symbiogenesis is the theory that evolutionary advances have in the past occurred as a result of one single-cell organism engulfing (or "swallowing") a different kind of organism. Some think it explains the origin of eukaryotic cells (which have a nucleus) from more primitive prokaryotic cells (which lack a nucleus).

Horizontal gene transfer is an "infective" process in which viruses or similar entities invade an organism and become incorporated into the genome of that organism. DNA transfer from one bacterium to another has been experimentally confirmed and could be involved in some cases of bacterial resistance to antibiotics. Some claim that a significant part of the human genome consists of DNA imported through infection by viruses.

[22] Mazur, Susan; *The paradigm Shifters*, (Caswell Books, New York, 2015).

[23] Marshall, Perry; *Evolution 2; breaking the deadlock between Darwin and design* (Ben Bella Books Inc., Dallas, 2015).

[24] https://www.theatlantic.com/science/archive/2017/06/its-like-all-connected-man/530532/

CHAPTER 8

With a little help from Mark Twain and his talking skeletons, this chapter considers how far fossil remains help us trace our human ancestry. We'll find that the neat progression from apes to humans, proposed by Darwinian "common descent" and presented as fact in our school books, is a myth of major proportions. That's not just this author's opinion but the sober verdict of many experts in palaeontology (the study of fossil remains). To find out for ourselves, we undertake an imaginary fossil-hunting trip to Ethiopia and discover "Fred," a hitherto unknown and equally imaginary skeleton that might just have been a human ancestor. But it proves impossible to place him in our family tree, and the reasons for our failure reveal in detail the problems always encountered in interpreting actual fossil finds. We need to treat with considerable caution the common belief that fossils tell their own unambiguous history. It's easy, like Mark Twain, to put words in the mouths of skeletons but in reality they cannot talk.

CHAPTER 8

DEM DRY BONES

What fossils really tell us about the rise of Man

And those who husbanded the golden grain,
And those who flung it to the winds like rain,
Alike to no such aureate earth are turned
As buried once, men want dug up again.

EDWARD FITZGERALD, *RUBAIYAT OF OMAR KHAYYAM OF NAISHAPUR*

Fitzgerald's verse has the ring of truth but it wouldn't appeal to a paleoanthropologist. What are paleoanthropologists? They are scientists who specialize in digging up human remains in the hope of discovering the secret of our origins (*paleo* means "ancient" and *anthropology* is the study of Man). Since it's such a mouthful, I'll call paleoanthropology "PA," and one who practices it "a PA."

To a PA, any fossil footprint, skeleton, or even isolated bone or tooth is truly "aureate" (worth its weight in gold) if it is deemed to throw light on human antiquity. PA doesn't concern itself only with humans and their supposed ancestors (known as *hominins*) but also explores the wider world of *hominids* (the great apes including humans and all their supposed ancestors).[1]

The American humorist Mark Twain wrote a short story[2] in which, one foggy night, he met and conversed with a succession of skeletons. They were making their way from an old burial ground to a new one—each carrying its coffin and complaining bitterly, though politely, about the way their original resting place had been commandeered for housing development. The graveyard desecration was real but the skeletons were not; Twain was simply putting his own words of protest into the mouths of the long-departed. And here lies the problem—it is all too easy for the discoverers of ancient fossils to make them "say" what they want them to say, namely, whatever fits their current theory or enhances their academic reputation. Bones can't speak for themselves. Their place in the history of humanity can only be inferred or guessed from their morphology, age, and condition—together with cultural clues such as tools, the use of fire, and the remains of lunch.

And that's where PAs come into their own. It is their task to study such fossil finds, assess their age, catalogue their similarities, relate them to known races of man, trace their supposed ancestors, evaluate their culture (if any), and assign them a place in mankind's family tree. In doing so, they invariably make the assumption that modern Man has evolved in a Darwinian manner from more primitive races, and ultimately from some kind of ape. In this chapter we are going to consider what "dem bones" really do tell us, and whether or not they support the evolutionary scenario. Note that in doing so I shall for convenience use the commonly accepted "geological timescale" for the ages of rock strata, although I have argued elsewhere that it involves unjustified assumptions that exaggerate these ages.[3,4]

Is man just an animal?

There can be no doubt that man is an animal. Our skeletons resemble those of the great apes, at least superficially. We share with mammals, birds, and reptiles a common body plan (head, four limbs, five fingers on each hand—that kind of thing). Our internal organs are similar in structure and function to those found in other animals which, like us, reproduce sexually (as do other organisms including plants). Many animals have brains and nervous systems analogous to our own. In short, we recognize a multitude of similarities among the "pheno-types" of living creatures (the way those organisms look and behave). Likewise, as we have seen, many of our genes bear a close resemblance to those of mice, monkeys, and marsupials (not to mention earth-worms, *etcetera*). Like other animals, we are conceived, born, grow up and grow old. Like them we eat, drink, sleep, get sick, and eventually die. "Dust you are and to dust you shall return," said the book of Genesis some 3500 years ago. Nothing much has changed.

But is Man *only* an animal, or is he something more? That is the question addressed in this book, and we must now consider what answers can (and cannot) be found by sifting through fossil remains. The negro-spiritual "dem bones, dem bones" celebrates the prophet Ezekiel's Old Testament vision—in which a valley full of scattered human bones came to life, bone by bone, until a great army stood upon its feet. It was, of course, a parable of God's ability to raise ancient Israel from its fallen condition. So might fossils help us piece together the story of mankind? Perhaps, but PA faces formidable difficulties.

I am not referring to the well-known fallacies and frauds that have bedeviled PA from its inception as a serious science in the late nineteenth century. For example, the first Neanderthal remains were identified by one anthropologist as a bow-legged Cossack, while an erstwhile "missing link" between apes and humans was conjured up on the basis of a single tooth and christened "Nebraska Man."[5] The tooth turned out to belong to a peccary (a piglike animal). The most famous fraud of all was "Piltdown Man"—an alleged missing link cunningly constructed from a human skull and the jawbone of an orangutan, which fooled the PA establishment for forty years.[6] While such errors and deceits make amusing and cautionary reading, they tell us nothing about the validity or otherwise of PA as a means of discovering Man's origins. But they do, perhaps, alert us to the difficulties of the PA enterprise.

FORMIDABLE DIFFICULTIES

The first thing to remember is that PA is necessarily a *historical* science, not an experimental one. I don't mean that experiments can't be done on fossil remains—they can. For example, DNA fragments can sometimes be extracted from fossil bones and yield valuable information about origins and relationships.[7] But by "experimental science," I mean science that can reproduce (in the laboratory or field) the events that we seek to explain by our hypotheses and theories. Historical sciences can't do that because they study unique past events that cannot, by definition, be repeated. These studies closely resemble crime-scene investigations, in which detectives try to reconstruct what happened during an unrepeatable criminal event. Archaeology is another example of historical science, as it examines ancient ruins and artifacts in the hope of reconstructing the history, politics, and lifestyles of ancient human societies.

Perhaps the most important consequence of all this is that PA, along with other historical sciences, relies much more heavily upon *interpretation* than do experimental sciences. With the latter it is usually possible to devise new experiments to test which of two (or more) possible explanations of the data is correct, but such luxury is not available to the historical sciences. New information may come to light if fresh discoveries are made, but this is usually a matter of chance and is seldom under the control of the scientist. It shouldn't surprise us, then, that PA is a subject where different experts offer different interpretations, and the debates often grow heated. Personal reputations are at stake and access to fossil remains may be denied to anyone who challenges the fossil owner's interpretation.

Interpretation-heavy sciences suffer a further problem: interpretations are strongly influenced by prevailing paradigms (patterns of ideas). We all try to fit new information into our existing view of things, "reading" our experiences in a way that harmonizes with our existing beliefs and comfort zones. It's difficult to break the mold in which our ideas have been cast, even when new information challenges those ideas. Again, therefore, we need to be willing to question "received" interpretations that are often presented to us as unassailable scientific facts.

As an introduction to the serious stuff, let me to take you on a flight of fancy. Our destination is Ethiopia and our purpose is to uncover a variety of what I will call "paleoanthropological pitfalls" (the difficulties facing PAs as they seek to interpret their finds).

DO-IT-YOURSELF PALEOANTHROPOLOGY

Imagine that you, as an amateur, develop an overwhelming desire to discover the *real* missing link between apes and humans. You read up on PA and persuade your incredibly rich uncle Fred to finance an expedition to Ethiopia (ancient name, "Afar"). You set up camp near a crumbling cliff where assorted bones have previously been found and put your hired laborers to work. It isn't long before you experience an outlandish degree of beginner's luck—you uncover the almost complete skeleton of a human-looking creature. The skull is fragmented and its other bones are disarticulated (no longer joined up). Some are missing, but by PA standards your discovery is amazingly complete. You call it "Fred" in honor of your uncle.

Someone asks how old the fossil is, and you suddenly realize that the bones themselves may tell you nothing about their antiquity. So, remembering what you have read about dating such remains, you hastily gather several barrow-loads of soil and stones from the site, and look around for an outcrop of volcanic (*igneous*) rock that can be dated by radiometric means (see later). There's nothing really close, but 50 meters away you do find such rock, so you chip off samples for age measurement. Fred's remains are labeled, packed with due reverence, and taken home—where you submit your discovery to anatomical experts and await their verdict.

First, the good news. The bones generally resemble human remains, but the arms are too long and seem to be adapted for swinging from branches, that is, for tree-dwelling. The bad news is that since the bones had fallen apart, it's difficult to say exactly how the pelvis articulated with the leg-bones—affecting whether or not Fred walked upright (had a bipedal gait). Furthermore, several attempts to reassemble the shattered skull come up with drastically different estimates of cranial volume, making the animal's brain size difficult to estimate. Nevertheless, in spite of these uncertainties, you believe you have found an ancestor of modern Man. You christen it *Homo afarensis fredericki* (meaning "man from Ethiopia, dedicated to Frederick") and set out to establish its place in the human family tree. This is where your problems really begin.

One expert who examines the remains declares that it was just a modern human being with a long-arm deformity and is irrelevant to human evolution. You disagree but have no way to challenge this idea because your fossil is the only one of its kind. To another expert, the bones are those of a giant extinct species of chimpanzee; the creature (he says) walked with bent knees; all the versions of the reassembled skull are wrong[8] and the creature actually had a tiny apelike brain. He renames it *Australopithecus afarensis fredericki* ("southern ape from Ethiopia dedicated to Frederick"). A third expert claims that one of his own finds bears the title *fredericki* and you have no right to use it, while a fourth says he found this kind of fossil twelve years ago, long before you did, but won't let you (or anyone else) see his own discovery because he hasn't yet written the definitive scientific paper about it. He says you have no right to name the fossil since he discovered it first, but declines to identify its role in human evolution.

DATING FRED

Perhaps dating your discovery will clarify the muddy anthropological waters? So you submit a bone to a Carbon 14 (abbreviated ^{14}C) dating lab, the soil and stones to geological experts, and the volcanic rock sample for radiometric dating. The results eventually come through. The ^{14}C measurement is inconclusive. It gives an age of around 3000 years (recent by PA standards) but the bone is porous and the lab suspects that live bacteria may have contaminated the specimen with their own ^{14}C. The bone could be almost any age. The radiometric dating of the volcanic rock puts its age at two million years or so, but the experts point out that this rock may have no age-related connection with the fossil you found. If a fossil lies *below* a stratum of igneous rock, it is reasonable to assume that it is older than the rock in question, but this neat arrangement doesn't apply to your skeleton. Even if it did, radiometric dating doesn't necessarily give correct ages for rock, as we shall see presently.

What about the soil and stones? They can't date the skeleton radiometrically, because they are erosion products from more ancient rocks—which could predate the creature by any amount of time. But there is one interesting piece of news—among the stones are "index" fossils that are typically found in rock strata from the "Pleistocene period" which (according to the accepted geological timescale) lasted from 2.58 million to 11,700 years ago. Could this mean that Fred is of similar age? Perhaps, but perhaps not. The index fossils occur in water-worn pebbles, and even if the pebbles were deposited during Fred's lifetime, they could have derived from much older virgin rock. They put an upper limit on Fred's geological age but leave the lower limit undefined.

Finally, what seems to be an ancient sharpened flint "knife" is found among the stones. Could this suggest that Fred used tools to skin and cut up food? Or might it indicate that humans hunted Fred and his tribe for their lunch? No one knows the answer. Also, the "knife" might just be a broken flint that just happens to resemble a crude tool. Or, like the pebbles, it could be much older than Fred. Or again, it might have been transported from a more recent location the last time the cliff suffered a rock fall.

However, you have faith in Fred and decide to opt for the radio-metric rock-sample date, even though the rock measured was some distance from his final resting place. Armed with this tentative age, you find a copy of the latest evolutionary family tree for hominids and consider where in that tree you should put Fred. Do you succeed? You'll find out at the end of the chapter.

Beginner's luck

The story related above is, of course, fiction but it isn't pure fiction. It was designed to illustrate some important real-life pitfalls in interpreting fossil remains, which we'll now look at more closely.

The first thing is why I said you had extraordinary "beginner's luck." A major problem for PA is that the fossil evidence on which it works is usually scarce. When an airline suffers too many "no-show" passengers, it responds by overbooking. Something similar can happen in PA, when inappropriate fossil candidates are recruited to fill the "no-show" ancestral gaps. Casey Luskin[9] cites two telling quotations from evolutionary pundits. Writing in 1996, PAs Donald Johanson and Blake Edgar admitted that "about half the timespan in the last three million years remains undocumented by any human fossils—only a handful of undiagnostic fossils have been found."[10] Again, Harvard Zoologist Richard Lewontin admits that the relevant fossils are generally so fragmented and disconnected that "no fossil hominid species can be established as our direct ancestor."[11]

Skull and other reconstructions

In his famous book *The Panda's Thumb*, palaeontologist Stephen Jay Gould points out that "most hominid fossils, even though they serve as [the] basis of endless speculation and elaborate storytelling, are fragments of jaws and scraps of skulls."[12] The fact that the key fossil evidence is usually fragmentary means that a lot of reconstruction is needed to assemble a fossil capable of being interpreted. We all know the fate of Humpty Dumpty in the nursery rhyme. Even though the pieces of that shattered egg-person were all available, "all the king's horses and all the king's men couldn't put Humpty together again."

PAs have an even greater problem when it comes to putting skeletons together using scattered or even isolated bones. Occasionally an almost complete skeleton is found but this is rare; reconstruction is almost always required.

This leads to a number of problems, including the real possibility that reconstructed fossils may inadvertently incorporate remains from different individuals and different species, creating an imaginary species that never actually existed. This may have happened in the case of a fossil species known as *Homo habilis* ("handy man") which allegedly represents an intermediate between *Australopithecus* ("southern ape") and Man. Fragments of a skull and extremities discovered by Louis Leakey in the 1960s were claimed to represent this new species, while ten years later his son Richard found a skull vault consistent with a cranial volume approaching that of Man. However, other experts believe that the original remains were those of an ape (*Australopithecus africanus*) and that Richard Leakey's later find was fully human. Combining these various remains into the single "handy-man" species obviously advanced the claims of human evolution but may well be an artefact of interpretation.[13] Even when the danger of composite reconstructions is avoided, the way PAs fit fragments together can dramatically affect the final result, leading to a skeleton that seems to exhibit features it never really had. Henry Gee, editor of the esteemed journal *Nature*, admitted in 2001 that "fossil evidence of human evolutionary history is fragmentary and open to various interpretations."[14]

A case in point is the fossil *Ramapithecus*, constructed from a few teeth and bones. Two separate sections of jawbone and teeth were initially reconstructed at an angle that made the complete tooth array ("tooth arcade") look somewhat human—suggesting that the fossil might be a human ancestor. But the same pieces were later rearranged more correctly at a different angle to resemble the tooth arcade of an ape, removing the earlier implication.[15] A further reconstruction *faux pas* relates to a fossil whose discovery caused great excitement in the PA world—the so-called *Ardipithecus* species. When first announced this specimen was said to have "the head of a hominim" but in reality the skull was crushed to fragments and was beyond reassembly. According to *National Geographic Magazine*, the bones were "so fragile that they would turn to dust at a touch."[16] Although it was alleged that *Ardipithecus* walked upright, a primatologist writing in the journal *Science* declared that "all of the *Ar. ramidus* bipedal characters cited also serve the mechanical requisites of quadrupedality...."[17] In other words, it isn't possible to tell whether the creature walked on two or four feet. Humanlike characteristics were "read into" the fossil when it was almost certainly an ape. Casey Luskin documents in some detail the chequered history of *Ardipithecus* and other fossils of interest in *Human Origins and the Fossil Record*.[18]

NAMING SPECIES: "PITHECUS" OR HOMO?

As noted in our make-believe fossil hunt, naming a PA discovery can be difficult. The Latin name given to a fossil has two main parts, the first indicating the "genus" of the creature and the second specifying the species. So, for example, you and I are labeled *Homo sapiens*, meaning that we belong to the genus *Homo* ("Man"; the genus is always capitalized) and to the species *sapiens* ("wise"). According to this way of classifying living things, a particular *genus* (plural "genera") may contain several or even many different *species*. Fossils of interest to PA fall into two categories; (1) the genus *Homo* meaning "man" and (2) genera that contain the word "pithecus" meaning "ape." For example, the genus *Australopithecus* means "southern ape" (the word *Pithecus* is never used alone). This distinction is important because it immediately shows the layperson whether the experts consider a creature to have been an ape or a human. Although apes are often presented as alleged ancestors of humans, correct classification always distinguishes them from humans. As evolutionary biologist Ernst Mayr admits:

> "The earliest fossils of Homo, *Homo rudolfensis* and *Homo erectus,*
>   are separated from *Australopithecus* by a large unbridged
>   gap. How can we explain this seeming saltation [evolutionary
>   jump]? Not having any fossils that can serve as missing links,
>   we have to fall back on the time-honored method of historical
>   science, the construction of a historical narrative."[19]

For "historical narrative," you could read "made-up story."

For a time there was an apparent exception to this classification rule, namely, bones (a tooth, a thigh bone, and a skull cap) found in Java in 1892 by a Dutch doctor, Eugene Dubois. He called his discovery *Pithecanthropus erectus* ("upright ape-man"). It became known as "Java Man" and was considered to be a genuine link between apes and humans. Later work[20], however, showed the remains to be much less apelike than Dubois believed and they were eventually reclassified as *Homo ergaster* ("working man"). The term "ape-man" no longer appears in the PA vocabulary.

The scarcity of fossil material creates a particular problem in deciding whether a fossil find represents a new species or just a variation within a known species. As anthropologist C. Quintyn explains:

> "Thousands of hominin fossil bones have been recovered over the
>   years, but only a few individuals have been identified within

each putative species. Rebecca Ackermann *et al.* (2006)
add that comparative patterning of skeletal variation does
not exist in the hominin fossil record because only single
individuals can be sampled, not biological populations. All of
this indicates that the identification of fossil species should be
at best difficult and at worst futile."[21]

Jealously guarded bones

Our next problem is discussed at length by Marvin Lubenow in the
opening chapter of his book, *Bones of Contention* (2004), and I will not
elaborate it here except to quote a couple of extracts. He writes:

"One would assume that those who have the proper academic
credentials and are able to travel to where the original fossils
are housed would have access to them. However, this is not
always the case. Science writer Roger Lewin quotes Donald
Johanson, the discoverer of *Lucy*, as agreeing that "only those
in the inner circle get to see the fossils; only those who agree
with the particular interpretation of a particular investigator
are allowed to see the fossils."

Lubenow continues:

"This lack of access—has important implications for the study
of human origins. It means that paleoanthropology is in
the strange situation of being a science in which most of its
workers do not have access to the material upon which their
science is based."[22]

Of course, plaster casts of these jealously guarded fossils are sometimes available, so why make a fuss about the originals being kept

from view? Lubenow gives an eye-opening reply. Less than half of the most important fossil material is available in the form of plaster casts, and there is a general feeling among PAs "that casts should not be used as resource material for a scientific paper" (a quote from Becky Sigmon of Toronto University[23]). When a rare (indeed, unique) exhibition of over forty important original fossils was held at the American Museum of Natural History in New York in 1984, the precision mounts for the original fossils were prepared using plaster casts supplied in advance. But when the original fossils were placed in these mounts, most of them did not fit.[24] Plaster casts are no substitute for originals!

Carbon 14 dating

Want a date with Fred? If you try Carbon dating, you'll be disappointed. Carbon 14 (^{14}C) is a radioactive form of carbon that is constantly being generated in the atmosphere as cosmic rays bombard nitrogen atoms (it is therefore called "radiogenic" carbon). These radiogenic carbon atoms react with oxygen to form carbon dioxide (CO_2) which is then taken up by plants and enters the food chain. As a result, all living things incorporate the same small proportion of ^{14}C as is found in the atmosphere—about one part per trillion. However, its atmospheric concentration varies over time. It was, for example, doubled in the 1960s by atomic bomb tests but has since dropped again by a third.

When an organism dies it stops taking up CO_2 from the atmosphere, and the radioactive ^{14}C it contains starts to decay in a predicable manner, reducing by half every 5700 years. The ^{14}C remaining in a sample can therefore be measured and the time since death calculated. However, after about 40,000 years[25] the radiogenic carbon has virtually all gone, so the method cannot date anything older than that. There are also other possible problems arising from such things as bacterial action, water leaching, and sample contamination, which mean the results may be inaccurate. There is, finally, the more basic difficulty for very old materials—having to assume that ancient atmospheric concentrations of radiogenic carbon were similar to today's values. This is something we simply do not know.

It is interesting that ^{14}C dates, even of pure carbon-containing materials like diamond, are often disputed on account of possible contamination, background radiation, and instrumental errors.[26] The chances of getting reliable dates from fossil bones are remote. So what do the ^{14}C results tell you about your discovery? Sadly, very little. Using this method, your skeleton appears to be only 3000 years old. Bacteria may have been at work in the porous bone and have contributed more ^{14}C than the bone itself. The age is indeterminate. To be fair, recent work on ^{14}C dating of soft tissue from an extinct giant marine lizard claims that other tests show that the ^{14}C they measured is original and not due to contamination.[27] But since the lizard is said to be more than 66 million years old, there shouldn't be any ^{14}C left to measure. Someone's interpretation has gone awry.

Any better luck with the soil and stones? Geologists tell you that the strata in the crumbling cliff come from the Cenozoic geological era (66 million years ago to the present) but warn you that a confusion of index fossils makes closer dating impossible. However, since your discovery is clearly a hominid of some kind they are sure it must belong to the Holocene epoch (the last 12,000 years). You recognize that this is a somewhat circular argument, but you go along with it for want of anything better. After all, you have one more chance—the much more scientific technique of radiometric dating.

RADIOMETRIC DATING

Although ^{14}C dating uses radioactivity to measure age, the term "radiometric dating" is normally reserved for methods used to determine the age of "igneous rocks"—rocks that have solidified from a molten state. An important proviso is that they must have remained impermeable to water, which otherwise could falsify results by removing or infiltrating the trace elements that are fundamental to the technique. This dating method can't therefore be used to measure the age of either fossil bones or sedimentary rock deposited from water, such as the crumbling cliff in our story. Also, while ^{14}C dating measurements are only meaningful for geologically young materials, radiometric dating techniques by contrast are only effective for very ancient rocks.

The most common dating technique for such rocks is the potassium-argon method. The element potassium, present in many rocks, has a radioactive form. This "isotope" (written ^{40}K) is present at 0.0117 percent of total potassium and decays over time into either argon or calcium. The decay process is so slow that it would take 1.25 billion years for 50 percent of a sample of ^{40}K to decay, with only 10.9 percent of decay events resulting in the formation of argon atoms (rather than calcium). Argon is a gas, and the method assumes that any of this substance initially present in the molten rock will escape rapidly once it reaches the open air. So when a rock solidifies (for example, when volcanic lava cools and hardens), it should contain no argon, and any of the gas found *subsequently* in the rock is assumed to have arisen by radioactive decay of potassium. By accurately measuring both the potassium and argon contents of the rock, therefore, researchers can calculate the time since solidification. This is what is meant by the "age" of a rock.

There are, however, a significant number of problems. Firstly, potassium compounds are highly soluble in water, so that potassium can be lost even from apparently solid rock. Secondly, the assumption that no argon is present in newly solidified rock may be false because the gas could be picked up from the atmosphere. Alternatively, argon initially present in the molten rock may not escape before the rock solidifies. To test the reliability of potassium-argon dating, geologist Andrew Snelling [28] collected thirteen samples of lava formed during eruptions of the Mt. Ngauruhoe volcano in New Zealand in 1949, 1954, and 1975. Without revealing that the rocks had solidified so recently, he sent the samples to a respected commercial dating organization, Geochron Laboratories, in Cambridge, Massachusetts, where they were dated by the potassium-argon method. The following results were reported;

Four samples were found to be "less than 270,000 years old"; one sample was "less than 290,000 years old"; one was dated at "800,000 years old; three were "one million years old"; one was "1.2 million years old"; one was "1.3 million years old"; one was "1.5 million years old"; and the last sample was dated at "3.5 million years old." The margin of error in all cases was given as plus or minus 20 percent. To be absolutely clear, there was nothing wrong with the laboratory's measurements. The problem lay in the assumptions made about the amounts of argon and potassium present in the magma when it solidified into lava. This doesn't mean that other methods of radiometric dating might (or might not) have given more accurate results; all it tells us is that these methods always involve assumptions that cannot be verified. (For expert readers, this also applies to so-called "isochron" methods which claim to eliminate such assumptions but where obviously false dates have also been obtained.[29])

TOOLS AND ARTIFACTS

African tribes and rainforest denizens tend to settle their disputes with machetes and blowpipes, rather than guided missiles and helicopter gunships. In that sense they are more primitive than the Pentagon. But that doesn't mean they belong to a lower species of humanity (or subhumanity). Their primitive weaponry tells us nothing about their biological nature. Taken from their cultural surroundings and given an education, they may be perfectly capable of matching the skills of modernity. So tools found (or not found) with fossil remains don't really tell us anything about human origins.

FINDING FRED A PLACE IN THE FAMILY TREE

Let's begin with a cautionary quote from Henry Gee, editor of the scientific journal *Nature*. "We have all seen the canonical parade of apes, each one becoming more human. We know that, as a depiction of evolution, this lineup is tosh (i.e. nonsense). Yet we cling to it. Ideas of what human evolution ought to have been like still color our debates."[30]

In evolutionary thinking, the "family tree" that concerns us here consists of a trunk representing the unknown common ancestor of all apelike creatures (including Man) and main branches, each of which represents a major division among hominids. Then secondary branches, sprouting from the main branches, represent subdivisions of these major groups, and so on, till one reaches the outer envelope of the tree's leafy canopy. Obviously, all extant species, like modern Man, chimpanzee, gorilla, orangutan, and so on will be found on this outer envelope. They are the outermost twigs of the tree. But where do you put fossilized creatures that have no modern counterpart? It depends entirely on your theory of descent!

An extinct species will still belong among the outermost twigs if it was not ancestral to any extant species. On the other hand, if it was ancestral to a modern species, it belongs deeper in the canopy—with its descendants (and their descendants) moving progressively outwards till they reach the outer envelope. How can anyone tell whether Fred was an ancestor of modern chimpanzees or modern humans, or was simply home-alone—an evolutionary dead-end with no known antecedents and no known descendants?

The age of a fossil, even if known, doesn't solve this dilemma. If modern chimpanzees suddenly went extinct they wouldn't become candidates for human ancestry just because they died out and humans didn't. Yet if PAs are still in business a thousand years hence, they might easily classify the extinct chimps as human ancestors because of their early demise. It's quite possible. After all, many PAs think that the last common ancestor of chimps and humans was rather like a chimp. Again, for many years Neanderthals were thought to be ancestral to modern man—until it was shown that they interbred with *Homo sapiens* and must have coexisted with them. The arrangement of hominid fossils in an evolutionary family tree, with one branch leading ultimately to Man, requires many assumptions.

Some will no doubt argue that there are early hominid fossils but no early human fossils, so Man must have come on the scene more recently than apes. But this may not be the case. If (for whatever reason) human populations were historically small, they may have left no trace in the fossil record during earlier times. But even if Man did arise later than apes, that doesn't mean they *descended* from apes. The belief that they did assumes, rather than proves, an evolutionary relationship.

So, with apologies for another quotation, I will finish this chapter with one more example. Jeffrey H. Schwartz, professor of biological anthropology at the University of Pittsburgh, writing in *Newsweek* on 9th October 2015, explains the case of a recently discovered fossil.[31]

> "Enter the newly announced species, *Homo naledi*, which is claimed to be our direct ancestor because it has features of australopiths [*australopithecus*] and *Homo*. Why is it a species of *Homo*? Because some specimens seem to be like us. Why australopith? Because other specimens have some of their features. Why do all belong to the same species? Because they were found in the same cave. But the published images tell a different story.... Viewed from the side, two partial skulls are long and low, with a long gently sloping forehead that flows smoothly into the brow—nothing like us...."

Professor Schwartz goes on in similar vein, considering differences among the remains between teeth and leg bones, before asking, "What to do?" Declaring that *Homo*'s taxonomy has become a confused "mess," he calls on the PA community to restudy the human fossil record without its current commitment to preconceived ideas.

Perhaps "dem bones" should be rephrased "dumb bones." They certainly have very little to tell us about human origins.

ENDNOTES:

[1] http://australianmuseum.net.au/
hominid-and-hominin-whats-the-difference.
"The most commonly used recent definitions are: Hominid – the group consisting of all modern and extinct Great Apes (that is, modern humans, chimpanzees, gorillas and orangutans plus all their immediate ancestors). Hominin – the group consisting of modern humans, extinct

human species and all our immediate ancestors (including members of the genera Homo, Australopithecus, Paranthropus, and Ardipithecus)."

2   Neider, Charles (editor); "A Curious Dream" in *The Complete Short Stories of Mark Twain* (Doubleday, USA, 1957) p. 32.

3   Andrews, Edgar; *From Nothing to Nature* (Evangelical Press, Darlington, 1978) pp. 57–74.

4   Andrews, Edgar; *God, science and evolution* (Evangelical Press, Darlington, 1980) pp. 108–127.

5   https://en.wikipedia.org/wiki/Nebraska_Man

6   http://www.bbc.co.uk/history/ancient/archaeology/piltdown_man_01.shtml

7   Ross, Alison; Better DNA out of fossil bones (BBC News) http://news.bbc.co.uk/1/hi/sci/tech/4260334.stm

8   Before Piltdown Man was shown to be fraudulent, early reconstructions of its fragmented human skull by two different experts showed enormous differences in cranial capacity. See http://www.nhm.ac.uk/our-science/departments-and-staff/library-and-archives/collections/piltdown-man.html

9   Luskin, Casey; in *Science and Human Origins* (Discovery Institute, Seattle, 2012) p. 46.

10 Johanson, Donald, and Edgar, Blake; *From Lucy to Language* (Simon & Schuster, New York, 1996) pp. 22–23)

11 Lewontin, Richard, *Human Diversity* (Scientific American Library, New York, 1995) p. 163

12 Gould, Stephen Jay; *The Panda's Thumb: More Reflections in Natural History* (W. W. Norton & Company, New York, 1980) p.126.

13 Junker, Reinhard; *Is Man Descended from Adam?* (Hannsler-Verlag, Neuhausen-Stuttgart, 1998). English translation p. 19.

14 Gee, Henry; *Return to the Planet of the Apes. Nature*, 412; 12 July 2001, pp. 131–132.

15 Junker, Reinhard; *loc. cit.* p.12.

16 Shreeve, Jamie; 'Oldest skeleton of Human Ancestor Found,' *National Geographic*, 1 October 2009, p. 1001

[17] Sarmiento, Esteban; "Comments on the Paleobiology and Classification of *Ardipithecus ramidus*," *Science*, 328, 28 May 2010, p. 1105b

[18] Gauger, A., Axe, D., and Luskin, C.; *Science and Human Origins* (Discovery Institute Press, Seattle, 2012) pp. 45–83

[19] Mayr, Ernst; *What Makes Biology Unique?* (Cambridge University Press, 2004) p. 198.

[20] https://en.wikipedia.org/wiki/Java_Man

[21] Quintin, C.; *Journal of Comparative Human Biology*, 60, 2009, pp. 307–341.

[22] Lubenow, Marvin, *Bones of Contention* (Baker Books, Grand Rapids, 2004) p. 26.

[23] Sigmon, Becky, and Cybulski, Jerome, (editors); *Homo erectus; papers in honor of Davidson Black* (Toronto University Press, 1981) p. 5.

[24] Delson, Eric (Editor); *Ancestors; The Hard Evidence* (Alan R. Liss Inc., New York, 1985) p. 4.

[25] The latest techniques claim to extend the usefulness of ^{14}C dating to around 100,000 years by detecting extremely small levels of radiogenic carbon, but the problems of contamination also become acute at these low concentrations.

[26] https://biblescienceforum.com/2014/11/02/carbon-14-in-diamonds-not-refuted/

[27] http://journals.plos.org/plosone/article?id=10.1371%2Fjournal.pone.0019445

[28] Snelling, Andrew; "Radioactive dating failures," *Creation* 22 No.1 (December 1999–February 2000) pp. 18–21.

[29] Mark, R. K. *et. al.*; *Geol. Soc. Amer. Abstracts with Programs*, 6, 1974, p. 456.

[30] Gee, Henry; *Nature* 478, 6 October 2011, p. 34.

[31] Schwartz, Jeffery; http://www.newsweek.com/homo-naledihomo-naledi-foundhomo-naledi-discoverydr-jeffrey-schwartzjeffrey-600437

CHAPTER 9

What is the relationship between the physical human brain and the non-material human mind? Psychologists and philosophers refer to this as "the hard question" because no convincing naturalistic explanation can be given. In this chapter, we explore the problem in a reader-friendly way by using an analogy in which the brain is represented as a house and the mind as its occupant. In the present chapter, three realtors inspect the house and its grounds, each offering a different opinion, sometimes amusing and sometimes alarming. (We'll meet another two of them in Chapter 10.) The realtors represent the various theories held by different schools of thought, which claim respectively that (1) there is no such thing as mind; (2) that mind is just a by-product of brain activity; (3) that mind has emerged from the brain in the course of human evolution; and (4) that mind is distinct from brain states ("dualism"). We evaluate them and expose the illogicality that most of them display. Finally we'll see how only one view is fully consistent with Christian theism—the belief that God, being a Spirit, possesses mind but no material brain, while Man, being made in the image of God, also has a "spiritual" mind that transcends his physical brain.

ARISTOTLE AND THE SNOWBALL

On human consciousness

"It seems to me immensely unlikely that mind is a mere by-product of matter. For if my mental processes are determined wholly by the motions of atoms in my brain, I have no reason to suppose that my beliefs are true. They may be sound chemically, but that does not make them sound logically. And hence I have no reason for supposing my brain to be composed of atoms. In order to escape from this necessity of sawing away the branch on which I am sitting, so to speak, I am compelled to believe that mind is not wholly conditioned by matter."

J. B. S. HALDANE, 1927[1]

How would you like to live in an ultramodern high-tech house, with its own beautifully laid-out yard and private gardens? Built on four levels, it has a basement, ground-floor living accommodation, a mezzanine entertainment suite, and a top-floor bedroom level. On the ground floor there are a variety of windows that look out on the world around you. The same is true of the mezzanine level—except that there the window-glass is colored, affecting the way you see the wider outside world. The bedrooms don't have windows, only video wall displays that can be changed at the touch of a button. The basement contains things you seldom use, together with an automatic heating plant and a lot of quiet machinery that keeps the house in tip-top working order, without you having to do anything or even being aware of it. How about the grounds? They are tended by robots controlled automatically from the basement complex. The lawns are cut, watered, and fertilized whenever sensors buried in the turf signal a need for attention; the trees are pruned and their fruit picked as required; the vegetable garden and greenhouse yield produce without any conscious effort on your part. Would you like to live there? I hope so, because you already do.

I'm not, of course, referring to a timber-bricks-and-mortar home but to the human body and mind that each of us inhabits. The garden represents your body, the house represents your brain, and you, the occupant, represent your mind. Note well the distinction between mind and brain, since it is a distinction that many neuroscientists deny, as we shall see. As you relax in your sitting room, you can mentally survey the contents of the ground floor and observe the activity in progress there—the *internal* things that you are actually conscious of. Or you can gaze out of a window and watch objects and events in the landscape beyond your property. Let's call this outside world "reality." The cellar is stacked with things that occupy your subconscious mind, along with the brain-controlled machinery that keeps your blood flowing, your lungs breathing, and your whole body functioning smoothly without conscious effort on your part.

On the mezzanine floor you keep your beliefs, morals, prejudices, opinions, convictions and suchlike things that constitute your "worldview." Like the window glass in our illustration, these things color your understanding of reality (the landscape of the world around you). This coloration, in turn, affects your attitudes and actions, sometimes without you realizing it. Finally, you can go upstairs to sleep, where you lose all consciousness of your surroundings—even though you brain is still as busy as ever, running the machinery of life and sorting out your tangled thoughts in nonsensical dreams.

Let's call this house-and-garden illustration the "Analogy," with a capital letter to distinguish it from other analogies.

EXPLANATIONS AND DEFINITIONS

We'll meet Aristotle and the snowball later in the chapter, but before we go any further, I want to make several things clear.

Firstly, please understand that the Analogy is *not* a theory of human consciousness or mind/body interaction. It is simply a device to help us understand the issues covered in this chapter. Secondly, unless otherwise stated, I shall use words like "mind," "intelligence," and "consciousness" to refer exclusively to human beings. This is not to deny that animals and even lower organisms have nervous systems, brains, intelligence, the capacity to observe, learn and communicate, the ability to react to stimuli, and so on. They obviously do possess these things, sometimes weakly, sometimes to a high degree. But in our quest to discover "what is Man," our focus here is on the human dimension and I would rather not have to qualify every reference to minds and brains by adding the descriptor "human."

Thirdly, I use the word "mind" to signify the sum of a person's self-awareness (identity), conscious thoughts, will, desires, memories, beliefs, abstract concepts, and emotions—plus anything else that has *no material or physical existence*. It thus includes such things as soul and spirit—terms I won't develop in this chapter but which we'll consider later under the biblical view of Man.

Fourthly, we need to be aware of the various theories of human consciousness and the so-called "mind/body problem," so we are going to consult some realtors or estate agents (I'll use "realtor" for brevity). Huh? Don't worry, I'm just extending the Analogy. In real life, the realtors and house agents we shall meet represent various schools of philosophical thought. Just like realtors, they may be good, bad or mediocre, and we need to learn to tell the difference.

WHAT'S YOUR LIFE WORTH?

Pursuing the Analogy, then, you decide to find out what your home is worth. Being a careful sort of person, you will seek opinions from three different realtors, but will also be prepared for their estimates to differ profoundly. I'll summarize here and work out the details later. Realtor 1 walks into your house ignoring you completely. When you ask why he is behaving so badly he replies, "Why should I take any notice of you, seeing that you don't exist? This property is just an unoccupied machine, and mind is a myth."

Realtor 2 is much nicer but she seems doubtful about the house. "I don't think it's worth much; but it would be different if it wasn't haunted."

"Haunted?" you splutter. "What do you mean, haunted? Show me the ghost!"

"Well," comes the apologetic reply, "I'm talking to it. You may think you're a real person but you are actually just a kind of emanation from all that machinery downstairs. You do exist but only as a by-product of the house. You have no *independent* existence—no strength, control, influence or power over the house or its grounds. You're just some kind of radiation field emitted by the house."

Realtor 3 is more to your liking. In his opinion you actually exist as a person; you own and enjoy the property and you can, if you choose, exercise some control over the machinery in the basement. What is more, you have the capacity to leave your home and go elsewhere without losing your identity or ceasing to exist.

Hopefully, the foregoing sketches will help us understand the *personal implications* of the actual theories of human consciousness (or some of them) that are on offer today. So we are going to consider these theories in turn and try to work out which of them make the most sense.

REALTOR 1: DOES YOUR MIND EXIST?

The view that only material objects are ultimately real is called "materialism," though other names such as "physicalism," "monism," or "reductionism" are also used. A material object can be defined as a publicly observable object, accessible to everyone in spacetime. Materialism therefore denies the existence of genuine nonmaterial entities such as mind, spirit and soul, while treating consciousness as an illusion arising from the operation of a material organ, the brain.

Materialism is based on the idea that every effect, including every human experience, must have a *physical* cause. John Haldane (1892–1964), whose comments provide our chapter-head quote, was a geneticist and religious skeptic who vigorously promoted Darwinian evolution. Yet in our quote he concludes that "mind is *not* wholly conditioned by matter"—and neatly sums up the dilemma facing those who claim that consciousness is merely a by-product of the physical brain. His opinion ought to carry weight with all of us, whatever our beliefs, but sadly it leaves materialists unmoved. For example, Francis Crick, codiscoverer of the DNA double helix, begins his book *The Astonishing Hypothesis* (reviewed by Bill Webster, of Monash University, in the journal PSYCHE[2]) with the following words:

> "The astonishing hypothesis is that 'You,' your joys and your sorrows, your memories and your ambitions, your sense of personal identity and freewill, are in fact no more than the behavior of a vast assembly of nerve cells and their associated molecules. As Lewis Carroll's Alice might have phrased [it]: 'You're nothing but a pack of neurons.' This hypothesis is so alien to the ideas of most people today that it can truly be called astonishing."[3]

Perhaps so, but the belief that mind is nothing more than a by-product of brain activity is widely held and vigorously promoted by many neuroscientists and popular science writers today. They ignore the self-evident problem highlighted by Haldane (among others) and claim that mind has no independent existence but is simply our awareness of the activity of our physical brains (our "pack of neurons"). For example, respected psychologists Malcolm Jeeves and Warren Brown declare:

> "We believe it is no longer helpful or reasonable to consider mind a nonmaterial entity that can be decoupled from the body ... [it is] a functional property of our brain and body."[4]

SNAKES AND STICKS

Patricia Churchland is an analytical philosopher noted for her work on the philosophy of mind. Unfortunately she is also an aggressively anti-Christian materialist, which colors her arguments and degrades her scientific objectivity. In her popular-level book *Touching a Nerve; Our Brains, Our Selves,* she explains that our brain circuitry is organized to provide neural models or maps of the outside world, adding:

> "When I consult a road map, there is the map in my hand and, quite separately, there is me. The map in my hand and I are not one. In the case of the brain, there is just the brain—there is no separate thing, me, existing apart from my brain ... no separate *me* that reads my brain maps."[5]

In the Analogy, this is like saying that the house (representing the physical brain) goes about its sophisticated automated functions but remains unoccupied. You, the owner, simply do not exist. She argues that external influences, imported by the physical senses, create physical maps of the external world in our physical brains, and our brains then formulate appropriate responses which issue in suitable behavior. In her materialistic scheme, no metaphysical "self" is needed to create the brain maps, read them, or initiate responses. She continues:

> "The 'designer' of brain organization is not a human cartographer, but biological evolution. If an animal's brain misrepresents its domain, mistaking a rattlesnake for a stick ... the animal will probably be killed before it can reproduce."

Thus (she claims) natural selection ensures that appropriate behavior is rewarded and inappropriate behavior is punished—causing brains to further evolve their capacity to make wise (that is, reproductively helpful) behavioral decisions.

But do neurons, neural circuits, or any of the physical hardware of the brain, have any capacity to make decisions that lead to one form of behavior rather than another—regardless of whether the decision is wise or unwise? For evolution to design the kind of system she describes, each decision would need to be random (if it were purposeful or preprogrammed, her materialistic thesis would collapse irretrievably). Granted that a decision to grab the snake could prove fatal (unless you're a mongoose), how can a *random* decision *not* to grab the snake help you next time you meet one? The only way you will avoid taking liberties with serpents in future is if you (or others you observe) survive such encounters and you learn not to risk another brush with death. In other words, a learning process is involved, and learning requires *conscious* activity.

No doubt someone will object to this last statement, pointing out that nonconscious robots and computers can learn. For example, that expensive voice-recognition software you bought for your computer had to learn the way you personally pronounce words before you could use it. Of course computers can learn, *but only if they have been preprogrammed to do so by a conscious agent*! The necessity of conscious action in learning is preserved. That's why you had to buy the expensive software; your conscious dog quickly learned to recognize your voice but your nonconscious computer would never have done so on its own. In using simplistic evolutionary arguments, Churchland is surely hiding behind a form of "psychological behaviorism"—which is defined as the belief that:

"Behavior can be described and explained without making ultimate
reference to mental events or to internal psychological

processes. The sources of behavior are external (in the environment), not internal (in the mind, in the head)."[6]

Or to put it simply, Churchland sidesteps any attempt to explain *how* brain states influence our actions and merely asserts that they do. That's fair enough, but she then smuggles in the claim that this eliminates the *need* for a conscious agency to be involved—a claim that reduces all living organisms to preprogrammed robots. Most school kids these days could design a simple robot that detects an obstacle and changes course to avoid a collision. But living organisms are more than robots.

REALTOR 2: ARE YOU A GHOST?

Your second visitor was friendlier but hardly more reassuring. On this view, consciousness is an "epiphenomenon"—something arising from the activity of the physical brain but having no independent existence, power, or significance. Yes, you do exist as a self-conscious person, but only as a helpless emanation from the material brain. When I walk into my utility room, I often hear the gentle hum that tells me the freezer is working. The hum comes and goes, of course, since the freezer motor only runs when the temperature rises in the cabinet. But this intermittent operation is itself an indication that all is well. Thus the hum does have a function but it isn't a *necessary* function; a soundproofed freezer would work equally well. The hum has no power to influence the operation of the equipment—it can't change the cabinet temperature or alter any of its other settings. It is simply a by-product (or even waste-product) of the freezer machinery, an inessential, insignificant, incidental and accidental emanation. In the more technical language of the *Stanford Encyclopedia of Philosophy*:

"Epiphenomenalism is the view that mental events are caused by
physical events in the brain, but have no effects upon any
physical events. Behavior is caused by muscles that contract
upon receiving neural impulses, and neural impulses are
generated by input from other neurons or from sense organs.
On the epiphenomenalist view, mental events play no causal
role in this process. Huxley (1874), who held the view,
compared mental events to a steam whistle that contributes
nothing to the work of a locomotive."[7]

What I have just described is an extreme form of the popular belief
that mind "emerges" from the physical brain, and we shall meet more
moderate versions of this idea below. But either way, you will often
come across the claim that mind is somehow unreal—"the ghost in
the machine." An article in *New Scientist* (August 2016) puts it thus:

"René Descartes was convinced that the body and conscious mind
are two different substances: the first is made of matter, the
latter is immaterial. His ideas influenced neuroscience until
a few decades ago, but the field has moved on. Today, it is
widely accepted that our brains give rise to consciousness. But
how? That is a raging debate."[8]

Descartes may be dead but he isn't buried (at least, some of his ideas
survive). Philosopher Keith Ward (former Regius professor of Divinity
at Oxford University) writes:[9]

"The metaphor of a ghost in the machine has worked well as a
rhetorical device to make people think that we all know the
brain (the machine) is real, whereas talk of a mind other than
the brain, or of mental events in addition to brain events, is

talk about something peculiar, not quite real, and probably illusory (a ghost). [But] ... talk of mental events is the most real thing we humans know. We know we have sense experiences, bodily sensations, thoughts, feelings and images. We know we experience things in ways that are unique to us and never wholly communicable to other people.... Mental events are real and to deny them would deprive us of all knowledge. They are not ghosts or hallucinations at all."

In the next section we shall see that the nonmaterial mind is far from powerless, having the capacity to modify brain activity and physical and emotional responses.

REALTOR 3: WHAT'S IT LIKE TO BE A BAT?

Your third valuer obviously subscribes to Haldane's conclusion, cited in our chapter-head quote: "*I am compelled to believe that mind is not wholly conditioned by matter.*" The things that makes you a self-aware person, having a continuous existence—your thoughts, personality, spirit, soul, memories, desires, ambitions, emotions and free will—are more than the unalterable and fatalistic output of your genes and neurons. In other words, Realtor 3 teaches that *dualism* (the belief that mind and physical brain are distinct) best describes the relationship between consciousness and brain, in spite of the fact that it creates what is often called the "hard problem." This is described by *New Scientist* magazine as follows:

"At its heart is what philosopher David Chalmers at New York University termed the 'hard problem' of consciousness: *how can physical networks of neurons produce experiences that appear to fall outside the material world?* As Thomas Nagel,

also at New York University, put it in the 1970s, you could
know every detail of the physical workings of a bat's brain, but
still not know what it is like to be a bat[10] (emphasis added).

Two dualistic answers can be offered to the "hard problem." Firstly, some argue that as brains evolved and became incredibly complex machines, something having a decidedly nonmaterial nature *emerged* from the machine. And this "something" was not just a helpless ghost but a mind capable of controlling the machine (at least to some extent). This is the answer offered by Raymond Tallis, whose intriguing book *Aping Mankind* we met in Chapter 1. He proposes that the evolution of the opposable thumb in an ape of some kind led to such a forward leap in dexterity that its brain underwent an evolutionary surge—causing the emergence of mind from the physical brain and producing Man as a unique kind of animal, capable of controlling its own destiny. Reverting for a moment to the Analogy, this is like saying that your house (the brain) built itself by the random accumulation of timber, bricks and glass, and then somehow accidentally created an intelligent architect who took over the management of its construction. Silly as this may seem, it lies at the heart of the emergent-mind thesis, which also predicts that computers will one day become intelligent in their own right (and, presumably, discover what it's like to be a bat; sorry, that should be "computer").

There is an amusing irony in this idea. We shall see presently that one of the strongest arguments used against dualism is that a non-physical entity such as mind could have no influence on a physical object like the brain. Why not? Because by definition, mind lacks physical properties such as mass or energy, and cannot therefore interact with a material object like the brain. Yet those who reject dualism are often the very same people who claim that nonphysical mind must have emerged in some way from the physical brain. In the Analogy, the architect is spawned by the house and completes his redesign, transforming it from ape accommodation to human habitation. He then steps outside to admire his work, forgets to take the key, and locks himself out. The mind/brain interface can be an open door, but it can't logically be a one-way turnstile.

The second and alternative dualistic view is that Man was equipped from the outset with both a material body (including a physical brain) and a nonmaterial mind. He differs from all animals by virtue of having *originated* as a thinking, self-aware, and moral creature. This, of course, is the biblical view of Man and we shall address it in Part 3 of this book. In what remains of this chapter we'll confine ourselves to examining dualism and its implications. Let's begin by recognizing that even nonemergent dualism comes in two different versions.

ARISTOTLE AND THE SNOWBALL

What is the connection between Aristotle and a snowball? Answer— hylomorphism. What's that? It's a Greek compound word meaning literally "matter form." Greek philosopher Aristotle (384–322 BC) taught that all physical objects have two basic properties, namely, matter (the stuff they are made of) and form (the way they look or are shaped; this includes such things as color, texture, and flavor). The snowball is a perfect example of hylomorphism, being made of snow (its matter) and shaped like a ball (its form). By calling it a "snow-ball" we spell out its hylomorphic nature explicitly.

Aristotle himself (who probably never saw a snowball) illustrated his theory by a lump of wax and applied it to the mind-body problem in Man. Michael Egnor explains:

"Human beings are composites of soul and body, integrated form
and matter, like (in Aristotle's phrase) the shape of wax and
the matter of the wax are just different aspects of one thing—
the wax itself. The scholastics didn't believe there was a Hard
Problem."[11]

Egnor believes that by returning to hylomorphic dualism, we could
explain consciousness in a very straightforward way, but I'm not so
sure. I think there are major problems with this view of consciousness
and mind.

Firstly, Aristotle's theory applies only to physical objects in space
and time (like snowballs and wax candles). On what grounds can
we justify its transfer to living creatures and specifically Man? How
can my nonmaterial self (or mind) become the "form" of my physical brain, so as to integrate my soul and body into a single entity?
It's easy to see how snow or wax can be formed into different shapes
without changing the substance being molded, but no such relationship exists between the "stuff" of the human brain and the "form" of
the human mind. It is OK to claim that body and mind are simply
different *aspects* of a unitary being, but we knew that already. The
hylomorphic concept sheds no light on the "hard problem" of how
these two aspects of the human person are related and interact. In this
context, hylomorphism is merely an assertion, not an explanation.

Secondly, the hylomorphic concept handcuffs mind and body
together in a way that no theist can logically accept. Going back to
the Analogy, it means that you (the mind) who occupy the house (the
brain), are simply part of the furniture. According to materialism, you
either don't exist at all or else you are purely decorative (powerless).
Aristotle certainly improves on that, but it leaves our mind as part of
the fabric of the house, just like the basement machinery. It may be

that the mind is a different *kind* of machine from those that pump our blood or digest our food. We could for example liken the mind to an electrical system which controls the mechanical machinery that performs such basic tasks. But can that be all? If so, the mind would be just as controlled by our physical genes and brain cells as the physical parts of our body. Furthermore, any distinction between Man and other animals would be lost and dualism would fail (as many think it does).

Most serious of all, the idea that our minds are merely a nonmaterial aspect of our integrated persons means that the mind cannot exist without a body (although a body can theoretically exist without a mind, producing a zombie). But a theist is one who believes that God himself is a spirit, possessing mind but *no physical form or constitution.* If God exists, then mind can exist without being joined to a body. Furthermore, Christian theists also believe that since Man is made in the image of God, our human minds continue to exist when our bodies die. As Paul declares, "To be absent from the body is to be present with the Lord."[12] Clearly, biblical Christianity requires that our nonmaterial minds are capable of existing apart from our physical bodies, and hylomorphic dualism doesn't offer that option.[13]

SUBSTANCE DUALISM

Fortunately, there is another kind of dualism, based on the teaching of French philosopher René Descartes (1596–1650) and known as "substance dualism." It is fair to say that most philosophers either reject it outright or view it with suspicion, but several respected authorities have recently rallied to its support, including J. P. Moreland[14] and Keith Ward. The latter writes:

"Dualism, the original sin of Descartes, is not yet dead. Dualists can
be found hiding in the philosophical undergrowth, slightly
cowed perhaps but still defiant. The heart of dualism, in the
sense relevant to this discussion, is that mind and matter
are two distinct sorts of things. Minds do not exist in space,
whereas matter is defined in terms of its location and extent in
space. Minds think, feel, and perceive and matter does not."[15]
(The reference to "original sin" is, of course, a joke.)

Both Tallis and Ward (among many others) point out that what are
often called "qualia" (a technical term derived from "qualities") exist
only in so far as they are *experienced* by conscious minds. These
qualia include such familiar things as pleasure, pain, sadness (and
emotions in general) together with the *perception* of sounds, colors,
tastes, odors, and other things—detected by the physical senses but
only *experienced* in the mind.

Besides qualia, there are other categories of mental activity that
are clearly nonmaterial. Firstly, there are abstract concepts accessible
to our minds such as shapes, numbers, and mathematical operations. These can, of course, be copied down on paper or some other
medium, thus seeming to be material objects. But they don't have to
be written down; they can be thought up and manipulated entirely in
the mental realm. They are *essentially* nonmaterial, occupying neither
space nor time. Finally, there is the human capacity to imagine things,
whether they exist materially or don't exist at all. In material terms,
we can build castles out of stone or sand, but mentally we can build
"castles in the air." This ability to think *about* things whether or not
we are currently *experiencing* them, or even if they don't actually exist,
is sometimes called "intentionality."

Finally, the awareness of ourselves as persons, enjoying continuity over time and distinct from other human persons, is a nonphysical mental experience. Unlike qualia which are transient, self-awareness tells us that our childhood memories and lifetime histories were just as much *ours* as our current experience of reading this book. Although we age and change with the passing years, the healthy mind has a sense of continuing identity, the belief that it belongs to a single enduring person. Keith Ward argues that even if such a mind had emerged from a complex physical brain, the fact of its *emergence* would necessarily make it something composed of nonmaterial "stuff"—a different kind of "substance" from the physical substances that make up our brains and bodies. Emergence implies, he adds, "that minds are different from matter. They could in principle be decoupled from matter …."[16] We have already seen, of course, that the idea of mind emerging from brain actually offers no explanation of the relationship between the two, but even if it were true it would do nothing to solve "the hard problem." But in spite of these fairly obvious reasons for treating mind and matter as two different things (or "substances"), vociferous objections are raised against substance dualism. I'll deal with the three strongest arguments here.

LIBET'S EXPERIMENT

Consider first an experiment first conducted in 1983 by neurologist Benjamin Libet.[17] He attached "brainwave" detector electrodes to the scalps of volunteer subjects and asked them to flex their fingers or wrists at a time of their own choosing. He also provided them with the means of recording the moment they became aware of the decision to flex. He found that brainwave activity associated with the act of flexing could be detected a third of a second (or more) *before* the subjects were conscious of their decision to initiate movement. The experiment has been verified in various laboratories, some using "functional MRI" scans instead of electrodes to detect brain activity. A delay is consistently found between the onset of brain activity and the subject's awareness that they have made the decision to activate movement. Opponents of dualism claim that when subjects think they are making a conscious (and "freewill") decision of mind, they are actually just obeying instructions that originate earlier in their material brains. Mind, they argue, has no power of its own but simply follows the dictates of neurons and electrical circuits in the brain. How else could the results be explained? Quite easily, as it happens.

Libet himself thought that the preconscious brain activity he observed was simply preparatory to conscious action. That is, the subjects know they are going to flex their fingers at a time of their own choosing, and it is this knowledge that is reflected in brain activity prior to the decision being made. When athletes run races, before the starting gun is fired, they are made ready by instructions to be "on your marks" and "get set." Their decision to "go" isn't made until they hear the gun (they get disqualified if it is), but their bodies are tensed in anticipation several seconds before the gun fires and they leave their starting blocks. Libet's and similar experiments provide no support for the idea that our conscious minds are slaves of our neurons.

How can mind interact with matter?

The second objection raised against substance dualism is that no one can explain how a nonmaterial mind, having no material properties, could influence the material (electrical and chemical) processes of the brain. However, just because we cannot explain something doesn't mean it can't happen. In fact, there is ample evidence that nonmaterial mind can and does influence the brain, often profoundly. Mario Beauregard, of the Neuroscience Research Centre, University of Montreal, sets out a comprehensive case for this contention in his 2012 book *Brain Wars*.[18] He details scientific studies of many mental phenomena that have been shown to influence the workings of the brain. These include neuro-feedback and meditation techniques to control brainwaves and the moods associated with them, mental pain control, and the medical use of hypnosis and "suggestion." (More controversially, he also cites "near-death experiences" to support his case.) Here, space allows me to give just a few examples, though I deal with the subject at greater length in *Who Made God?*[19]

How thinking can change the brain

You have probably heard of the "placebo effect" in medicine. Patients given an inactive substance but told that they are receiving a new drug developed to treat their illness usually show clinically significant improvements in their condition. As a consequence, all new drugs are now subject to double-blind trials, in which neither the patient nor the prescribing doctor knows whether the drug or an inactive placebo is being administered. Not infrequently, the placebo confers the same benefit as the experimental drug (which then, of course, is pronounced a failure). But the phenomenon is not limited to medicines.

Baba Shiv, a professor of marketing at Stanford Business School, gave the same wine to a group of people but the first time they received it he told them it cost $45 a bottle and the second time $5.[20] Unsurprisingly, the group declared that the "more expensive" wine tasted better. However, he also used "functional" MRI brain scans to examine the pleasure centers of his subjects' brains and found that these centers "lit up" more strongly when they thought they were drinking expensive wine. The volunteers' false beliefs really did affect their brain activity—not the other way around.

A second example[21] was a study at the Garvan Institute in Sydney, Australia. Volunteer recreational athletes were given either growth hormones or inactive placebos—without knowing which they were taking. After eight weeks, the volunteers who *thought* they were taking performance-enhancing drugs but were only taking placebos actually outperformed everyone else in the trial. The strong relative performance of the placebo takers could not be due to the attention they were receiving, because all participants in the trial received the same treatment. But even if care and attention was responsible in some way, this in itself is significant. We all know that encouragement stimulates improvements in performance, whatever the field of endeavor. But why? It can only be that the mind, motivated by *nonphysical* encouragement, induces *physical* changes in the brain—that then result in greater effort being made. Either way, the trial showed that believing that you are receiving a performance-enhancing drug improves performance—even when the belief is false. These results can mean only one thing—the nonmaterial mind (belief) can change the brain (the ultimate physical source of improved performance).

No one is really sure how or why the placebo and similar effects influence the brain, but they undoubtedly do. Perhaps the most likely answer involves the exchange of *information* between the mind and the brain. Everything we have considered in this and some earlier chapters shows that there is two-way traffic between the nonmaterial mind and the material brain (and thence onwards to experiences and/or physical actions). The physical brain responds to the input of nonmaterial information (both true and false) and stores that information in memory. The absorbed information must then become physically encoded in the brain, perhaps through epigenetic changes or in the brain's physical circuitry. But either way we can envisage nonmaterial information and the physical brain working together in harness to produce human experience and activity.

THE ROLE OF INFORMATION

Having introduced the concept of information, we are now ready to deal with the third objection to substance dualism. It is deceptively simple. If a human brain is damaged or destroyed, the mind associated with that brain is also damaged or destroyed. Doesn't this prove that mind and brain are just different aspects of the same thing? It is true that in life, the mind "shelters" in the brain and cannot function without it. In the Analogy, the occupant needs the shelter of the house, but this doesn't mean that the occupant is part of the furniture. A different analogy might help us here.

If the book you are reading is burned to ashes, the information it contains vanishes with it. Before it is destroyed, the nonmaterial information "shelters" in the material paper and ink of the physical book. But obviously, the information is not made of paper and ink; it has an existence quite apart from the medium on which it is stored. If this were the only copy of the book in existence, the information would be irretrievably lost (a mind would die with the associated brain and cease to exist). But suppose that the author of the book had perfectly memorized the text. Then the information would continue to exist even though the only physical medium containing it had been destroyed. If, therefore, every human mind is archived in the mind of God, every such mind survives the destruction of the brain in which it once resided. This is the clear implication of the Bible's teaching on the survival of the soul, the resurrection of the dead, the final judgment, and everlasting life.

So can information exist without residing in a physical organ? Undoubtedly. And can information be encoded and utilized by physical organs? Of course; there would be no such thing as life if that were not so. Is mind, then, composed of information? Yes, in one sense, but it must also possess the ability to evaluate, manipulate, and use that information. And mind must also have further dimensions of a moral, rational, and transcendent nature—as we shall see in the final section of this book.

ENDNOTES:

1   Haldane, J.B.S.; "When I am dead" in *Possible Worlds and Other Essays* (1927; Chatto and Windus, London, 1932 reprint, p. 209. There is a 2001 reprint by Transaction Publishers).

2   PSYCHE, 2(18), July 1995 http://psyche.cs.monash.edu.au/v2/psyche-2-18-webster.html
    Review of; Francis Crick (1994) *The Astonishing Hypothesis: The Scientific Search for the Soul.* New York: Charles Scribner's Sons.

3   Crick, Francis; *The Astonishing Hypothesis* (1994) p. 3.

4   Jeeves, Malcolm, and Brown, Warren; *Neuroscience, Psychology and Religion* (Templeton Press, West Conshohocken, PA, 2009) p. 52.

5   Churchland, Patricia, Touching a Nerve; Our Brains, Ourselves (W. W. Norton & Co., New York & London, 2013) p. 34.

6   https://plato.stanford.edu/entries/behaviorism/

7   https://plato.stanford.edu/entries/epiphenomenalism/

8   https://www.newscientist.com/article/mg23130890-300-metaphysics-special-what-is-consciousness/

9   Ward, Keith; *More than Matter?* (Lion Hudson, Oxford, 2010) p. 23.

10 https://www.newscientist.com/article/mg23130890-300-metaphysics-special-what-is-consciousness/

[11] Egnor, Michael, What is consciousness? http://www.evolutionnews.
org/2016/07/what_is_conscio102995.html

[12] 2 Corinthians 5:6–9.

[13] Note that mediaeval theologians such as Duns Scotus and Thomas
Aquinas did develop Christian applications of hylomorphism but their
arguments become very complicated and unconvincing. For a brief but
comprehensive discussion of these matters, see https://en.wikipedia.
org/wiki/Hylomorphism

[14] See e.g. Moreland, J. P.; *The recalcitrant Imago Dei* (SCM Press, London,
2009).

[15] Ward, Keith, loc. cit. pp. 112–113.

[16] Ward, Keith, loc. cit. p. 116.

[17] http://www.informationphilosopher.com/freedom/libet_experiments.
html

[18] Beauregard, Mario; *Brain Wars* (Harper-One, New York, 2012).

[19] Andrews, Edgar; *Who made God? Searching for a theory of everything*
(3rd edition; EP Books, Welwyn Garden City, 2016) p. 260.

[20] Kealey, Terence; *The Times* (London), 25 February 2008, p. 16.

[21] Reported in *The Times* (London), 18 June 2008, p. 24.

CHAPTER 10

In a now-defunct internet blog, atheist Richard Dawkins once described me as a "wingnut," which can be freely translated as "a crazy person" or someone "lacking mental abilities." Why? You'll have to ask him, but I suspect it was because he couldn't get his head around the fact that, as a highly qualified research scientist and university teacher, I nevertheless believed the Bible. Would he, I wonder, say the same of intellectual giants and Christians such as Isaac Newton (who discovered the laws of gravity and motion), Michael Faraday (who gave us electricity in a usable form), Clerk Maxwell (whose electromagnetic field theory first explained light and radiation), Werner Heisenberg (who originated quantum mechanics), and Arno Penzias (radio astronomer and 1978 Nobel Prize winner)?

The huge philosophical gulf between Dawkins and Bible-believing scientists arises from their respective worldviews. To an atheist, a scientific worldview is utterly incompatible with a religious worldview. To a Christian, a biblical worldview embraces both science and faith in a God who has created all things and continues to sustain them. So in this chapter we shall discuss worldviews (what they are and how they differ) before explaining the essential features of a biblical worldview. The chapter therefore serves as a bridge, linking our earlier explorations of humanity to the Bible's teaching on the nature of Man.

WORLDVIEWS AT WAR

On the nature of reality

"Even more purposeless, more void of meaning, is the world which Science presents for our belief. Amid such a world, if anywhere, our ideals henceforward must find a home. That Man is the product of causes which had no prevision of the end they were achieving; that his origin, his growth, his hopes and fears, his loves and his beliefs, are but the outcome of accidental collocations of atoms; ... all these things, if not quite beyond dispute, are yet so nearly certain that no philosophy which rejects them can hope to stand. Only ... on the firm foundation of unyielding despair can the soul's habitation henceforth be safely built."

BERTRAND RUSSELL, 1903.[1]

"God so loved the world that he gave his only begotten son, that whoever believes in him should not perish but have everlasting life."

THE APOSTLE JOHN, CIRCA AD 68.[2]

The picture on the birthday card showed a spherical goldfish bowl containing two goldfish and a mobile radio miraculously working underwater. The conversation went as follows:

> Radio: "Liverpool have just scored from a corner!"
> First fish: "What's a corner?"
> Second fish: "I've no idea."

"Liverpool," of course, means UK's Liverpool Football Club, and you will find the joke either hilarious or incomprehensible. If the latter, you'll have to ask a soccer fan or a philosopher. You find the soccer fan and I'll provide the philosopher—specifically, Immanuel Kant (1724–1804) the German philosopher who invented the term "worldview" (German *Weltanschauung*) to describe the way we interpret the world around us—both as regards what it means and how we relate to it. The goldfish have no concept of a "corner" because their world (the spherical bowl) contains no such thing. There's no place for corners in their worldview.

But the birthday card humor is not really about goldfish bowls, it's about us. It offers a shrewd commentary on the fact that we human beings differ greatly among ourselves in the way we perceive the world around us. This is starkly demonstrated by the two quotations that head this chapter. Bertrand Russell's atheistic, almost nihilistic, worldview offers no hope for a meaning in life, but John's God-centered worldview holds out the prospect of love, deliverance, and eternal life for those who embrace it.

The purpose of this chapter, then, is to provide a bridge between the first two parts of this book and the final part. In Chapters 1–9, we have examined in some detail how secularism, materialism, and atheism seek to explain "life, the universe, and everything." I hope I have shown that by leaving God out of the equation, all such theories and speculations (together with the worldviews they support) actually offer no ultimate explanations at all. But what is the alternative?

In this chapter, I am going to introduce a biblical worldview that in my opinion, both as a scientist and a Christian, does provide answers to ultimate questions. It also explains why, as argued in earlier chapters, attempts to airbrush God out of the picture always end up in scientific and philosophical blind alleys.

WORLDVIEWS AND AXIOMS

Of course, our two chapter-head worldviews exist alongside an almost continuous spectrum of possible alternatives. But wherever you stand on that spectrum, three things must be obvious: (1) whether we know it or not, each of us has a worldview of some kind; (2) not all worldviews can be true; and (3) the worldview we adopt will have a profound impact on our life.

Every belief system has its own worldview, even those belief systems that believe they have no beliefs. However, I distinguish between a belief system and a worldview in the same way as we distinguish between a house and its foundations. That is, I'm using "worldview" to mean the underlying assumptions (or presuppositions) on which any belief systems must be built.

A worldview consists of ideas we perceive to be "true" or self-evident, even though we can't prove their truth to other people. Science and mathematics are built on the foundation of assumptions called "axioms."[3] Scientific axioms include the beliefs that the natural world is governed by laws that do not change from day to day or place to place, and that humans possess the ability to comprehend the natural world. In mathematics, an axiom is a starting point from which other statements can be logically derived. Similarly, religions are based on what some philosophers call "warranted beliefs"[4]—our personal convictions that certain things are true and others false. Valid beliefs and axioms are those that can be reinforced by experience, even though they cannot be *proved* by formal logic or mathematical theorems.

Thus Bertrand Russell's worldview was based on a belief that God does not exist, while John's rested on the opposite conviction that he does. In both cases, an appeal is made to experience. Russell asserts that there is no *scientific* evidence of God's existence—which is plainly not so, as we saw in Chapter 2 where we considered the origin of the laws of nature. His stance also involves the further (and obviously false) assumption that science is the only valid source of genuine experience and true knowledge. On the other hand, John presents his personal experience of the life and teaching of Jesus Christ as evidence for the reality of God—explaining that he wrote his Gospel "that you might believe that Jesus is the Christ, the son of God, and that believing you might have life in his name."[5] Neither claim will satisfy everyone, because different people's worldviews are built on different assumptions. A person's worldview can change, of course, but only as a result of *personal* experience or *personal* reasoning, by which their basic assumptions are replaced by new ones. But how are we to know which assumptions are true and which are false? Or to put it another way, how can we recognize which basic assumptions (if any) represent *reality* as distinct from error or illusion? Let's ponder the question for a while.

CAN WE ACCESS REALITY?

I hope you haven't forgotten the Analogy of Chapter 9 because we need to revisit it. Not totally satisfied with the verdicts of Realtors 1,

2, and 3, you decide to consult a couple more. But realtor 3, who lifted your spirits, is followed by realtor 4 who gets you worried again. She arrives at your garden gate but declines to enter the property. Why? She explains that the house is a private world that only you yourself can experience. No one else can enter and look around, nor can you visit anyone else. Like her, you are denied access to other properties, imprisoned forever in your own thoughts. If, in the last analysis (she argues), we can only believe things on the basis of our own subjective observations, how can we be sure that these observations provide access to the *same* reality as others see and talk about? According to cosmologists Stephen Hawking and Leonard Mlodinow in their book *The Grand Design*, we can't be sure. They write:

> "These examples bring us to a conclusion that will be important in this book: there is no picture-[independent] or theory-independent concept of reality. Instead, we will adopt a view that we will call model-dependent realism; the idea that a physical theory or world-picture [worldview] is a model ... and a set of rules that connect the elements of the model to observation. This provides a framework with which to interpret modern science." [6]

They continue: "According to model-dependent realism, it is pointless to ask whether a model is real, only that it agrees with observation."[7] So according to Hawking and his coauthor, our observations can never connect us with reality (whatever that may be) but can only help us build models that may or may not represent reality. They would argue (correctly) that we believe in electromagnetic waves not because we can see them oscillating in the void but because they offer a coherent explanation of the colors we see, the heat we feel, and the radio signals we hear when we turn on our TVs. Our direct sensations allow us to model these unseen electromagnetic waves, but whether or not the models correspond to reality (they say) we shall never know. Hawking and his coauthor don't seem to understand that their "model-dependent realism" is actually what philosophers have long called "antirealism"— the very opposite of realism which (according to the *Stanford Encyclopedia of Philosophy*) involves "the metaphysical commitment to the existence of a mind-independent reality."[8] So is there a real reality out there beyond our inner experiences? *How you answer that question will profoundly affect your worldview.* So let's think about it.

IS REALITY REAL?

Realtor 5 arrives. When you point out the excellent views you have over the world beyond your property, he says you are fooling yourself. This outside "reality" doesn't actually exist, he explains, but is manufactured by yourself every time you look out of your windows. When you aren't looking, it simply isn't there. When you protest that you see the same views whenever you do look, so they must exist even when unobserved, he smiles and asks how you intend to prove this claim. Ultimately, he argues, only mind exists, and matter is a figment of your imagination. He is clearly an antirealist, but could he be right?

Personally, I get a lot of help from philosopher George Berkeley (1685–1753) because he turned antirealism on its head. He began by reasoning (in agreement with Stephen Hawking and realtor 5) that we can only *know* that a material object exists when we *are perceiving* it by our senses. This argument is sometimes called "empiricism" and is neatly summarized in a limerick:

> There was a young man who said, "God
> must find it exceedingly odd
> when he finds that the tree
> continues to be
> when no one's about in the Quad." [9]

However, an anonymous versifier replies:

> Dear sir, your astonishment's odd.
> I'm always about in the Quad.
> And that's why the tree
> continues to be
> Since observed by, yours faithfully, God.

For a theist like Berkeley, of course, the latter verse expresses belief in a "real" objective universe that exists independently of mankind's perception of it but which, crucially, depends on the existence of a cosmic mind, namely God. In spite of Stephen Hawking's claims, all scientific endeavors rest on an axiomatic belief in objective reality—for unless there is a "real" universe out there, *independent of man's mind*, there is nothing for science to investigate. This harmonizes, of course, with Berkeley's ontological scheme, namely that the universe and all its contents exist in the mind of God, who is the ultimate observer. (It is of note that Stephen Hawking in the final chapter of his earlier book *A brief History of Time*, doesn't hesitate to refer to "the mind of God," mentioning it seriously eight times in its five closing pages.[10]) Berkeley doesn't deny that things exist when we don't perceive them, writing:

> "To me it is evident ... that sensible things [things we sense] can't
> exist except in a mind or spirit. From this I conclude, not

that they have no real existence but that—seeing they don't depend on my thought, and have an existence distinct from being perceived by me—there must be some other mind in which they exist. As sure as the sensible world really exists, therefore, so sure is there an infinite omnipresent Spirit who contains and supports it."[11]

While we must agree that much of our knowledge is inferential, Berkeley firmly roots our experiences and observations in a genuine, external, and unchanging reality—the reality of the mind of God. Without the existence of such a "real reality" to which our own observation and experience gives us at least partial access, the entire scientific enterprise rests on very shaky ground.

IS THERE A GENUINE BIBLICAL WORLDVIEW?

Is it possible, then, to formulate a biblical worldview? Many today deny that such a worldview is possible. They argue that the Bible, taken as a whole, is self-contradictory and offers no consistent picture of reality. After all, they say, the Old and New Testaments contain 66 separate books written over a period of some 1500 years by an indeterminate number of different authors, some known and some unknown. Furthermore, it encompasses a wide variety of styles and genres, including poetry and prose, history and allegory, prophecy and apocalypse, along with wisdom literature of various kinds. How can such a random compilation of ancient literature offer us any meaningful explanation of life, the universe, and everything today? Others, while seeming to embrace a biblical worldview, do so only by rewriting the Bible (they would call it reinterpretation). That is, they adjust what the Bible actually teaches to conform to their own personal perspectives or extrabiblical viewpoints. They are like a child who shoots an arrow at a barn door and then paints a target around it—guaranteeing a bull's-eye every time.

A genuine biblical worldview, then, must clearly respond to these criticisms, whether they are explicit or implicit. It does so in a radical manner—by setting out, as one of its basic elements, its own doctrine of divine inspiration. If we presuppose (1) that God exists, and (2) that he desires to communicate with mankind, how would he do this? It is likely that he would use methods and media available to humanity throughout its history. He wouldn't use the Morse code or the internet, for example. As regards methods, human languages would seem to be the ideal choice, being endowed with a high degree of portability, precision, and permanence. Teaching can, of course, be transmitted by word of mouth, but the written word (in whatever language) is more likely to survive in an unadulterated form. The existence of a written revelation is therefore entirely consistent with the basic tenets of theism.

It also follows that while such revelation originates with God, it would be entirely natural for it to be written down by human beings— requiring God to use human messengers in the process. This is exactly what the Bible claims. For example, King David wrote, "The Spirit of the Lord spoke by me and his word was on my tongue" (2 Samuel 23:1-2). The result? The greater part of the Bible's book of Psalms. In the New Testament, Peter explains the origin of the Old Testament writings as follows: "No scripture is of [in the sense of "exists by"] any private interpretation, but holy men of God spoke as they were moved by the Holy Spirit" (2 Peter 1:20). The context makes it clear that Peter is not referring here to the interpretation of *existing* scripture but to the "coming into being" of new scripture through a prophet's interpretation of God (literally, a "speaking between" God and man).

Paul likewise claims, "[These] things we also speak, not in words which man's wisdom teaches, but which the Holy Spirit teaches" (1 Corinthians 2:13) and tells Timothy that "All scripture is breathed out by God and is profitable for teaching, for reproof, for correction, and for instruction in righteousness" (2 Timothy 3:16 ESV).

The latter quote, although taken from the New Testament, refers primarily to the Old Testament, which constituted the "Bible" of the early church until the New Testament writings were in general circulation. It was only at this stage that the Bible as we know it today was completed. This is important because it demonstrates that first-century Christians saw *both* Testaments as revealed Scripture—one looking forward to the coming of the Messiah and the other looking back on his accomplished work of redemption. When we talk of a biblical worldview, therefore, we mean one which encompasses both Testaments and, crucially, harmonizes their teaching. For example, Jews might legitimately claim to hold an "Old Testament worldview" while rejecting the claims of Jesus Christ. But their OT worldview, while "biblical" in one sense, is not biblical in the sense I am using the term in this chapter.

CIRCULAR REASONING?

The Bible's claims to divine inspiration are, of course, made by the Bible itself, and so involve a measure of circular reasoning or "self-referral," but this is inevitable. By definition, "revelation" communicates information that is otherwise unknowable to those receiving it. It cannot, therefore, be verified independently (though in some cases it may be substantiated by subsequent events, as when prophecies are fulfilled at a later date). But remember what we have learned about axioms and presuppositions. Every worldview depends upon some unprovable assumptions, but can become a "warranted belief" by virtue of personal (including shared) experience. If, as Christians claim, the Bible (1) is consistent with Man's understanding of himself and of the cosmos; (2) has made verifiable predictions of future events; (3) passes the test of historical accuracy; and (4) often leads people into a personal experience of God through faith in Jesus Christ, then it is both rational and warranted for Christians to claim that the Bible's ultimate author is God rather than men.

With respect to (1), the Bible does indeed provide answers to the enigma of Man's nature, described so clearly in Alexander Pope's poem quoted at the start of Chapter 1. With respect to (2) the Old Testament both foreshadows and makes detailed predictions of the coming, Person, and work of Jesus Christ. In Luke's Gospel, chapter 24, we read that, "beginning at Moses and all the prophets, he [Jesus] expounded to them in all the scriptures the things concerning himself."[12] An outstanding example of this is the way Isaiah 53, written hundreds of years before Christ was born, describes in explicit detail the death of Christ and its redeeming purpose. There are also many other biblical prophesies that have been fulfilled historically long after they were made.[13] With respect to (3), archaeology and historiography both provide clear evidence of the historical accuracy of the Bible[14].

This last point is worth emphasizing. While most religions have their own "holy books" or scriptures, and some claim they are divinely revealed, the Bible is unique in that its message stands or falls on historical facts. These vary from such mundane things as place names, trade routes, and identified kings, rulers, and empires; to fact claims such as the physical resurrection and ascension of Jesus following his crucifixion. Paul writes, "If Christ is not risen, then our preaching is in vain and your faith is also in vain,"[15] but he also presents historical evidence for the resurrection: "He was seen [alive] by Cephas, then by the twelve. After that he was seen by over five hundred brethren at once, of whom the greater part remain to the present."[16] Skeptics, of course, will reject these claims but I submit that the divine authorship of the Bible, in both its Testaments, is a self-consistent warranted belief. There does exist, therefore, a coherent biblical worldview. So let's try to see what it is.

THE BIBLICAL WORLDVIEW

By defining reality as that which exists in the mind of God, George Berkeley has already brought us to the heart of the biblical worldview, which (in the words of the apostle Paul) tells us that "in him [God] we live and move and have our being."[17] But to break this worldview down into its component presuppositions, I'm going to use Paul's address to the Stoic and Epicurean philosophers at Athens as a kind of template. This passage is specially helpful because, although the apostle is talking to highly intelligent people, they were nevertheless polytheistic idol worshippers, having no knowledge of the Jewish faith or scriptures. So he could take nothing of his own viewpoint for granted and had to cover the most basic ideas about the God to whom he sought to introduce them. Here is what he said in Acts 17:22–31 (I retain the verse numbers for ease of reference in what follows):

(22) "Men of Athens, I perceive that in all things you are very
religious; (23) for as I was passing through and considering
the objects of your worship, I even found an altar with this
inscription: 'to the unknown God.' Therefore, the one whom
you worship without knowing, him I proclaim to you: (24)
God, who made the world and everything in it, since he is
Lord of heaven and Earth, does not dwell in temples made
with hands. (25) Nor is he worshipped with men's hands, as

though he needed anything, since he gives to all life, breath, and all things. (26) And he has made from one man every nation of men to dwell on all the face of the Earth, and has determined their pre-appointed times and the boundaries of their dwellings, so that they should seek the Lord, in the hope that they might grope for him and find him—though he is not far from each one of us; (28) for in him we live and move and have our being, as also some of your own poets have said, 'For we are also his offspring.' (29) Therefore, since we are the offspring of God, we ought not to think that the Divine Nature is like gold or silver or stone, something shaped by art and man's devising. (30) Truly, these times of ignorance God overlooked, but now commands all men everywhere to repent, (31) because he has appointed a day on which he will judge the world in righteousness by the man whom he has ordained. He has given assurance of this to all by raising him from the dead."

No doubt this is a synopsis of a longer speech, but that may actually help bring out the central ideas more clearly. What, then, according to Paul, are the basic building blocks of the biblical worldview?

GOD THE CREATOR

Firstly, there is a Creator who Paul calls "God" and who is responsible for the existence of "the world and everything in it." This was not universally accepted in Paul's day, any more than it is in ours. The old idea that the physical universe is itself eternal, and therefore had no need of a creator, goes back a long way. Aristotle argued for it, though certain Neoplatonists rejected the idea. Medieval philosophers also debated the matter, and modern theories of an eternal cosmos were discussed briefly in Chapter 2 and are still current. It is only in the last fifty years or so that most cosmologists, through the weight of evidence, have adopted a "standard model" of the universe which recognizes that it did have a beginning—just as the Bible has always said: "In the beginning God created the heavens and the Earth."[18] Aristotle reasoned that the physical cosmos could not have had a physical cause, since (being physical) any such "cause" would be part of the cosmos and thus incapable of creating it. That's fair enough so far, but then he drew the wrong conclusion, namely that the physical world had no cause at all and thus had no beginning. But Paul (following biblical teaching generally) solves Aristotle's dilemma at a stroke by attributing creation to a *spiritual* Being who is independent of the physical world.

Interestingly, this attribution has a necessary implication. If all physical or material entities are excluded as causes, it also means that the cosmos was created *ex nihilo* (out of nothing) and not from some precursor substances. In this respect, the biblical view is arguably unique among the multitude of mankind's creation stories. "Creation myths" abound, and almost every culture, tribe, and religion has its own story of how the world came to exist. In our modern scientific age, most of these myths are recognized as primitive, amusing, and often bizarre—futile attempts to explain mysteries, some of which remain unsolved today. But we need to remember that communities in various parts of the world still cling tenaciously to their creation myths, either as genuine history or as the embodiment of lasting wisdom. I quote below just three of many examples.[19]

- A cosmic ocean is a motif found in the Creation myths of many cultures and civilizations. The cosmic ocean is often seen as the entire universe in a dim and nonspecific past, and the first source of gods or the world. Often, the cosmic ocean is still considered to surround the present world.

- Egyptian creation stories variously feature a cosmic "egg," "primeval waters," or a "primeval mound." One version relates how the sun god emerged from the primeval mound, which itself stood in the chaos of a primeval sea.

- According to one Chinese creation myth, the universe began as an amorphous chaos. This collapsed to form a cosmic egg which remained for thousands of years while the opposing principles of Yin and Yang were balanced within it. Eventually a horned giant called Pangu emerged from the egg and began to create the world by dividing the "murky Yin" of Earth from the "clear Yang" of sky with a swing of his axe.

These and many other creation myths exhibit some interesting features. Firstly, common themes occur repeatedly even in widely separated parts of the world. One almost universal idea is that the Earth's surface was initially covered entirely by an ocean—out of which emerged not only geographical and biological features but even the gods who created them. The cosmic ocean is sometimes replaced or accompanied by a cosmic egg from which the world as we know it emerged. Implicit in these ideas is that some material stuff (whether water or "egg" or chaos) was eternal, having no beginning. Only rarely is eternal existence attributed to gods or sentient creators. Another point of interest is the way these ancient ideas live on in our scientific age. As we saw in Chapters 2 to 4, the search for extra-terrestrial life is dominated by the belief that such life is most likely to be found on planets (or even satellites) where oceans exist or have existed in the past, while the idea of an eternal cosmic egg has been resurrected as a quantum precursor of the Big Bang.

While ancient creation narratives sometimes echo the biblical account of creation, where waters also covered the Earth's surface initially, they differ in two fundamental ways. Firstly, the Bible's concept of *ex nihilo* creation is not found in any of these myths. The nearest thing is when "chaos" is presented as the primeval condition of the universe, but chaos is not "nothing." Secondly, the biblical Creator is one who stands outside of time ("with the Lord one day is as a thousand years and a thousand years as one day"; 2 Peter 3:8), but this concept is also absent from other creation stories. It is entirely fair to say, therefore, that the Bible's creation account is unique by virtue of these two sophisticated ideas. Skeptics may point to resemblances between the biblical account and the creation myths of other cultures and claim that the biblical narrative is just another of the same kind. But similarities, such as they are, could have an entirely different explanation. A creation myth might reflect certain basic creation facts that have been passed on from the dawn of human history by cultural transmission—even though they have become corrupted beyond recognition in other ways. The Bible's view of God as Creator, on the other hand, has survived the test of time—to a degree that made it possible for me, as a scientist in the twenty-first century, to write Chapter 2 of this book!

Lord of heaven and Earth (1) Providence

The next foundational element of Paul's worldview is that God not only "made the world and everything in it" (past tense), but is "Lord [or ruler] of heaven and Earth" (present tense; v.24). There are three issues here providing us with the second, third, and fourth elements of the biblical worldview, and we shall look at them in turn. They are the activity of God, the sovereignty of God, and the immanence of God ("immanence" means that God's presence permeates the material creation while being wholly distinct from it; compare Psalm 139). Let's start with activity (God's providence).

Many worldviews that acknowledge the existence of God nevertheless see him as uninvolved—being remote, unconcerned, or inactive in the world of human experience. Deists, for example, believe that God created all things but subsequently left his creation to its own devices—becoming the ultimate absent landlord. Many animistic worldviews also admit the existence of a Supreme Being but consider that humans need only concern themselves with the active spirits that inhabit rivers, forests, mountains, rocks, and so on, since only these spirits have any direct impact on people's daily lives. In Greek mythology, the gods were generally too busy fighting and scheming against one another to take much notice of lowly mankind, and so we could continue.

By contrast, the God of the Bible is profoundly active in the world. "He gives to all, life and breath and all things" (v.25). This activity can be called "the providence of God" and is referred to in innumerable Bible texts, such as Moses' assurance that "the eternal God is your refuge and underneath are the everlasting arms"[20]; the claim that God is the ultimate provider of our food ("You visit the Earth and water it ... you provide their grain ... You make it soft with showers, you bless its growth ..."[21]); and Paul's confidence that "all things work together for good to those who love God."[22]

Lord of heaven and Earth (2) Sovereignty

The third element of the biblical worldview is that, in spite of appearances, God is in control. Paul indicates that human political history is ordained by God, who has "made from one man every nation of men to dwell on all the face of the Earth, and has determined their pre-appointed times and the boundaries of their habitations" (v.26). More generally, he tells us elsewhere that God "works all things according to the counsel of his will,"[23] while even Nebuchadnezzar, a heathen Old Testament king, felt compelled to testify that God "does according to his will in the army of heaven and among the inhabitants of the Earth. No one can restrain his hand or say to him, "What have you done?""[24] We echo this teaching, of course, when we call God "almighty."

Admittedly, this creates a problem—if God is both good and almighty, why does he not prevent all evil, whether arising from natural disasters, human wickedness, or any other cause? A second concern is that the teaching could encourage fatalism, which is found in some religions but is decidedly nonbiblical. I'm going to offer answers to these question in Chapter 11; my purpose here is simply to assert that the sovereignty of God is a key element in the biblical worldview (though not always in other theistic worldviews).

Lord of heaven and Earth (3) Immanence

Fourthly, the biblical worldview includes the immanence of God in the material creation. This idea is contained in Paul's statement, "[God] is not far from each one of us, for in him we live and move and have our being" (vv. 27–28). While God is transcendent (not contained within the material creation), his Spirit nevertheless pervades the cosmos. Psalm 139 declares[25]:

"Where can I go from your Spirit?
Or where can I flee from your presence?
If I ascend into heaven, you are there;
If I make my bed in hell, behold you are there.
If I take the wings of the morning
And dwell in the uttermost parts of the sea,
Even there your hand shall lead me
And your right hand shall hold me."

Immanence is important because it means that God's activity, out-lined above, does not involve any kind of *intervention* on his part. He does not observe the world from afar and then intervene as necessary or in an arbitrary way. His immanence means that he is ever-present in the created order and does not need to be called in as a divine firefighter or emergency service. This, of course, fits well with the Berkelian concept of an ever-present God whose mind maintains all things in existence, and with the biblical teaching that Christ upholds all things by the word of his power.[26]

HUMAN SIN, ACCOUNTABILITY, AND CHRIST

There remain three more foundational elements that emerge from Paul's address. Firstly, that the human race derives from a histori-cal Adam, made in the image of God. Secondly, that human sin and accountability ensure the certainty of judgment. And thirdly, that Jesus Christ is central to the entire scheme of things. These issues are so important to the biblical worldview that we shall devote the final chapters of this book to them.

ENDNOTES:

1   Russell, Bertrand; *Why I Am Not a Christian,* ed. Paul Edwards (Simon and Schuster, New York: 1957) p. 107.

2   John 3:16. For date see www.chafer.edu/files/v14no2_date_of_john_s_gospel.pdf

3   https://en.wikipedia.org/wiki/Axiom. "An axiom or postulate is a statement that is taken to be true, to serve as a premise or starting point for further reasoning and arguments. The word comes from the Greek *axíōma* (ἀξίωμα) 'that which is thought worthy or fit' or 'that which commends itself as evident.' The term has subtle differences in definition when used in the context of different fields of study. As defined in classic philosophy, an axiom is a statement that is so evident or well-established that it is accepted without controversy or question. As used in modern logic, an axiom is simply a premise or starting point for reasoning."

4   http://www.oxfordscholarship.com/view/10.1093/0195131932.001.0001/acprof-9780195131932-chapter-6

5   John 20:31.

6   Hawking, Stephen, and Mlodinow, Leonard; *The Grand Design* (Bantam Press, 2010) pp. 42–43.

7   Hawking, Stephen, and Mlodinow, Leonard; *loc. cit.,* p. 46.

8   http://plato.stanford.edu/entries/scientific-realism/

9   McCracken, C.; "What *Does* Berkeley's God See in the Quad?" *Archiv für geschichte der Philosophie* Vol. 61 (1979) pp. 280–92.

10 Hawking, Stephen; *A Brief History of Time* (Bantam Press, 1988) pp. 171–175.

11 Berkeley, George; *Three dialogues between Hylas and Philonous in Opposition to Skeptics and Atheists* (Second dialogue, The Harvard Classics, 1909–14); www.bartleby.com/37/2/2.html

    Full quotation; "And pursuant to this notion of reality, you are obliged to deny sensible things any real existence: that is, according to your own definition, you profess yourself a skeptic. But I neither said nor thought the reality of sensible things was to be defined after that manner. To me it is evident for the reasons you allow of, that sensible things cannot exist otherwise than in a mind or spirit. Whence I conclude, not that they have no real existence, but that, seeing they depend not on my thought, and have all existence distinct from being perceived by me, there must be some other Mind wherein they exist. As sure, therefore, as the sensible world really exists, so sure is there an infinite omnipresent Spirit who contains and supports it."

[12] Luke 24:25–27.

[13] See Chapter 13 for further examples of OT predictions.

[14] Wilson, Clifford; article at https://answersingenesis.org/archaeology/does-archaeology-support-the-bible/

[15] 1 Corinthians 15:14.

[16] 1 Corinthians 15:5–6.

[17] Acts 17:28.

[18] Genesis 1:1.

[19] See article at https://en.wikipedia.org/wiki/List_of_creation_myths

[20] Deuteronomy 33:27.

[21] Psalm 65:9–13.

[22] Romans 8:28.

[23] Ephesians 1:11.

[24] Daniel 4:35.

[25] Psalm 139:7–10.

[26] Hebrews 1:3.

CHAPTER 11

It's now time to consider what really happened in the Garden of Eden. Did Adam and Eve actually exist, and were they truly the progenitors of the whole human race as the Bible claims? We consider (and reject) the idea that there must have been thousands of Adams and that the biblical couple stand proxy for an evolving population of apes. Was Eve really tempted by a talking snake? Was there actually a tree bearing forbidden fruit which Adam and Eve ate in defiance of God? Did their defiance bring about estrangement from God and human mortality? And what, if anything, is the significance of the "tree of life"?

It is popular today, even for Christians, to dismiss the opening chapters of the Book of Genesis as myths—perhaps offering spiritual lessons but having no historical reality. But the Bible, in both Old and New Testaments, is adamant in affirming the historicity of the narratives of the creation and fall of Man. We shall see how it also spells out the consequences of Adam's rebellion against his Creator, how those consequences affect us today, how they offer a compelling explanation of the human condition, and why Jesus Christ had to come into the world "to seek and to save that which was lost."

ADAM AND THE APPLE

The historicity and fall of Adam and Eve

*"Through most of the church's history Christians, like the Jews
from whom they sprang, have believed that the biblical Adam
and Eve were actual persons from whom all other human
beings are descended, and whose disobedience to God brought
sin into human experience."*

PROFESSOR C. JOHN COLLINS[1]

We've considered Aristotle and the snowball, but now we must
go back in time to address Adam and the apple (actually an
unspecified tree-fruit). If, as it claims, the Bible is God's message to
mankind, we shouldn't be surprised that Man occupies a central role
in the biblical worldview. His creation and fall from favor is described
in the Bible's opening chapters. But did the human race really begin
with Adam? And if it did, how many "Adams" actually existed? To

make it easier, I'll put it as a multiple-choice question: how many Adams were there?

(a) None; (b) One; (c) Two; (d) Three; (e) 10,000.

The right answer? It depends on who you ask. Skeptics choose (a), claiming that Adam is a myth and no such first man ever existed. The Bible says (b), for "The Lord God formed man of the dust of the ground and breathed into his nostrils the breath of life; and man became a living being."[2] This must refer to a single person, since we read later that "the Lord God said, 'It is not good that man should be alone.'"[3] On the other hand, answer (c) could be equally correct, because we are told that "God created man [Hebrew "*adam*"] in his own image; in the image of God he created him; male and female he created them."[4] So the first woman Eve must also be counted as an "Adam." But perhaps the Bible's full answer is (d) because the apostle Paul declares that "Adam … is a type [that is, a picture or pattern] of him who was to come [that is, Christ],"[5] and again: "The first man Adam became a living being; the last Adam [Christ] became a life-giving spirit."[6] The first Adam will concern us in this chapter and the next; after that we'll see why Christ is called "the last [that is, second] Adam" and what that means to us on a personal level.

Finally, both skeptics and theistic evolutionists argue that (e) must be the correct answer because the possibility of the human race arising from just a single couple is ruled out by population genetics. They claim that to explain the genetic variability among humans today, *Homo sapiens* must have emerged from a population of apelike ancestors that could be as high as 10,000.[7,8] However, the arguments and calculations that lead to this conclusion involve significant assumptions, so let's consider some of them.

THOUSANDS OF ADAMS?

Let me start by making one thing clear. It is theoretically possible for two parents to populate the Earth in relatively few generations. Suppose a woman bears four children before the age of forty. Assuming that two of the children are female and reproduce according to the same pattern as their mother, the next (second) generation will contain four fertile women who will bear eight females. If the same pattern is repeated consistently in future generations, the number of child-bearers in generation "n," where "n" is any number, will be 2^n (two to the power n). The world's population in 2017 was 7.5 billion and this figure would (according to this calculation) be reached in thirty-three generations. Counting each generation as forty years, this would take only 1320 years!

Of course, this calculation is ridiculously simplistic. We know that population sizes can shrink as well as rise. The calculation assumes an unrealistic constant reproductive pattern and ignores infant mortality, barrenness, maternal deaths, and catastrophic events—such as wars, ice ages, and the great flood recorded in Genesis (and in many other traditions worldwide). But my only purpose here is to point out that, given favorable conditions, you don't need all that many generations to produce huge populations.

However, the "10,000 Adams" scenario isn't based just on numbers, but on genetic diversity. The argument begins with the fact that a single individual has only two version of a given gene. These different versions are called "alleles" of the gene. For example, your eye color is largely determined by whether you have the alleles for blue eyes or for brown eyes, or one of each ("brown dominates "blue," so both your alleles need to be "blue" to give you blue eyes. Other alleles are also involved to a lesser extent). A single couple can therefore have no more than four different alleles of a given gene between them. If the four alleles of any gene possessed by Adam and Eve were passed on *unchanged* to all their descendants, we ought to find that only the same four versions of the gene are present in the entire human population. Instead, depending on the type of gene involved, there may be hundreds of different alleles of a given gene in the modern human genome. And although some of this variation could be explained by known genetic mechanisms, these would be hopelessly insufficient to account for most of it. Thus the whole human race can't have descended from a single couple, can it?

But notice the assumptions made in reaching this conclusion. Firstly, among all the mutations that evolutionists say will occur in a particular gene over the course of time, it is assumed that very few have led to the creation of a new allele. That is, almost every mutation in that gene has been either harmful (leading to the elimination of the altered gene) or neutral (producing no functional change in the allele). This leads to the conclusion that normal evolutionary processes are simply too slow to explain the genetic diversity of a race descended from a single pair. Yet macroevolution in its entirety rests on the *opposite* assumption, namely that *beneficial* mutations happen all the time, get fixed in a population by natural selection, and (on the same timescale as envisaged for the rise of Man) lead not just to new alleles but to whole new genes, genomes, and species! You really can't have it both ways.

A second assumption is that Adam and Eve had genomes just like ours today, whereas they could have been created with a vastly richer store of DNA than that of modern man, and in which the potential for many different alleles lay dormant. The only reason a given couple have four alleles of any gene between them is that they each receive two alleles from their parents, one from dad and one from mum. But if Adam and Eve were specially created beings, they had no parents and we have no idea how many alleles of a given gene they possessed. In other words, the starting point of four alleles is based on the assumption that Adam and Eve evolved from some earlier creature and the argument comes close to circular reasoning. If the progenitors of humanity were specially created with an enriched genome, this would also explain why intermarriage between their children didn't cause genetic problems through interbreeding. A third assumption is that no new alleles could have been produced rapidly by the epigenetic and other non-Darwinian processes we discussed in an earlier chapter. None of these assumptions can be considered sound.

Geneticist Ann Gauger and coauthors have given a detailed technical refutation of the 10,000 calculation.[9,10,11] Based only on known genetic processes, these calculations demonstrate how the whole human race could well have developed from a single pair. She concludes:

"But one thing is clear right now: Adam and Eve have not been disproven by science, and those who claim otherwise are misrepresenting the scientific evidence."

Her work is further supported by a sophisticated population model proposed by Fazale Rana[12] which, if correct, predicts that Adam was a real person who lived somewhere between 50,000 and 70,000 years ago. Yet further arguments leading to the same conclusion are advanced by John Bloom in his paper *On Human Origins*[13] and Richard Buggs in *Nature; ecology and evolution*.[14] An excellent summary of these arguments in favor of a single couple being progenitors of the human race is given in an essay by philosopher Lydia McGrew who concludes:

"What we're being told is that there is something analogous to
a video of the past showing, via highly reliable methods,
what appears to be an uninterrupted history of the natural
evolution of mankind from nonhuman ancestors—a history
of mankind that could not have begun with two individuals.
This is not true. Given the Scriptural evidence for the
existence of an historical Adam and Eve, the first and only
parents of mankind, Christians are fully justified in asking
for strong counterevidence. It doesn't seem to have been
forthcoming, despite all the fanfare."[15]

Taken together, these considerations mean that it is perfectly rational
and scientifically justified to believe that all humanity did indeed
stem from one original created pair, as the Bible asserts.

THE GENESIS GENRE

Our discussion of Adam and Eve leads to an obvious question. How
far does the biblical creation narrative as a whole reflect real history?
Opinion is, of course, divided, and the answer will depend on how we
identify the literary genre (the kind of literature) to which the Genesis
narrative belongs. We know the difference between J. R. R. Tolkien's
The Lord of the Rings and Edward Gibbon's *The Rise and Fall of the
Roman Empire*. That is, we are all familiar with the idea of genres and
easily distinguish between such categories as fiction and nonfiction,
poetry and prose, history and myth. But there are other less familiar
genres. For example, some books in the Bible (notably Daniel in the
Old Testament and Revelation in the New) employ an "apocalyptic"
genre in which information is conveyed using verbal symbols rather
than simple statements or propositions. The genre of a piece of literature will affect the way we interpret it, and here lies the problem

with the early chapters of Genesis (specifically, chapters one to eleven). The genre employed is ancient and may not fit into any modern category. Is it the same as employed in other ancient Near East writings and creation stories as some assert? That's doubtful considering the profound and self-evident differences between these stories and the biblical narrative, and becomes highly unlikely if (following the biblical worldview) we accept that the Bible is *revelatory* in character and *not* the fevered invention of ancient ignorance.

We must be careful to distinguish between myths and miracles. Myths are nonhistorical narratives but miracles may be real events that are, by their very nature, incapable of scientific explanation. Examples of miracles include the *ex nihilo* creation of the universe that we discussed in Chapter 2, and the resurrection of Jesus Christ following his crucifixion. Both are essential to the biblical worldview as historical events, not myths. In the same way, the Bible views the creation of Adam, and separately of Eve, as both miraculous and historical.

Most of the book of Genesis is plainly presented as historical narrative and there is no obvious discontinuity in style between the first eleven chapters and the rest. We shall also see below that all subsequent biblical references seem to assume that Adam and Eve did indeed exist historically and were the sole progenitors of the human race. In other words, the biblical scriptures, both Old and New Testament, view the genre of Genesis as historical and nonfictional throughout.

This does not mean that the "Genesis genre" is always *literal*. This is a word I dislike because its meaning is vague. For example, when Genesis 1 tells us that God said, "Let there be light" and proceeded to introduce each new creative act in similar terms, what language did he use? A literal interpretation would require him to speak audibly in some known or unknown tongue. But it makes much more sense to treat the word "said" as a metaphor, signifying that a command was given, not vocally, but in the mind of God. This latter interpretation is not literal but remains historical.

In the same way, a narrative may contain symbolism without losing historicity. Christians accept that Satan, a spiritual personage, is referred to as a dragon in the book of Revelation chapter 12, where the apostle John's obvious purpose is to describe real future history using symbolism. So the talking serpent who tempted Eve may represent Satan symbolically in the Genesis story, while (as discussed below) the two specific trees that feature prominently in the fall narrative are clearly symbolical. This doesn't mean that the serpent and the trees didn't actually exist, only that the story endows ordinary objects with spiritual significance. My point is that the inclusion of symbolism in the Genesis account does not destroy its historicity.

In the biblical worldview, then, Adam and Eve were historical persons, miraculously created by God, and all the events reported in the first eleven chapters of Genesis actually took place historically (whether reported literally, symbolically or by a mixture of the two). I believe this is the position taken, without exception, by the Bible as a whole.

SOLE PROGENITORS

Throughout the Bible, Adam and Eve are treated not only as real people but also as the sole progenitors of the human race. This belief is integral to the biblical worldview, as is evident from many passages in both old and new Testaments. To give just a few examples:

- The Bible contains three genealogies that trace historical personages back to Adam. The first is found in Genesis, where a detailed genealogy is interspersed with narratives of events. In Genesis 5:1–5, the line is traced from Adam to Noah; Genesis 10:1–32 records the descendants of Noah's three sons, including Shem; and Genesis 11:10–32 details the descent of Abraham from Shem. This single family tree has many side branches, including some leading to the origin of various tribes and nations, but its ultimate purpose is to link the historical figure of Abram (later renamed Abraham) to the first man, Adam. There can be no doubt that whoever compiled these genealogies had no intention of linking a succession of mythical characters to the historical person of Abraham. The Genesis family tree has a solid trunk that goes down to equally solid historical roots! A similar (but obviously independent) line of human descent from Adam to Abraham is described in 1 Chronicles 1:1–28, while the genealogy in Luke 3:23–38 traces Jesus' lineage back to Adam, "[the son] of God." Note that, unlike modern family trees, biblical genealogies were designed to show relationships and are seldom continuous; whole generations may be omitted.[16]

- The historical reality of Adam's sin undergirds the Bible's entire narrative of judgment and redemption, and lies at the heart of its teaching on evil, death, resurrection, heaven and hell. This is reflected particularly in Paul's statement in Romans 5:12–21 on sin (inherited from Adam) and redemption (accomplished by Christ): "For as by one man's disobedience many were made sinners, so also by one man's obedience many will be made righteous."[17] It features again in Paul's discussion of death and resurrection in 1 Corinthians 15: "For since by man [Adam] came death, by man [Christ] also came the resurrection of the dead. For as in Adam all die, even so in Christ, all shall be made alive." Finally, in his short epistle, Jude refers to a prophecy by Enoch, whom he calls "the seventh from Adam." Jude clearly expected the prophecy to be fulfilled, and this would not make sense if he thought Enoch and Adam were fictional characters.

- As a final example, the historical reality of Adam and Eve provide the basis for Jesus' teaching on marriage. He said: "Have you not read that he who made them at the beginning made them male and female and said; 'for this reason a man shall leave his father and mother and be joined to his wife and the two shall become one flesh'? So then, they are no longer two but one flesh. Therefore, what God has joined together, let not man separate."[18]

One crucial implication of the historicity of Adam and Eve is that all human beings are equal in the sight of God. There are many different "races" and conditions of humanity, but if, as Paul claims, "God has made from one [man] every nation of men to dwell on all the face of the Earth,"[19] there can ultimately be no distinction among them. The biblical worldview leaves no room for racism, tribalism, sexism, ageism, or any other "ism" that seeks to make some people morally or biologically superior to others. As we shall see in the next chapter, every human being bears the self-same "image of God."

THE FALL OF ADAM AND EVE

Why did Jesus Christ come into the world? He described his mission in these words: "The Son of Man has come to seek and to save that which was lost,"[20] and again, "I did not come to call the righteous, but sinners to repentance."[21] Paul adds that "God demonstrates his own love towards us, in that while we were still sinners, Christ died for us."[22] That is, Christ came into the world because human beings are spiritually "lost" and need to be saved from that condition. While the fall of an historic Adam is not explicitly mentioned by Jesus himself, it must surely be the only reason he would have given for the lost spiritual condition of our race. Certainly, the New Testament assumes the historical reality of Adam's rebellion against God's commandment. Paul writes, "Adam was formed first, then Eve. And Adam was not deceived but the woman, being deceived, fell into transgression" (1 Timothy 2:13–14).

Anyone who argues that the fall of Adam and Eve is a myth, designed only to describe (rather than explain) the sin-prone nature of human beings, is not embracing the biblical worldview. Some seek to explain the moral imperfections of human nature as a stage in the evolution of Man, who (they say) we should regard as a "work in progress"—incomplete but heading in the right direction. This certainly seems to be the once-popular view of Jesuit philosopher Pierre Teilhard de Chardin, who saw mankind as evolving progressively towards "point omega"—a Christlike condition of perfection and union with God.[23] De Chardin's theories have been kept alive and even revived recently by some Roman Catholic thinkers. There is, however, an impressive lack of evidence that mankind is improving biologically and morally with the passage of time (read your daily newspaper). So what, according to the Bible, actually happened in the paradise called Eden?

THE FALL: ITS NATURE

According to the Genesis account, Adam and Eve were created in the image of God as morally innocent, sinless beings. Before they arrived on the scene, God pronounced his work of creation "good." After their creation, he "saw everything that he had made, and indeed it was very good" (Genesis 1:25 and 1:31). If the arrival of Adam and Eve advanced the status of creation from "good" to "very good," we can safely assume that they met God's quality-control standards, morally and in every other way. But the image of God they bore had implications; like God himself they possessed (within their limitations as created beings) free will. That is, they were free agents designed to obey their Creator, not automatically but *willingly*. And they *needed* to obey, because God had laid upon them a single obligation: they were not to eat the fruit of "the tree of the knowledge of good and evil." If they disobeyed this commandment, they would "surely die" (Genesis 2:17).

How dreadfully draconian! Surely it was too severe a punishment for first offenders committing a victimless crime? Not at all. Had God given them fifty commandments or even just ten, breaking one might have been a minor misdemeanor, but he had only given them one. To break that single commandment was therefore the ultimate crime—equivalent to a person today committing treason or breaking every law on the statute book in a single criminal act. Their action was nothing short of a declaration of war against their Creator. They put their own desires (the fruit was "good for food … pleasant to the eyes, and a tree desirable to make one wise") above God's requirements, serving self in preference to their Maker. It was, *and remains*, the basic human sin, that "they worshipped and served the creature rather than the Creator" (Romans 1:25)—where the "creature" or "created thing" includes both ourselves (and our appetites) and the innumerable things human beings idolize and worship in the material world.

THE FALL: ITS DETAILS

So, according to the biblical worldview, what really transpired? The answer is symbolized by the two trees that feature in the narrative of Man's fall into sin—"the tree of the knowledge of good and evil" from which Adam and Eve ate in defiance of God, and "the tree of life," whose fruit would enable Adam and Eve to "live forever."[24] There is no reason to doubt that, to Adam and Eve, these were actual trees in an actual garden, but their importance resides in what they symbolized rather than any magical properties of their fruit. What is this symbolism?

The first tree, as we have seen, stood as a test of Adam's submission to his Creator. It could have been any tree, so long as God had designated it, and it alone, as forbidden. We are not told how this particular tree was marked for avoidance, but Adam and Eve were clearly in no doubt about which tree it was. The only clue we have is its location "in the midst [or middle] of the garden" (Genesis 3:3). Depending on the layout of the garden, this might have been sufficient both to identify it and to emphasize its central importance in God's economy. It was called "the tree of the knowledge of good and evil" (Genesis 2:17), but again this does not necessarily mean that its fruit possessed magical qualities. I would not be dogmatic about this, but the knowledge referred to might well have been acquired *by the act of disobedience* itself, rather than from any special properties of the fruit.

But what exactly was the knowledge they acquired? The phrase "knowing good and evil" is sometimes used in the Old Testament as an idiom for knowledge generally, and also for maturity as opposed to childhood (see Deuteronomy 1:39). In his commentary on Genesis,[25] Philip Eveson notes the childhood connection and argues that God's purpose in denying Adam and Eve "the knowledge of good and evil" was not to keep them in moral ignorance but to maintain their moral dependence upon himself—just as young children are (in a general sense) dependent on their parents. However, it is quite possible that these later idiomatic uses are generalizations of the Genesis account. That is, "the knowledge of good and evil" can be taken at its face value in Genesis and only treated as idiomatic in later usage. It is difficult to reconcile an idiomatic meaning in Genesis 1–3 with the fact that this knowledge brought moral corruption and physical death into human experience.

Certainly, Adam and Eve's rejection of God's commandment was an evil action and one they understood would be wrong. They had always known that to eat from that particular tree would be rebellious, meaning that they were already conscious of the difference between right and wrong. What changed when they ate was that they *experienced* evil personally for the first time. They discovered what it meant to be sinners, degraded by their defiance of God and consumed with a guilt that infused their being and permeated their self-awareness ("the eyes of both of them were opened and they knew that they were naked"; Genesis 3:7). Previously they had experienced only good at the hands of a benevolent Creator. Now, for the first time, they understood what evil really meant.

The second tree, "the tree of life," symbolized God's activity in imparting and maintaining life. As Paul tells the Athenian philosophers,[26] "[God] gives to all, life, breath and all things ... for in him we live and move and have our being." We read of the tree of life again in the final book of the Bible, where the apostle John sees a vision of heaven. "In the middle of its street, and on either side of the river, was the tree of life, which bore twelve fruits, each tree yielding its fruit every month. And the leaves of the tree were for the healing of the nations" (Revelation 22:2; see also Rev. 2:7 and 22:14). Clearly, John is taking up the Genesis references and teaching that the tree of life represents God's provision of healing for the soul—the gift of eternal life which Christ said he gives to those who believe in him: "My sheep hear my voice and I know them and they follow me. And I give them eternal life and they shall never perish, neither shall anyone snatch them out of my hand" (John 10:27–28).

Since every tree in the garden was permitted for food apart from the one forbidden to them, Adam and Eve had access to the tree of life throughout their time in Eden. It could be argued that this was, in fact, their source of immortality before the fall. What we do know is that they had to be removed from the garden to prevent them continuing to live forever in rebellion to God (and thus neutralizing the sentence of death he had passed upon them): "Behold, the man has become like one of us, to know good and evil. And now lest he put out his hand and take also from the tree of life and eat and live forever … therefore the Lord sent him out of the garden of Eden to till the ground from which he was taken" (Genesis 3:23; note that the plurality used to denote God could either be a reference to the Trinity or to spiritual beings generally, including angels).

THE FALL: ITS CONSEQUENCES

It is no exaggeration to say that the fall of Man plays a major part in shaping the biblical worldview, so we must finally consider its consequences, the first of which is human mortality and death. Philosopher Friedrich Nietzsche famously declared:

> "God is dead. God remains dead. And we have killed him. How shall we comfort ourselves, the murderers of all murderers?"

But the biblical claim is the mirror image of Nietzsche's lament. It is God who lives forever, and Man who is dead and remains in that state unless and until he is brought to life by God.

It is obvious that Adam and Eve did not drop dead under the forbidden tree, so what did God mean when he said, "you shall surely die"? Two things. Firstly, Man was sentenced to become mortal, that is, subject to physical death. Paul writes, "by man came death ... in Adam all die..." (1 Cor. 15:21–22, where the context requires that this refers to physical death). Secondly, however, estranged from God, Man is consistently described in the New Testament as being spiritually dead;

> "You ... were dead in trespasses and sins, in which you once walked
> [lived] ... but God, who is rich in mercy ... even when we
> were dead in trespasses, made us alive together with Christ
> (by grace you have been saved)." (Ephesians 2:1–5)

The death sentence pronounced by God was thus twofold, involving both physical mortality and spiritual death (estrangement from God). According to the New Testament, we all inherit from Adam and Eve not just their physical mortality but also their damaged morality. It was the mission of Jesus Christ to reverse both these forms of death, as we shall see in Chapters 13 and 14. His ability to do so is the core and kernel of the Christian gospel.

DEAD TO GOD

We all know what physical mortality means, but what does it mean to be "dead in trespasses and sins"? The word "dead," in this case, is a metaphor. When a person is fast asleep, or even deeply engrossed in some activity, we often say they are "dead to the world," meaning that they are unaware of their surroundings. In the same way, to be spiritually dead is to be unaware of God and of the fact that "in him we live and move and have our being" (Acts 17:28). The New Testament often describes our ignorance of God as spiritual blindness (another metaphor, of course). Being dead or blind to God doesn't necessarily mean that people have no religion. Indeed, a good case can be made out that we are all inherently religious, believing in something or someone that transcends our humanity. But it does mean that, by nature, we are all ignorant of the living God, the one who created and sustains both the cosmos and ourselves.

The phrase "dead in trespasses and sins" also describes the consequence of our ignorance of God. To trespass is to break (literally, to go beyond) God's laws; to sin is to fall short of the standards God has set for human conduct. They differ in that trespass is an action whereas sin is an attitude (that may of course lead to actions). The word "sinner" is still used in archery[27] to describe an arrow that fails to hit the target (the arrow falls short), and Romans 3:23 declares that "all have sinned and fall short of the glory of God." What, then, is the target we fail to reach? It is "the glory of God" as exhibited in the Person and life of Jesus Christ, as we shall see more clearly in Chapter 13. Seen in this light, it surely takes overweening pride to deny that we are sinners (and moral pride is, perhaps, the greatest sin of all!)

But there is more bad news. Adam and Eve, having believed Satan rather than obeyed God, found themselves in bondage to sin, unable to escape its influence. This is something else we inherit from our first parents. Until they believed the gospel, Paul tells the Ephesians:

"You were dead in trespasses and sins, in which you once walked according to the course of this world, according to the prince of the power of the air [that is, Satan], the spirit who now works in the sons of disobedience." (Ephesians 2:1–3)

At first, Adam's disobedience seemed to free him from the rule of God but it actually put him under the authority of Satan, and thus subject to the power of temptation and sin. One of Aesop's fables might help us understand what Paul is telling the Ephesians.

> "The Horse thought he had the plain entirely to himself but then a Stag intruded into his domain, demanding to share his pasture. The Horse, wanting to rid himself of the interloper's unwelcome presence, asked a man for help. The man replied that if the Horse would receive a bit in his mouth and agree to carry him on its back, he would pursue and kill the Stag. The Horse agreed and allowed the man to mount him. After the Stag has been dealt with, the Horse asked the man to get off his back and set him free. But the man refused to let him go and from that hour the Horse found himself enslaved to the service of man."[28]

Of course, we have to reassign the characters! In New Testament theology, the horse becomes Man, the pasture is Man's rebellious free will, the stag represents God's "intrusive" moral requirements, and the man in the fable is Satan ("the spirit who now works in the sons of disobedience" in the quote from Ephesians 2). Man may have freed himself from God's commandments but only at the cost of enslavement to Satan and to sin.

The theme of Man's bondage to sin is elaborated in Romans 6:16–23 where we read, "When you were slaves of sin you were free in regard to righteousness. What fruit did you have then in the things of which you are now ashamed? For the end of those things is death." And Jesus confirms this view of human sin: "Most assuredly I say to you, whoever commits sin is the slave of sin" (John 8:34). However, those who put their trust in Christ can declare that "the Father … has delivered us from the authority of darkness and translated us into the kingdom of the son of his love, in whom we have redemption through his blood, the forgiveness of sins" (Colossians 1:12–14).

THE BONDAGE OF THE NATURAL WORLD

The second consequence of the fall was the impact it had upon the natural world. Following Man's expulsion from the Garden of Eden, we are told that God cursed the ground for Adam's sake.

> "Because you have … eaten from the tree of which I commanded
> you, saying "You shall not eat of it," cursed is the ground for
> your sake; in toil you shall eat from it all the days of your life.
> Both thorns and thistles it shall bring forth for you and you
> shall eat the herb of the field." (Genesis 3:17–18)

The theme is developed by Paul in his letter to the Romans.

> "The creation was subjected to futility, not willingly, but because
> of him who subjected it in hope. Because the creation itself
> also will be delivered from the bondage of corruption into the
> glorious liberty of the children of God. For we know that the
> whole creation groans and labors with birth pangs together
> until now." (Romans 8:20–22)

Paul treats it as common knowledge that, since the fall, the created order has been subject to "the bondage of corruption," and he attributes this state of affairs to the deliberate action of God. However, this is a temporary situation, for these are "birth pangs" which will come to an end when Christ returns to judge the world in righteousness.[29]

Until then, "we who have the first fruits of the Spirit groan within ourselves, eagerly waiting for the adoption, the redemption of our body" (Romans 8:23; a reference to the physical resurrection that the Bible says will take place at the return of Christ). This is the "great hope" to which Christians can and should look forward; "denying ungodliness and worldly lusts, we should live soberly, righteously and godly in the present age, looking for the blessed hope and glorious appearing of our great God and savior Jesus Christ."[30]

The teaching summarized in the previous paragraphs is intrinsic to the biblical worldview. It accounts for the mortality of man, his sinful tendencies, his estrangement from God, and the "futility" or "corruption" of the natural world order—evidenced by the universal phenomena of death and decay, by nature "red in tooth and claw," and by the relatively inhospitable environment the Earth provides for life.

Clearly, much more could be said, and whole books have been written to explore these matters in greater detail. But since we are here considering the view of Man presented by the Bible, I'll leave it there. I appreciate that this will satisfy neither those who dismiss these early chapters of Genesis as total fiction, nor those who find in them a spiritually meaningful mythology while denying their historicity. But the position I have outlined is, I suggest, the only one that allows us to take seriously the biblical claims that we must now examine, namely: (1) that God created Adam and Eve in "his own image," and (2) that Jesus Christ came into the world to "seek and to save that which was lost." These two themes will occupy us in the remaining chapters of this book.

ENDNOTES:

1 Collins, C. John; *Did Adam and Eve really exist? Who They Were and Why It Matters* (Inter-Varsity Press, Nottingham, 2011) p. 11.

2 Genesis 2:7.

3 Genesis 2:18.

4 Genesis 1:27.

5 Romans 5:14.

6 1 Corinthians 15:45.

7 Biologos at http://biologos.org/blogs/dennis-venema-letters-to-the-duchess/does-genetics-point-to-a-single-primal-couple/ AND http://biologos.org/blogs/dennis-venema-letters-to-the-duchess/adam-eve-and-human-population-genetics-part-4-signature-in-the-snps

8 McKnight, Scott and Venema, Dennis; *Adam and the Genome; Reading Scripture after Genetic Science* (Brazos Press, Ada, MI, 2017).

9 Gauger, Ann; in *Science and Human Origins* (Discovery Institute Press, Seattle, 2012) pp. 105–122.

10 Hössjer, O; Gauger, A; Reeves, C; Genetic modeling of human history part 1: comparison of common descent and unique origin approaches. *BIO-Complexity* 2016 (3):1–15.

11 Gauger, Ann; in *Dictionary of Christianity and Science* (Ed. Paul Copan et al; Zondervan, 2017).

12 Rana, Fazale, with Ross, Hugh; *Who was Adam? A Creation Model Approach to the Origin of Man* (NavPress, Colorado Springs, 2005) pp. 55–75.

13 Bloom, John A.; *On Human Origins: A Survey* (Christian Scholars Review 27.2, 1997) pp. 181–203.

14 Buggs, Richard; https://natureecoevocommunity.nature.com/users/24561-richard-buggs/posts/22075-adam-and-eve-a-tested-hypothesis (2017).

15 McGrew, Lydia; http://www.whatswrongwiththeworld.net/2014/07/no_virginia_science_has_not_de.html

16 http://www.reasons.org/files/articles/The-Genesis-Genealogies.pdf

17 Romans 5:19.

18 Matthew 19:1–6.

19 Acts 17:26.

20 Luke 19:10.

21 Mark 2:17.

22 Romans 5:8.

23 Teilhard de Chardin's "point omega" concept is discussed at https://en.wikipedia.org/wiki/Pierre_Teilhard_de_Chardin#Teachings.

24 Genesis 2:16-17; 3:22.

25 Eveson, Philip; *The Book of Origins* (Evangelical Press, Darlington; 2001) p. 67.

26 Acts 17:25, 28.

27 See http://www.wordorigins.org/index.php/site/comments/trespass_sin_debt/. This article claims that the reference to "sinner" in archery had fallen into disuse by the first century, but Paul's clear use of the analogy in Romans 3:23 contradicts this opinion.

28 http://fablesofaesop.com/the-horse-and-the-stag.html

29 Acts 17:31.

30 Titus 2:12–13.

CHAPTER 12

Not without reason, Mark Twain declared, "I cannot help feeling disappointed in Adam and Eve." According to the Bible, they (and they alone) were created in the image of God and should surely have done better than they did. We explored the cause of their failure in the previous chapter, but we must now enquire what happened to the divine image they were supposed to bear. We will find that, in spite of everything, the image persists even in fallen humanity. But what, exactly, constitutes that image?

Some argue that the divine image in Man is no big deal, consisting only in the fact that Man is a social animal to whom God subcontracted the care of planet Earth. In this chapter, we shall beg to differ—rejecting this minimalist view and showing that humans do indeed have a special relationship with God. His image in us means that we alone among sentient creatures share the "communicable" characteristics of God. What are these shared attributes? We'll consider them under the following four headings: soul and spirit, language and logic, creativity and competence, and law and love.

CHAPTER 12

THE IMAGE OF GOD

Why Man is unique

"Then God said, 'Let us make man in our image, according to our likeness; let them have dominion over the fish of the sea, over the birds of the air and over the cattle, over all the Earth and over creeping thing that creeps on the Earth.' So God created man in his image, in the image of God he created him, male and female he created them."

GENESIS 1:26–27.

"I cannot help feeling disappointed in Adam and Eve."

MARK TWAIN IN *WHAT IS MAN? AND OTHER ESSAYS.*[1]

In Chapter 6 we considered *how* humans are unique among animals. In this chapter, we shall see *why* we are unique. Previously we assessed Man's relationship with the biosphere; now we must explore his relationship with God.

Why are human beings unique? I'll give the short answer now and we'll work it out in detail below. According to the Bible, we are unique because among created things *only Man bears God's image*. Nothing in the inanimate cosmos was made in the image of God. Nothing in the plant or animal kingdoms is imprinted with that image. Not even the angels were made according to the likeness of God.[2] You may believe that or not, but in this chapter I'm inviting you to think it through.

In writing this chapter and the previous one, I was in two minds as to which should come first. Logically perhaps, our discussion of the image of God should have preceded the story of Adam's fall into sin. But on the other hand, unless Adam, Eve, and the fall were genuinely historical, the idea that Man alone bears the image of God would be little more than a pious platitude. The great apes would surely object if they had the wit to do so, and at least some animal rights activists would be up in arms.

A SPECIAL RELATIONSHIP

But can we take it for granted that there *is* a special relationship between God and Man, other than that of Creator with creature? Perhaps Mark Twain, quoted above, had a point. How could two people, allegedly made in God's likeness, turn out so badly? I gave a partial answer to that question in the previous chapter, describing how Adam and Eve, of their own free will, chose to please themselves rather than obey God. However, we still need to investigate what it means that Adam and Eve were created "in the image of God" and *how far that image survived their fall* into sin. It is clear that the divine image *did* survive, because a few chapters later in Genesis 9, God prohibits murder in the following terms: "Whoever sheds man's blood, by man his blood shall be shed; for in the image of God he made man."[3] In spite of their rebellion and sin, therefore, human beings retain special value in the sight of God because they still bear his image. This stands in stark contrast to the animals, concerning which God said: "Every moving thing that lives shall be food for you."[4]

So what does it mean that Man bears the image and likeness of God? Clearly it cannot mean "physical image" because God is a Spirit[5] having no material substance. If he did possess such substance, he would be part of the material world he created, which is self-contradictory. (I'll deal with the incarnation of Christ in the next chapter.) Accordingly, some think the image of God in Man isn't the big deal it's made out to be. They say it just signifies that God, as Lord of heaven and Earth, deputed Man to be lord of Earth as his representative. In effect, God subcontracted the care and rule of the Earth to mankind, saying; "Be fruitful and multiply; fill the Earth and subdue it; have dominion over the fish of the sea, over the birds of the air, and over every living thing that moves on the face of the Earth."[6] Others go a little further and see the image of God as Man's ability to form relationships with God and with one another—relationships which support sophisticated social structures that lie beyond the capacity of other creatures.

But neither of these ideas does justice to the Bible's "image of God" concept, which must surely imply that humans actually *share* certain attributes or characteristics with their Creator. As philosopher J. P. Moreland points out, the lesser functions of being God's representative and building relationships require Man to possess Godlike *capacities*. He writes:

> "As image bearers, human beings have all those endowments
> necessary to re-present and be representative of God ... and
> exhibit the relationality in which they were meant to live, such

as endowments of reason, self-determination, moral action,
personality and relational formation. In this sense, the image
of God is straightforwardly ontological…."[7]

In this context, "ontological" means that the image shares something
of the "being" or *nature* of the divine Original, not just his functions
(like ruling) and abilities (like language). This does not mean that
Adam and Eve were mini-gods: they were, after all, *creatures* (created
things). But it does mean that they were uniquely designed to know
and have fellowship with God.

This ontological relationship between God and Man is further
implied by the incarnation of the Son of God—the man Christ Jesus
who is "the image of the invisible God"[8] and "the express image of
[God's] Person."[9] Of course, the word "image" means different things
in different contexts, but it is no accident that Man (male and female)
and Christ are both said to bear God's image. Luke's genealogy of
Jesus, working backwards in time, ends thus: "Cainan the son of Enos,
the son of Seth, the son of Adam, *the son of God*" (Luke 3:38, emphasis
added; note that in each case the words "the son" are not in the original but are obviously implied). Thus according to Luke, Adam was
God's offspring as truly as Seth was Adam's—though Adam's relationship with God was obviously spiritual rather than physical.

Jesus Christ is also called the "son of God."[10] The word "son" has
a whole new meaning when applied to Jesus. But nevertheless, the
divine Christ obviously desired to identify with our humanity, and
during his days on Earth he actually preferred the title "son of man."[11]
This further suggests that Adam bore the image of God in the ontological sense defined above. In this chapter we'll focus on Adam and
Eve, but Jesus Christ, the ideal man, will occupy us in the next.

In what sense, then, did Adam and Eve share the nature of God?

Clearly, there are some divine attributes that created beings cannot share (they are "incommunicable")—such as God's self-existence, omniscience, omnipresence and omnipotence. But other divine characteristics can be shared (they are "communicable")—like intelligence, wisdom, love and mercy. So in seeking to understand what it means that humans bear the image of God, I'm going to consider four duplex attributes, to which I'll attach easily remembered names. They are (1) soul and spirit, (2) language and logic, (3) creativity and competence, and (4) law and love. I call them "duplex" because the two members of each pair are closely related. These things may not exhaust the meaning of God's image in Man, but I think they go a long way towards explaining it.

More importantly, they demonstrate the unique privilege and role assigned to Man in creation, and point forward to a future for humanity that the apostle Paul describes in unforgettable terms: "Eye has not seen, nor ear heard, nor have entered into the heart of man, the things that God has prepared for those who love him."[12] That God has planned such a future for those who (on account of their fallen nature) do *not* love him, constitutes the "amazing grace" celebrated so eloquently in John Newton's famous hymn—and which lies at the heart of the Christian gospel.

SOUL AND SPIRIT

God's image in Man is seen firstly, then, in our possession of soul and spirit. What do these words mean? In Genesis 2:7 we read: "And the Lord God formed Man of the dust of the ground and breathed into his nostrils the breath of life; and Man became a living soul." Some translations render "soul" (Hebrew *nephesh*) as "being," and this is perfectly legitimate—because throughout the Old Testament the word "soul" is descriptive of the whole person, not some inner component of a person. In many references it is used collectively to simply mean "people." However, it is only rarely (eleven times) applied to any creature except Man (nearly 500 times). Just a handful of times it is also applied to God himself, when it can only mean "whole being" and is best regarded as an anthropomorphism. Almost always, therefore, it signifies the whole *human* being. Although a human soul has a physical body and in that respect is unlike God, it also possesses nonmaterial elements such as mind and spirit. It is these nonmaterial and "spiritual" aspects of the soul that humans share with God and which set them apart from all other living things.

The New Testament occasionally refers to body and soul (Greek *psuche*, from which we get our word psychology) as separate entities. For example, Jesus tells his disciples, "Do not fear those who kill the body but cannot kill the soul"[13], and asks, "What is a man profited if he gains the whole world and loses his own soul?"[14] Does this mean that body and soul are separable? Yes, but the separation envisaged in these texts only *follows* bodily death. In life, souls always possess bodies. Generally, then, in both Old and New Testaments, "soul" refers to the whole person and includes both material and nonmaterial elements. The important point is this. In the biblical worldview, humans are not totally physical beings, as claimed by materialistic philosophy, but possess both physical and spiritual natures. It is this combination that makes them souls rather than mere animals. Furthermore, the Bible also teaches that there will be a final resurrection in which these two elements will be finally reunited.

THE HUMAN SPIRIT

I have begun to use the word "spiritual" and we must now examine what it means that human beings possess a "spirit." What is the difference between a soul and a spirit? Just this: as a human being made in God's image, you *are* a soul but you *have* a spirit. Furthermore, while our soul determines our personal identity from the cradle to the grave, our spirit can undergo change. For example, Paul prays for the Ephesians, "that God would *give you the spirit* of wisdom and revelation in the knowledge of him, the eyes of your understanding being enlightened..." (emphasis added).[15] He is not talking here about the Holy Spirit but about wisdom, insight, understanding and attitude. Put simply, my human spirit determines the kind of person I am. Meanness and generosity, selfishness and thoughtfulness, cruelty and kindness, reliability and waywardness—all such things constitute and reflect the spirit of a person and are open to change.

According to the Bible, the greatest change that can happen to a human spirit occurs when a person receives the Spirit of God and is "born again" as a result. The apostle John reports a conversation between Jesus and the scholarly Jewish counselor Nicodemus, to whom he says:

> "Most assuredly, I say to you, unless one is born of water [that is, naturally[16]] and the [Holy] Spirit, he cannot enter the kingdom of God. That which is born of the flesh is flesh, and that which is born of the Spirit is spirit. Do not marvel that I said to you, 'You must be born again.'"[17]

Nicodemus, of course, already had a human spirit like everyone else. But in order to enter into a saving relationship with God, it was necessary for the Holy Spirit to open his spiritual eyes and take up residence within him. Such an event would be tantamount to a spiritual "new birth" and would transform his human spirit. As Paul says elsewhere, "You received the Spirit of adoption by whom we cry out 'Abba, Father!'—the [Holy] Spirit *bearing witness with our spirit* that we are children of God" (emphasis added).[18] And again: "If anyone is in Christ he is a new creation; old things have passed away; behold, all things have become new."[19] I'll explain further what this all means in our final chapter, but here we just need to note that such transactions with God through faith in Jesus Christ can only happen because Man, being made in the image of God, possesses a human spirit in the first place. It's not a privilege open to chickens or chimpanzees.

LANGUAGE AND LOGIC

Among the most important divine attributes shared with Adam and Eve is the ability to use language and logic (I use "logic" in the general sense of the possession and operation of mind). As we shall see, language and logic are inseparably linked. I'll start with language because that's where God himself begins! According to Genesis 1, the Creator "spoke" the world into being, saying, "Let there be light ... let there be a firmament [an expanse; the sky] ... let the dry land appear ..." and so on. In the New Testament, we also read that Christ is continually "upholding all things by the word of his power"[20]—indicating that God used or uses language both in creating and sustaining the cosmos. Language is also God's chosen method of communicating with mankind. As the opening verses of Hebrews put it: "God, who at various times and in different ways spoke in time past to the fathers by the prophets, has in these last days spoken to us by his Son."[21] It makes perfect sense, therefore, that God was able to converse with Adam and

Eve (probably by thought transfer rather than vocal speech) from the moment of their creation, as is repeatedly asserted in Genesis 1 and 2.

Let me clarify what I mean by "language." I do not necessarily mean any particular human language, or even spoken language, but rather *the capacity to express our thoughts in a structured manner.* To give a simple illustration: if my mind tells me I have injured my leg, a cry of "Ouch!" doesn't qualify as language. But the statement, "Doctor, it hurts here," does qualify, because it conveys a message that has a grammatical and meaningful structure. The minimum requirements of language, then, are:

1. A set of symbols (usually words or signs) that have defined or agreed meanings.
2. Grammar (a set of rules governing the way the symbols should be used in combination).
3. Syntax (the arrangement of the symbols to convey meaningful messages or information).

As indicated earlier, when God is said to speak, the biblical writers are using speech as a metaphor to picture "something-that-God-does," whether in creating and upholding the cosmos or communicating with Man. But a metaphor is only valid if it resembles the thing described, so the "something-that-God-does" must share certain characteristics with language, such as the *expression* of thoughts, desires and intentions, along with the *exercise* of will and the *implementation* of purpose. When God is doing these things, it is entirely appropriate to say that he is "speaking."

Language is more than communication. All animals communicate in one way or another. As I point out elsewhere:

"Many—perhaps all—animals communicate using codes, which
range from simple alarm cries or a hen's call to her chicks,
to the complex array of whistles by which dolphins keep in
touch. Honey bees perform a 'dance' to tell the hive where
nectar is to be found, the 'steps' in the dance indicating
both the direction and distance of the hoard.... Animal
scents may also provide a primitive communication system
between members of a species. Ant colonies, for example, use
pheromones to pass information around."[22]

But language is far more than a means of communication. It is the
unique human ability by which our thoughts are not only articulated
but also *formulated*. Try thinking of something without assigning
names or describing actions, or without joining names to actions in
some way. You can, perhaps, picture or imagine things nonverbally
but you cannot *think* about them without the help of verbal structures
(language)—as we shall see further in a moment.

THE ORIGIN OF LANGUAGE

If language is an aspect of the image of God in Man, its origin is self-
evident. Man was created from the outset with this unique ability.
But, of course, many seek to explain the phenomenon of language
without reference to God, and invariably do so using an evolutionary
framework. But that's about as far as agreement among them goes.
The origin of language has been described as the "hardest challenge
to science" and some have suggested that it lies beyond the capacity of
science to resolve. One commentator puts it thus:

"[The] shortage of empirical evidence [on the origins of language]
has led many scholars to regard the entire topic as unsuitable

for serious study. In 1866, the Linguistic Society of Paris banned any existing or future debates on the subject, a prohibition which remained influential across much of the western world until late in the twentieth century. Today, there are numerous hypotheses about how, why, when, and where language might have emerged. Despite this, there is scarcely more agreement today than ... when Charles Darwin's theory of evolution by natural selection provoked a rash of armchair speculation on the topic."[23]

So what happened in the late twentieth century to change this situation? The answer is Noam Chomsky who, as a graduate student at Penn State University, proposed a radically new theory of language. His idea was that language was not learned but that humans are born with a "language organ"—a capacity resident in the brain that is just as physical as the heart and liver, and which begins to function at birth. As a chick doesn't have to be taught to peck its way out of the egg, so humans possess an instinctive capacity to use language. Whatever its nationality, a child's language organ (possessing elements Chomsky calls "deep structure," "universal grammar," and a "language acquisition device") equips him or her to express thoughts from an early age, constructing sentences and using correct grammar. Of course, there must be a process of learning ("language acquisition") in early childhood, but it is rapid and effortless, because the required mental equipment is in place from birth.

It's like learning to ride a bicycle. As a small boy it took me time to master the technique, but I eventually succeeded because I had the equipment. But before I acquired the bicycle as a birthday present, riding on two wheels was beyond my power. In the same way, according to Chomsky, nonhuman creatures lack the necessary mental equipment and cannot therefore use language (though some do learn to ride bicycles). In further support of Chomsky's ideas, a group of deaf children were discovered to have evolved a sophisticated sign language of their own. Writing in the *Psychological Science Journal*, Ann Senghas and Marie Coppola, explain:

> "The present study investigated the language production of a generation of deaf Nicaraguans who had not been exposed to a developed language. We examined the changing use of early linguistic structures ... in a sign language that has emerged since the Nicaraguan group first came together. In under two decades, sequential cohorts of learners systematized the grammar of this new sign language.... Thus, sequential cohorts of interacting young children collectively possess the capacity not only to learn, but also to create, language."[24]

Chomsky probably overemphasized the physicality of his "language organ" and it is unlikely to consist of a lump of brain tissue. It is more likely a distributed functionality involving many areas of the brain. But his idea of an innate human capacity appears to be entirely valid (though not everyone agrees[25]).

CHATTERING CHIMPS

Attempts to teach spoken language to chimpanzees fall somewhat short of the attainments of a talking parrot. Significantly more success has, however, been obtained with sign language, where intense efforts have taught chimps to use gestures to ask for food. In a detailed survey of the field, a paper[26] from the "Animal Communication Project" concludes:

"Though none will argue that any animal has the full capacity of humans for language, none should deny that at least some animals have quite impressive competencies for language skills, including speech comprehension."

However, this conclusion is based on observations of a single bonobos ape, and the paper also quotes psychologist Steven Pinker, author of *The Language Instinct*, as declaring, "No chimpanzee has learned sign language.... They've certainly learned some gestures, but sign language is not just a system of gestures. It's a full, grammatical language with its own systematic grammar, like Latin."

In spite of these failures to teach language to apes, Chomsky and his supporters still think that language originally evolved by Darwinian processes, emerging somewhere and somehow between ape antecedents and *Homo sapiens*. They just can't explain how it could possibly have happened. And, of course, Chomsky's theory of an *innate* language apparatus in humans is entirely consistent with special creation and the image of God in Man.

LOGIC

Let's move on to logic (I use the word in a general sense). Logic involves the formulation, contemplation, and manipulation of ideas—something that can only be done using language and grammatical structures. For thought to be logical, objects must be labeled and described (nouns and adjectives), actions must be specified (verbs and adverbs), while relationships between these language elements must be constructed (grammar and syntax). Canadian sinologist G. Pulleyblank puts it this way:

"Our capacity, through language, to manipulate the mental world
and so deal imaginatively with the world of experience,
has been a major factor, perhaps the major factor, in giving
humans the overwhelming advantage over other species in
terms of cultural, as opposed to biological, evolution."[27]

To put it simply, we cannot think without using words (or equivalent symbols) that have defined meanings. Since languages such as Chinese are based on pictograms (formalized pictures that represent individual words) some people can, no doubt, think in symbols. But there is no essential difference between these symbols and the words we use in most languages, and which allow us to construct an almost infinite range of meaningful statements and speculations. Without language, rational thought would be impossible. You can watch a mental video clip but you can neither describe nor evaluate what you are seeing without using language. Your mind is more than a TV screen.

And this raises a classic "chicken-and-egg" question: which came first, logic or language? It seems to me that one cannot exist without the other, so they are either both innate, manifesting the image of God in Man, or they have evolved together. The problem with the evolutionary answer is that evolution isn't supposed to work that way. Each evolutionary step is allegedly the result of a random mutation that gets fixed in a population because it has a beneficial impact on reproduction. No one knows how many such steps would be required to generate a perceptible survival benefit from either logic or language, nor how long each step would take to become fixed. But one thing is certain—random mutations, even if beneficial, are not noted for cooperating to provide the coevolution of such different traits as logic and language.

CREATIVITY AND COMPETENCE

The third duplex attribute that humans share with God is creativity and competence—the ability to design and construct. This ability applies both to material things (like the universe and a garden shed) and to nonmaterial things (like the laws of nature or a piano concerto). Of course, some animals possess the ability to design and construct—witness the nest of a bower bird, a termite hill, or a beaver dam. But these are instinctive activities involving no evidence of planning, invention, or original thought. Animal instincts are frequently amazing but they cannot be described as creative.

On God's part, *creatio ex nihilo* is the ultimate act of material creativity, as we saw in Chapter 10. Some commentators argue that the doctrine is not taught unambiguously in the Bible, and was the second-century invention of well-meaning theologians seeking to combat certain heresies. But apologist Paul Copan has dealt with this in great detail[28] and shows convincingly that "creation from nothing" is indeed taught in the Bible and means exactly what it says. As Psalm 33:6 declares, "By the word of the Lord the heavens were made, and all the host of them by the breath of his mouth."

So let's think for a moment what kind of creativity was involved in the origination of the universe.

Before anything else could happen, laws must have been put in place to govern space and time, matter and energy, and the way these things interact. As we saw in Chapter 2, these "laws of nature" are essentially mathematical, rational, and consistent. Then, of course, the material elements that make up the physical universe were created by unimaginable power as God declares: "I *am* the LORD, who makes all things, who stretches out the heavens all alone,"[29] and again, "He who sits above the circle of the Earth ... stretches out the heavens like a curtain and spreads them out like a tent to dwell in."[30]

But God's creativity is not limited to the material creation and its laws. Throughout the Bible he is revealed as active in the affairs of men and nations: "He gives to all life, breath and all things,"[31] and works "all things according to the counsel of his will."[32] In Acts 17, Paul speaks of "every nation of men [who] dwell on all the face of the Earth," asserting that God has "determined their preappointed times and the boundaries of their habitation."[33] In other words, human national and political history also lies under the sovereign control of God.

The apostle James declares that "every good gift and every perfect gift is from above and comes down from the Father of lights [that is, from God]."[34] So God's creativity is seen not only in creation itself but also in providence—the way God provides for and directs his creation on a day-by-day basis. "I know the thoughts that I think towards you, says the Lord; thoughts of peace and not of evil, to give you a future and a hope."[35]

It is evident that Man shares something of God's creative urge. From childhood onwards we love to imagine things, plan things, invent things, make things, and enjoy the products of our creative activity. Children delight in building sandcastles, drawing pictures, inventing games, and imagining adventures, while adults build houses, design gardens, invent spacecraft and plan business ventures—or simply find satisfaction in cooking a special meal. Such creativity is unique to Man, and the only rational explanation I can offer is that we are made in the image and likeness of God.

And that brings us to the second point, namely, competence. To imagine and plan is one thing, but to convert our ideas into reality is quite another. God, of course, is ultimately competent, for he has the ability to fulfill every desire and purpose he intends. In this respect, humans fall immensely short of perfection. Many of us love music but will never master a musical instrument. We admire art but our efforts with a paintbrush are pathetic. Others, of course, do possess the competences we lack, but might be unable to bake a cake, give a talk, or run a marathon. We are at best only partly competent to turn resolutions into results. But even so, what an enormous gap there is between ourselves and the most intelligent of nonhuman animals, especially when we approach the matter collectively! That is, there do arise among us men and women whose competence, in one field of human endeavor or another, is simply breathtaking and even incomprehensible. Every generation and most cultures have their brilliant musicians, mathematicians, inventors, sporting heroes, artists, writers, poets, politicians, teachers, doctors, scientists, and so on. Is this the outcome of mindless evolution or the outworking of the image of God? I will leave the reader to judge.

LAW AND LOVE

I'm again using words in a broad sense to label categories of human experience. Thus by "law" I mean not only our perception and use of rules and regulations, but also our possession of a moral nature—without which laws would be meaningless to us (I imagine we've all seen pictures of a Kingfisher perched hungrily on a "no fishing" river sign). By "love" I mean the ability to relate to others in sophisticated interpersonal and social structures. We shall see that there is a close interplay between law and love.

I devoted two whole chapters in *Who Made God?* to the subject of law, both in society and in science, so I will only summarize here. I argued that human society is characterized (both formally and informally) by the existence of laws or rules that govern the way we interact with our fellow human beings. Without such rules, society cannot exist, for they provide it with its fundamental structure. Similarly, the natural cosmos functions in conformity with the laws of nature, which are stable in space and time and thus allow science to be practiced. I pointed out that the laws of nature (being rational and even mathematical in character) could not have just "happened" and must rather have their origin in a rational and mathematical mind (as we saw also in Chapter 2). Less obviously, the laws of society can be traced back to the principle of *Patria Potestas* (paternal power) according to which social laws and norms of behavior originally stemmed from the authority vested in heads of families and tribes. The ultimate head of the human family, according to the Bible, is the God who created us and who still sustains and provides for us. Thus ultimately the source of all law, whether in science or society, is the mind of God—and Man, being made in God's image, is the only creature capable of understanding, embracing, and applying it. Unfortunately, this also means that we are capable of breaking social laws when it suits us, though happily the laws of nature are beyond our reach.

LOVING LAW

To the modern mind, law and love may seem strange companions. Too often today, love is viewed as an *alternative* to law as that which should govern our relationships with other people. The Beatles pop group famously sang;

> *There's nothing you can do that can't be done.*
> *Nothing you can sing that can't be sung.*

*Nothing you can say but you can learn how to play the
    game.*
It's easy.
Nothing you can make that can't be made.
No one you can save that can't be saved.
*Nothing you can do, but you can learn how to be you in
    time.*
It's easy.
All you need is love.
All you need is love.
All you need is love, love
Is all you need.

Sadly, of course, the song became the anthem of a generation that despised law, reveled in disobedience, and rejected the norms of social behavior. Why? Because the "love" celebrated in the song is not the love of one's neighbor which undergirds society, but the love of self which undermines it. But genuine love loves law, and that for good reason. Addressing God, the Psalmist wrote: [36]

Oh, how I love your law; it is my meditation all the day!
*You, through your commandments make me wiser than my
    enemies;*
For they [the commandments] are ever with me;
I have more understanding than all my teachers,
For your testimonies are my meditation.

Far from restricting our liberty, laws (especially moral laws) underlie a whole range of human freedoms. The Psalmist discovered that God's law provides freedom from ignorance—a principle that Jesus also proclaims, "If you abide in my word [that is, obey my teaching] you are my disciples indeed, and you will know the truth and the truth will make you free."[37]

Civil law also provides precious freedoms because (among other things) it requires us to respect legitimate authorities and the rights of our fellow citizens, encouraging us to express our love towards others by doing to them what we would have them do to us. A society that functions according to "the rule of law," while never perfect, is nevertheless a peaceful and healthy society, where freedom has a chance to flourish. But one in which the rule of law has broken down rapidly becomes degenerate, dangerous, and destructive. If society is a train, laws are the tracks on which it runs. If it stays on the rails, it can take its passengers safely to rewarding destinations, but if it leaves the track it becomes a train crash in which everyone suffers. It is the height of wisdom, therefore, to love law.

THE LAW OF LOVE

I argued earlier that all law has its origins in God, and the same is true of love. The apostle John boldly proclaims that "God is love."[38] This doesn't mean that God has no *other* attributes, but that love finds its *definition* in the nature of God. I think John meant it to apply both ways, as if he had written, "God is love and love is God." That is, firstly, that love is an outstanding and manifest property of the One who is also holy and "dwells in unapproachable light."[39] And secondly, that love can only be fully understood by reference to the character of God.

When asked to state God's greatest commandment, Jesus replied, "You shall love the Lord your God with all your heart and with all your soul and with all your mind. This is the first and great commandment.

And the second is like it; you shall love your neighbor as yourself."[40] On another occasion a questioner asked him, "But who is my neighbor?" and Jesus answered by telling the story of the Good Samaritan[41]—the foreigner who showed costly and outstanding kindness to an injured Jew, despite the fact that Jews and Samaritans despised and even hated one another. The message is crystal clear: we are commanded by God to love our fellow men and women, regardless of who they are, and seek to do them good, not harm. Why should we do that? Because we all bear the same image of God and are thus members of the same human family. This is the law of love.

Sadly, in our fallen state, we find it impossible to consistently obey this law, although at times it does surface above the murky waters of our sin, revealing itself in acts of self-denial, sacrifice, and compassion—and reminding us that as human beings we still possess the capacity to love. Even more sadly, while we sometimes manage to obey the second commandment (to love our neighbor), our sinful nature prevents us totally from observing the first (to love the Lord our God). But, as we shall see in the next two chapters, even this failure can be reversed—for "God demonstrates his own love towards us, in that while we were still sinners, Christ died for us."[42] The power of the law of love is demonstrated supremely in the Person and redeeming work of the Son of God, by which the image of God can be renewed in those who put their trust in him.

ENDNOTES:

[1] Twain, Mark; *What is Man? And other essays* (Loki's publishing, Sunnyvale, Ca.; Amazon UK edition) p. 80.

[2] Hebrews 1:7,14; 2:16. Angels are called 'sons of God' in Job 1:6 and 2:1 but 'sons' is used there in the idiomatic sense of any group led by

a father figure. For example, 1 Samuel 10:12 refers to the leader of a group of prophets as 'their father.'

3   Genesis 9:6.

4   Genesis 9:3.

5   John 4:24.

6   Genesis 1:28.

7   Moreland, J. P., *The recalcitrant Imago Dei* (SCM Press, London, 2009) p. 4.

8   Colossians 1:15.

9   Hebrews 1:3.

10   For example, Matthew 16:16–17 and many other places.

11   For example, Matthew 9:6 and many other places.

12   1 Corinthians 2:9.

13   Matthew 10:28.

14   Matthew 16:26.

15   Ephesians 1:17–18.

16   Some see "born of water" as a reference to baptism, but the following clause "that which is born of flesh is flesh" makes it clear that Jesus is using the Hebrew poetical device of repeating a statement using different words.

17   John 3:1–8.

18   Romans 8:15–16.

19   2 Corinthians 5:17.

20   Hebrews 1:3.

21   Hebrews 1:1-2.

22   Andrews, Edgar; *Who made God? Searching for a theory of everything* (EP Books, Welwyn Garden City, 3rd ed.,2016) p. 179.

23   From a detailed examination of the origin of language at https:// en.wikipedia.org/wiki/Origin_of_language

24   Senghas, Ann, and Coppola, Marie; *Psychological Science Journal* (July 1, 2001); http://journals.sagepub.com/doi/ abs/10.1111/1467-9280.00359

25   Wolfe, Tom; The Kingdom of speech (Jonathan Cape, London, 2016).

A journalist build a case against Chomsky but on rather slender foundations.

26 http://acp.eugraph.com/apes/

27 Pulleyblank, Edwin G; "The meaning of duality of patterning and its importance in language evolution," in *Studies in Language Origins* (John Benjamin, Philadelphia, 1989) Vol. 1, pp. 53–65.

28 Copan, Paul; *Trinity Journal* 17.1 (Spring 1996): 77–93. https://earlychurch.org.uk/article_exnihilo_copan.html

29 Isaiah 44:24.

30 Isaiah 40:22.

31 Acts 17:25.

32 Ephesians 1:11.

33 Acts 17:26.

34 James 1:17.

35 Jeremiah 29:11.

36 Ps. 119:97-99.

37 John 8:31–32.

38 1 John 4:8.

39 1 Timothy 6:16.

40 Matthew 22:35–40.

41 Luke 10:25–37.

42 Romans 5:8.

CHAPTER 13

Has there ever been a perfect human being? In spite of the praise and adoration we lavish on our heroes, saints and pop idols, the answer has to be "No." The Bible, however, claims a single exception to this rule. Jesus Christ, it maintains, was the perfect man who shows us what humanity would look like if Adam and Eve had not fallen into sin. But even more important, he shows us what humanity will, one day, become—when those who trust in his redeeming work will escape condemnation and live with him in "new heavens and a new Earth in which righteousness dwells."

Many mock this biblical vision of the future as "pie in the sky by and by," but who is right, the Christian church or an unbelieving world? The whole issue turns, of course, on the Person of Jesus Christ. Did he really exist and, if so, who was he? Was he an ill-fated reformer, a deluded romantic, a master conman or (as he and his disciples claimed) the incarnate Son of God? C. S. Lewis pointed out that we have to choose between three options: Jesus was either mad, bad, or God (to paraphrase Lewis' famous "trilemma"). In this chapter we shall try to find answers. We'll consider his historical reality, his own claims, the beliefs of his followers, the moral magnificence of his teaching and, crucially, some of the factual evidence that supports his extraordinary claims.

THE SECOND ADAM

Jesus Christ, the perfect man

"O loving wisdom of our God! When all was sin and shame, a second Adam to the fight and to the rescue came."

JOHN HENRY NEWMAN (D. 1890)

This book borrows its title from Psalm 8, which celebrates the creation of Man in glowing terms:

"What is Man that you are mindful of him, and the son of man that you visit him? For you have made him a little [or for a little while] lower than the angels and you have crowned him with glory and honor. You have made him to have dominion over the works of your hands; you have put all things under his feet."

The New Testament, however, quotes the psalm and adds a proviso: "But now we do not yet see all things put under him, but we see Jesus, who was made a little [or for a little time] lower than the angels, for the suffering of death, crowned with glory and honor."[1] The message is clear: with regard to Adam's descendants, Psalm 8 is an unfulfilled prophecy, but in regard to Jesus Christ, it has been both vindicated and fulfilled. He alone has lived up to expectations. He alone is the "second Adam" who shows us what humanity should look like. He alone was the perfect man. And that, according to the Bible, has both cosmic and personal implications, as we shall see.

WHO WAS JESUS CHRIST?

An obvious starting point is the Person of Christ. Did he even exist historically? And if he did, who was he and what claims did he make? No serious historian, whether Christian or non-Christian, doubts that Jesus of Nazareth existed—the son of a working class family in first-century Roman-occupied Israel, who became an itinerant Jewish Rabbi and founded the Christian religion. He is mentioned by both Jewish and Roman historians of the first and second centuries, specifically Josephus (AD 37–100), Tacitus (AD 56–120), Pliny the Younger (AD 61–113), and Lucian (AD 125–180). There may also be references to Jesus in the Babylonian Talmud (AD 70 onwards) but they are not as clear as in the aforementioned sources. All these writers were more or less hostile to Jesus and the early Christian church, yet they still testified to his existence, crucifixion, and ongoing influence. What they actually wrote about Jesus is examined and discussed in detail by Michael Gleghorn.[2]

In spite of this evidence, some skeptics (called "mythicists") deny his existence, claiming that Jesus was a purely fictional character—either reassembled by his disciples from various heathen myths, or projected from their "astral" dreams and visions. Mythicists place great emphasis on the fact that the four gospels were not written till twenty to fifty years after the events they describe, and then not (they allege) by eye-witnesses of those events. The first argument is unconvincing because most people have excellent recall of things they experienced fifty years ago, and the second unconscionable because it would make liars of Matthew and John, as well as Peter and James (Jesus' brother) in their letters. The fact that all the New Testament documents were in circulation so *soon* after the events they describe is actually unique among historical documents of that era. To give just one example, almost everything we know about the Emperor Tiberius (d. AD 37) comes from *The Annals* written eighty years after the emperor's death by Roman historian Tacitus.[3] John Dickson, honorary fellow of the Department of Ancient History at Macquarie University, writes: "Anyone who dips into the thousands of secular monographs and journal articles on the historical Jesus will quickly discover that mythicists are regarded by 99.9 percent of the scholarly community as complete 'outliers,' the fringe of the fringe"[4] (note the word "secular" in this quote).

THE DEITY OF CHRIST

So let's move on from the ridiculous to the sublime (to reverse the proverbial phrase). It is one thing for scholars to agree *en masse* that Jesus of Nazareth really existed, but quite another for Christians to claim that he was God in human flesh and born of a virgin. Yet this, of course, is precisely what the New Testament does maintain—not as a side issue but as the indispensable core of the biblical worldview. I appreciate that there are some who accept the Bible but reject the deity of Christ, such as Jehovah's Witnesses and Unitarians generally, but their position calls for considerable exegetical ingenuity. Mainstream Christianity has always held firmly and unapologetically to the incarnation and virgin birth.

Nor can these two doctrines be separated. If Jesus had been conceived normally, he would have been just like you and me—an heir of Adam and of his fallen nature. He could not then have been the sinless son of God in human flesh. On the other hand, if Jesus was indeed God incarnate, a miraculous birth would surely have been mandatory. The two ideas hang together logically, but is there any supporting evidence for these amazing claims? Yes, a considerable amount. Perhaps the foremost evidence is that, following his crucifixion, Jesus rose from the dead, but we will consider that later. What else can be said?

BAD, MAD, OR GOD

We face a "trilemma" if we are compelled logically to choose between three alternatives. One such trilemma, popularized by C. S. Lewis, offers us three options on the character of Jesus Christ. "You must make your choice" writes Lewis. "Either this man was, and is, the Son of God, or else a madman or something worse."[5] "Something worse" would be that Christ was a fraud, the most successful confidence trickster of all time. But if Jesus was bad or mad, how can we explain why, by common consent, his moral teaching is unsurpassed?

Clearly, the force of the trilemma lies in the ethical system taught by Jesus and set out particularly in his "Sermon on the Mount" (Matthew's gospel, chapters 5 to 7). Why do I say that this system is unsurpassed? Because it goes beyond any other ethical teaching of which I am aware. Consider some examples. Firstly, we saw in Chapter 12 that love lies at the heart of God's message to mankind, and that the two great commandments, derived from the Old Testament, are (1) to love God with all our heart soul, mind and strength, and (2) to love others as we love ourselves. But to these ancient precepts Jesus adds a staggering and unprecedented third: "Love your enemies, bless those who curse you, do good to those who hate you ... that you may be sons of your Father in heaven; for he makes his sun rise on the evil and on the good, and sends rain on the just and on the unjust."[6]

Secondly, while most moral codes outlaw adultery and murder, none apart from Christ's apply these principles to our thoughts as well as our actions. In his teaching, to lust is to commit adultery;[7] to hate or despise another person is to commit murder.[8] And God holds us accountable for these sins, even if they remain unobserved and hidden in our hearts.

Thirdly, Jesus' instructions to go the second mile[9] and turn the other cheek[10] are contrary to all our natural inclinations. They call for a sublime trust in God's care for us, and are not commonly endorsed, even by the most worthy among us. The matchless and radical morality taught by Jesus Christ must surely eliminate the possibilities that he was either mad or bad (or even sincerely mistaken) when he laid claim to deity.

THE CLAIMS OF CHRIST

Some suggest, however, that Jesus never actually claimed to be God, and that his aura of divinity was created by the adoring disciples. But if (either intentionally or by honest mistake) the disciples falsified the New Testament records concerning Christ's *claims*, how can we logically accept what they wrote about his *teaching*? It is extremely unlikely that the same disciples could get it so wrong about Christ's person and so right about his moral authority. And if they *did* succeed in doing both, it would leave us with no reliable source for the highest ethical system known to man. It comes down to the historical credibility of the New Testament—a credibility that is powerfully defended by

Dr. Craig Blomberg in his magisterial study *The Historical Reliability of the New Testament.*[11]

I find it interesting that the New Testament documents record the claims of Christ in several ways: (1) by reported sayings from his own lips; (2) by the authors expressing their personal beliefs; and (3) in the writings of some, like Luke and Paul, who never knew Christ during his Earthly lifetime. I don't know about you, but if I were making up a story about a fictional character, I would attribute all the claims directly to the hero, because they would then come across as firsthand and not secondhand. And I would certainly never include the testimony of anyone who was not an eyewitness! In other words, my fairy-tale would look nothing like the New Testament.

In what follows, I set out some of the identical claims made equally by Christ himself and by the disciples (some relying on the testimony of others). Personally, I find this rather messy mixture of attributions has the ring of reality rather than conspiracy. So what did Jesus claim about himself, and what are the parallel claims by others in the New Testament? (I restrict myself to six categories and one or two examples of each; there are many more.)

- *He claimed the authority to forgive sin.*

Jesus: "Seeing their faith, Jesus said to the paralytic, 'Son, be of good cheer; your sins are forgiven…. But that you may know that the Son of Man has power on Earth to forgive sins,' then he said to the paralytic, 'Arise, take up your bed, and go to your house.'"[12]
Others: "If we confess our sins, he is faithful and just to forgive us our sins and to cleanse us from all unrighteousness."[13]

- *He claimed that God was his Father (in an obviously unique sense).*

Jesus; "I and my Father are one."[14] "He who has seen me has seen the Father ... do you not believe that I am in the Father and the Father is in me?"[15]

Others: "In him [Christ] dwells all the fullness of the Godhead bodily."[16] "God ... has spoken to us by his Son, whom he has appointed heir of all things ... who being the brightness of his glory and the express image of his person, and upholding all things by the word of his power, when he had purged our sins sat down at the right hand of the Majesty on High."[17]

- *He claimed to be sinless.*

Jesus: "Because I tell the truth, you do not believe me. Which of you convicts me of sin? And if I tell the truth, why do you not believe me?"[18]

Others: "For we do not have a High Priest who cannot sympathize with our weaknesses, but was in all points tempted as we are, yet without sin."[19]

- *He claimed (and demonstrated) the power to heal all manner of diseases.*

Jesus: "He went into the synagogue on the Sabbath day, and stood up to read. And He was handed the book of the prophet Isaiah. And when He had opened the book, He found the place where it was written: 'The Spirit of the Lord is upon me, because he has anointed me to preach the gospel to the poor; he has sent me to heal the broken-hearted, to proclaim liberty to the captives and recovery of sight to the blind, to set at liberty those who are oppressed; to proclaim the acceptable year of the Lord....' And He began to say to them, 'Today this Scripture is fulfilled in your hearing.'"[20]

Others: "Then His fame went throughout all Syria; and they brought to him all sick people who were afflicted with various diseases and torments, and those who were demon-possessed, epileptics, and paralytics; and He healed them."[21]

- *He claimed (and demonstrated) the power to raise the dead*

Jesus (before raising Lazarus from the dead): "I am the resurrection and the life. He who believes in me, though he may die, he shall live. And whoever lives and believes in me shall never die."[22]

Others: "When he came near the gate of the city, behold, a dead man was being carried out, the only son of his mother; and she was a widow.... When the Lord saw her, he had compassion on her and said to her, 'Do not weep.' Then he came and touched the open coffin ... and he said, 'Young man, I say to you, arise.' So he who was dead sat up and began to speak."[23]

- *He claimed to give eternal life to those who believe in him*

Jesus: "My sheep hear my voice, and I know them, and they follow me. And I give them eternal life, and they shall never perish, neither shall anyone snatch them from my hand."[24]

Others: "For the wages of sin is death, but the gift of God is eternal life in Christ Jesus our Lord.[25] And this is the testimony: that God has given us eternal life, and this life is in His Son."[26]

- *He claimed to be truth, life, and the only way to God.*

Jesus: "Jesus said to him, 'I am the way, the truth, and the life. No one comes to the Father except through me. If you had known me, you would have known my Father also....'"[27]

Others: "Nor is there salvation in any other, for there is no other name under heaven given among men by which we must be saved.[28] For if when we were enemies we were reconciled to God through the death of His Son, much more, having been reconciled, we shall be saved by His life."[29]

FULFILLED PROPHECY

Jesus of Nazareth fulfilled many Old Testament prophecies that we know were made hundreds of years before his birth. There is no shortage of examples—for according to Luke's gospel, "Beginning at Moses and all the prophets, [Jesus] expounded to [his disciples] in all the Scriptures the things concerning himself."[30] It has been suggested that there are more than 300 Old Testament prophecies that were fulfilled by Jesus Christ during his life on Earth but we have space to consider only a small selection of the most significant.

Most of these prophecies look forward to the coming of the "Messiah," which means "the anointed one." The Greek equivalent is "the Christ," which is a title rather than a personal name. These prophecies do not necessarily imply that the Messiah would be God in human form. Indeed, most Jews were expecting a political Messiah who would restore the Davidic kingdom and national pride. But some of the prophecies fulfilled by Christ go much further and bear witness to his divinity. In either case, the prediction, hundreds of years in advance, of events in the life of Jesus of Nazareth testify to the miraculous nature of his birth, life, ministry, death and resurrection. So let's spend time considering some of them.

THE BIRTH OF CHRIST

When the wise men from the East arrived in Jerusalem bringing gifts of gold, frankincense, and myrrh to the infant Jesus, they asked the experts where the newborn "King of the Jews" could be found.[31] The priests and scribes had no hesitation in quoting the Prophet Micah (8th century BC): "But you, Bethlehem Ephrathah, though you are little among the thousands of Judah, yet out of you shall come forth to me the one to be ruler in Israel, whose goings forth have been from of old, from everlasting."[32] The priests used a watered down version of the quotation, so I have cited the verse as it appears in the Hebrew Old Testament. Jesus was indeed born in Bethlehem Ephrathah, near Jerusalem (there was another Bethlehem in Zebulun, Northern Israel[33]), but Micah refers not only to his birthplace but also to his "everlasting" nature and activity ("goings forth").

According to Matthew 1:23, the virgin birth of Christ was also predicted. Isaiah 7:14 says "Behold the virgin shall conceive and bear a son and shall call his name Immanuel" (the name means "God with us"). Objections have been raised to this claim, specifically: (1) the context requires a contemporary fulfillment, and (2) the Hebrew word in Isaiah can just mean "young woman." In response it can be said (1) that Old Testament prophecies do quite often have both contemporary and future fulfillments, and (2) that Matthew uses a word that undoubtedly means "virgin." Also, the birth in Isaiah is given as a *sign*, so it must refer to some unusual event, not just to a young woman having a baby. The name "God with us" is also highly significant, of course, with respect to Jesus' nature.

THE TIMING OF CHRIST'S COMING

The book of Daniel was written in the fifth century BC and gives first-hand testimony to events in the reigns of rulers well known to secular history, such as Nebuchadnezzar, Belshazzar, Darius, and Cyrus. But it is also remarkable for its prophecies of future events—so much so that skeptics, rejecting the possibility of such prophecies being fulfilled, date the book as late as 165 BC. The earlier date has much supporting evidence[34] but either way, everyone agrees that it was written several hundred years before the death of Christ. Daniel writes:

> "Seventy weeks are decreed about your people and your holy city,
>> to finish the transgression, to put an end to sin and to atone
>> for iniquity; to bring in everlasting righteousness ... Know
>> therefore and understand that from the going out of the word
>> to restore and build Jerusalem, to the coming of an anointed
>> one, a prince, there shall be seven weeks. Then for sixty-two
>> weeks it shall be built again with squares and moats, but in
>> a troubled time. And after the sixty-two weeks, an anointed
>> one shall be cut off and have nothing. And the people of the
>> prince who is to come shall destroy the city and sanctuary."[35]

This part of the book of Daniel is written in an "apocalyptic" genre and thus needs careful interpretation, but no one doubts that the word "week" [literally, "seven"] represents seven years (one apocalyptic day is one actual year). The "word to restore and build Jerusalem"—following its destruction by Nebuchadnezzar and the seventy-year captivity of Israel in Babylon—can only sensibly refer to the edict of Artaxerxes l in 457 BC (referred to in Ezra 7:13 and not to be confused with the earlier edict of Cyrus to rebuild the *temple* in Jerusalem). The first prince mentioned, who comes forty-nine years after Artaxerxes' edict, is not easily identified, but could be Ezra the priest. Although Ezra is referred to only as a "skilled scribe in the law of Moses,"[36] the letter given to him by Artaxerxes II (and reproduced in Aramaic in Ezra 7:12–26) shows the high esteem in which he was held by the king. This might well justify the title "prince," and the timing of "seven sevens" (forty-nine years after the edict of Artaxerxes I) fits well with one possible date for Ezra's expedition to Jerusalem to reestablish Mosaic principles of worship and government.

Then follows a further sixty-two sevens which, added to the "seven sevens" just mentioned, brings the date to AD 26 (69 sevens or 483 years after the 457 BC edict)—after which "an anointed one [Hebrew, *Messiah*] shall be cut off." We are not told how long it is *after* the 69 sevens have expired that the Messiah is cut off. But notice that the prophecy begins by saying, "*seventy* weeks [not sixty-nine] are decreed about your people and your holy city, to finish the transgression, to put an end to sin and to atone for iniquity; to bring in everlasting righteousness." There is, therefore, a period of seven years to be added to the 483 years before atonement is accomplished and everlasting righteousness brought in—which brings us to AD 33, the commonly accepted date of Christ's crucifixion. According to the New Testament, what Daniel describes here is *precisely* what Jesus Christ accomplished by his death and resurrection.

Needless to say, those who reject the biblical worldview find many alternative interpretations of Daniel's "seventy weeks" prophecy, omitting Christ completely from the story. Some Christian interpretations differ somewhat from my own. But quite apart from the calculation of dates (which are seldom precisely known), there are remarkable similarities between Daniel's prophecy and established history—including the death of the Messiah (Christ), the subsequent sacking of Jerusalem in AD 70 by the Roman general Titus, and the destruction of the temple. The latter event is accurately predicted by the words, "And the people of the prince who is to come [Titus] shall destroy the city *and sanctuary*" (emphasis added). The Jewish temple was a special target for the Romans because they rightly saw it as the emblem of Jewish nationhood. The fact that the prophecy specifies the destruction, not just of the city but also of a temple in the city, is significant support for its accuracy and authenticity.

THE NATURE AND MINISTRY OF CHRIST

The prophecy of Isaiah was written during the eighth century BC, though some argue that the last 15 chapters were penned 150 years later by another hand. Either way, it was complete long before the time of Christ, yet it contains several remarkable prophecies that were fulfilled by Jesus of Nazareth. We'll look at three of them. In Isaiah 9:6–7 we read:

> "For unto us a Child is born, unto us a Son is given; and the
> government will be upon His shoulder. And His name will be
> called wonderful counselor, mighty God, everlasting Father,
> prince of peace. Of the increase of His government and peace
> there will be no end; upon the throne of David and over
> his kingdom, to order it and establish it with judgment and
> justice, from that time forward, even forever."

It is impossible to identify anyone other than Christ who even begins to fulfill this prophecy, but according to the New Testament he fulfilled it in every respect. Isaiah predicts that one would come (note future tenses after the first line) as a child born of woman, yet also as a son given. Hebrew poetry often takes the form of a statement followed by its repetition in different words, so there might be no double meaning here. But on the other hand, the same poetic convention does frequently introduce a meaningful difference between the statement and its repetition, and such a difference would be an exact match of the New Testament claim that, although Jesus was Mary's child by birth, he was also God's son sent from heaven. And clearly, the remainder of the verse is consistent with this New Testament view.

Isaiah next identifies the coming one as a ruler, the heir to David's vacant throne. This is a consistent messianic theme in the Old Testament and firmly attaches the prophecy to the coming Christ. First-century Jews, including Jesus' own disciples, expected the Messiah to establish an Earthly kingdom, restoring freedom, peace and prosperity to national Israel. But Isaiah speaks here of an *everlasting* kingdom, established on principles of "judgment and justice," something that could never be said of an Earthly kingdom. Much closer to the prophecy were the angel's words to Mary;

"You will conceive in your womb and bring forth a son, and shall
call his name Jesus. He will be great and shall be called the
son of the highest, and the Lord God will give him the throne
of his father David. And he will reign over the House of Jacob
for ever, and of his kingdom there will be no end."[37]

Indeed, so closely do these words match Isaiah's prediction that skeptics accuse Luke of tailoring his story to fit the prophecy. But Luke is generally acknowledged to be a careful historian, and there is unanimity among New Testament writers that Christ did not come to establish a temporal Earthly kingdom, but the eternal and spiritual kingdom of God.

Isaiah isn't finished yet! He next attaches four names to the messianic child, titles that leave us in no doubt what kind of person he would be: "Wonderful Counselor, Mighty God, Everlasting Father, Prince of Peace." The first title celebrates his wisdom as a man, the second his divine power, the third his deity, and the fourth his mission to reconcile sinful people to a holy God. The whole New Testament asserts that these amazing titles belong alone to Jesus of Nazareth, the Son of Man; the Son of God. As far as I am aware, such comprehensive claims have never been made on behalf of any other historical person.

CHRIST'S ATONING DEATH

One of the most detailed messianic prophecies is found in Isaiah 52:11 to 53:12, which speaks of the "suffering servant" of God. Whole books have been written on this prophecy and it will be impossible to examine it in depth here, but if you have never read this passage I suggest you take a moment to do so (an internet search for the cited verses will quickly find it). Let me summarize its predictions, adding in brackets brief notes on the way Jesus fulfilled them:

- His was marred beyond recognition by suffering. (Jesus was scourged with whips and tortured with a crown of thorns. He was too weak to carry his cross.)
- He would, nevertheless, "sprinkle" many nations. The word "sprinkle" is borrowed from the Mosaic ritual of sprinkling ashes and water to effect ceremonial cleansing. Spiritually, it speaks of cleansing the conscience from sin.[38]
- He would be "despised and rejected by men, a man of sorrows and acquainted with grief."
- "We esteemed him stricken, smitten by God ... but he was wounded for our transgressions [not his own] and bruised for our iniquities." (The innocent dies for the guilty.)

- His sufferings on our behalf bring peace with God and healing for our souls.
- "All we like sheep have gone astray, we have turned every one to his own way, and the Lord has laid on him the iniquity of us all." (Christ is our substitute and sin-bearer.)
- "He was taken from prison and from judgment and ... cut off from the land of the living. For the transgressions of my people he was stricken." (Jesus was imprisoned and tried before being crucified.)
- "He made his grave with the wicked but with the rich in his death." (Jesus was crucified with two criminals but then buried in a rich man's tomb.)
- "It pleased the Lord to bruise him; he has put him to grief." (It was God's plan that Jesus should suffer for our sins.[39])
- "When you make his soul an offering for sin, he shall see his seed [spiritual children], he shall prolong his days [he will live again beyond the grave], and the pleasure of the Lord shall prosper in his hand [God's plan of redemption will succeed]."
- "By his knowledge [experience] my righteous servant shall justify many, for he shall bear their iniquities ... he bore the sin of many and made intercession for the transgressors." (In the New Testament, Hebrews 7:25 declares that Jesus "is able to save to the uttermost those who come to God through him, since he ever lives to make intercession for them.")

The fulfilled prophecies outlined above need an explanation. Skeptics advance the idea that the New Testament writers deliberately constructed false accounts of Christ's life around Old Testament prophecies. But I suggest that this "conspiracy theory" objection demands far greater credulity (unjustified belief) than just accepting the New Testament claims as true.

There remains the greatest claim of all—that Jesus rose from the dead following his crucifixion. This is so important that we need a new (and final) chapter to consider it. We'll do so under three headings: "the claim," "the evidence," and "the implications."

ENDNOTES:

1   Hebrews 2:6–9.
2   http://www.bethinking.org/jesus/
    ancient-evidence-for-jesus-from-nonchristian-sources
3   http://www.abc.net.au/religion/articles/2014/12/24/4154120.htm
4   Also from http://www.abc.net.au/religion/
    articles/2014/12/24/4154120.htm. See also https://en.wikipedia.org/
    wiki/Tacitus#History_of_the_Roman_Empire_from_the_death_of_
    Augustus
5   Lewis, C. S.; *Mere Christianity* (Collins, London, 1952) pp. 54–56. (In all
    editions, this is Bk. II, Ch. 3, "The Shocking Alternative.")
6   Matthew 5:44–45.
7   Matthew 5:27–28.
8   Matthew 5:21–22.
9   Matthew 5:41.
10 Matthew 5:39.
11 Blomberg, Craig; *The Historical Reliability of the New Testament* (IVP
    Academic, 2nd edition, 2007). https://www.amazon.com/Historical-
    Reliability-New-Testament-Evangelical-ebook/dp/B01MSUCJ66/
    ref=tmm_kin_swatch_0?_encoding=UTF8&qid=1498992547&sr=8-1]
12 Matthew 9:2–7.
13 I John 1:9.
14 John 10:30.
15 John 14:9–10.
16 Colossians 2:9.

17 Hebrews 1:1–3.

18 John 8:45–46.

19 Hebrews 4:15.

20 Luke 4:16–21.

21 Matthew 4:24.

22 John 11:25–26.

23 Luke 7:11–17.

24 John 10:27–28.

25 Romans 6:23.

26 1 John 5:11.

27 John 14:6–7.

28 Acts 4:12.

29 Romans 5:10.

30 Luke 24:25–27.

31 Matthew 2:1–12.

32 Micah 5:2.

33 http://www.keyway.ca/htm2001/20010514.htm

34 "Documents written in 5th century BCE Egypt (~495 BCE to ~402
    BCE) reveal unique textual and linguistic styles from that era. These
    documents are called the Elephantine Papyri. By comparing the texts of
    the Elephantine Papyri to the texts of Daniel, scholars have concluded
    that the textual style of Daniel places the book within the era of the
    5th century BCE. Even Naturalists accept that the style of writing would
    place the book of Daniel centuries earlier than the 2nd century BCE."
    [http://harvardhouse.com/Daniel_date-written.htm]

35 Daniel 9:25–26 (ESV).

36 Ezra 7:6.

37 Luke 1:30–34.

38 See Hebrews 9:13–14.

39 See Acts 2:23.

CHAPTER 14

The claims of Christ culminate in one final astounding prediction: "I lay down my life that I may take it again. No one takes it from me but I lay it down of myself. I have power to lay it down and I have power to take it again" (John 10:17–18). In this final chapter, we are going to see if the claim and its fulfillment stand up to the tests of history, consistency, and logic.

How can we know whether or not Christ really did rise from the dead following his crucifixion? Such a unique event cannot be reproduced in a scientific experiment but can only be verified (or disproved) by appeal to historical documents, by the mutual reinforcement of the testimony and behavior of eyewitnesses and early commentators, and by the logical consistency between the resurrection and the claim that Jesus was indeed the incarnate Son of God.

We shall therefore look firstly at the evidence for the resurrection and secondly at its four main implications, namely: (1) that faith in Christ brings justification to sinners and the forgiveness of their sins; (2) that Christ is alive today, building his church and actively promoting the unfolding purposes of God; (3) that he will return to Earth to implement the final judgment; and (4) that God's ultimate purpose for mankind will be fulfilled.

THE RESURRECTION: FACT OR FICTION?

The claim, the evidence, and the implications

"I know of no one fact in the history of mankind which is proved by better and fuller evidence of every sort, to the understanding of a fair inquirer, than the great sign which God [has] given us that Christ died and rose again from the dead."

THOMAS ARNOLD, FORMER CHAIR OF MODERN HISTORY AT OXFORD UNIVERSITY.[1]

In his magisterial letter to the Romans, the apostle Paul leaves us in no doubt concerning his belief in the resurrection. He begins by referring to the "good news" of Christ as follows:

"The gospel of God [is that] which he promised before through his prophets in the holy scriptures, concerning his Son, Jesus Christ our Lord, who was born of the seed of David according to the flesh, and declared to be the Son of God with power, according to the Spirit of holiness, by the resurrection from the dead."[2]

The ultimate proof of Jesus' deity—for every New Testament writer—is his physical resurrection three days after he died by crucifixion. This isn't just Paul's opinion: it was first declared publicly by Peter on the day of Pentecost, just seven weeks after Christ's death and long before Paul's Damascus Road conversion:

> "Him, being delivered by the carefully planned intention and
> foreknowledge of God, you have taken by lawless hands, have
> crucified and put to death; whom God raised up, having
> loosed the pains of death, because it was not possible that he
> should be held by it."[3]

Why was it impossible for Christ to remain dead? Peter explains by quoting Psalm 16, where David writes:

> "You will not leave my soul in Hades [the place of the departed]
> nor will you allow your Holy One to see corruption. You have
> made known to me the way of life; you will make me full of
> joy in your presence."[4]

Peter points out that King David himself *did* die, stay dead, and "see corruption." So David wasn't speaking of himself but of the Messiah, the descendant who would one day occupy his throne forever. According to the book of Acts, the result of Peter's speech that day was the conversion of about three thousand people to faith in Christ and the beginning of the historic Christian church.[5] Had any of these people doubted Peter's interpretation of Psalm 16, or the fact of Christ's resurrection, they could easily have checked it out. They could have walked a short distance to the tomb or sought a second opinion from the Jewish priests, or asked the Roman authorities for their side of the story. Perhaps some of them did. But in spite of the opportunities they had to investigate or question the resurrection claim, we are told that these early converts:

> "continued steadfastly in the apostles' teaching and fellowship, in the breaking of bread and in prayers ... praising God and having favor with all the people. And the Lord added to the church daily those who were being saved."[6]

THE RESURRECTION OF CHRIST: THE EVIDENCE

What, then, is the evidence that Jesus did rise from the dead? Whole books have been written on the subject. They range from scholarly works by Christian theologians[7] to gripping accounts by authors who set out to disprove the resurrection but became convinced of it by the evidence[8]. Many people, of course, deny the very possibility of Christ's rising from the dead, including those who speak for non-Christian religions such as Judaism and Islam, and offer alternative theories to account for the Bible's historical accounts of the event. However, my purpose here is only to outline the main evidences that have been presented and argued in depth by Christian believers down the centuries. For a longer, yet concise and well-reasoned treatment of the subject, including answers to the aforesaid alternative theories, I recommend Dr. John Blanchard's forty-page booklet, *Jesus: Dead or Alive?*[9] Here I will just summarize the basic evidence in favor of the resurrection.

Before doing so, however, let me deal with one objection that is sure to be raised, namely that all the evidence for Christ's resurrection is derived from the Bible itself and must therefore be considered suspect. Isn't it rather like a criminal's mother giving evidence in court that her son is innocent? However, this objection is based on two misunderstandings.

Firstly, since the resurrection of Christ was a unique event that occurred (or, if you are skeptical, did not occur) 2000 years ago, the only evidence possible is historical in nature. Regardless of their content, the New Testament writings are known to be genuine and dateable *historical documents*. They must therefore be received and evaluated as admissible sources of evidence. That's important to grasp, since there are virtually no secular documents that mention the resurrection *either way*. Some will take this to mean that it never happened, while others, like me, will wonder why Jewish and Roman historians refrained from attacking it. After all, the resurrection claim was of such public importance that Christ's followers were bitterly persecuted for teaching it. This persecution, documented in the Acts of the Apostles and amply confirmed by secular history, shows that opponents had every *reason* to advance arguments and evidence against the resurrection. Indeed, they should have been falling over one another in their eagerness to do so. Their silence on the subject suggests they had no evidence to offer.

Secondly, the arguments set out below do not depend on accepting the New Testament at face value, because they actually rebut the charges that its testimony might be deliberate falsehood or superstitious error. How do they do this? By providing uncontested *circumstantial* evidence for the validity of the biblical account. Two decades acting as an "expert witness" in the British High Court and courts in North America taught me one thing at least. While an individual can easily lie in the witness box, circumstantial evidence is extremely difficult to fabricate, since that requires control of the "crime scene" environment and/or the willing cooperation of other people.

So what are the evidences for Jesus' resurrection?

- In the space of seven weeks, the disciples were transformed. A group of fearful men who ran away when Jesus was arrested[10] and hid from the Jews behind locked doors[11] became fearless advocates of the resurrection of Christ, even accusing the populace of murdering their Messiah. Following the resurrection, the apostles were willing to die rather than deny it.
- The empty tomb. If Christ's body had been stolen by grave robbers or spirited away by the authorities to prevent the tomb becoming a shrine, or mistakenly placed in a different tomb, then the Jews and Romans would have quickly found it and put it on display. That would crush once for all the belief that Christ had risen. Instead, *they admitted that the body had disappeared* by accusing the disciples of removing it (in spite of the guard placed on the tomb and the despondent attitude of those same disciples before the empty tomb was confirmed).
- The New Testament contains no eyewitness account of the actual resurrection event. A concocted story would surely have included one.
- The first witnesses to the empty tomb were women. Among first-century Jews, a woman's testimony was considered almost worthless and was accorded a low rating by law courts. In harmony with this, even the apostles at first dismissed the women's account as idle tales[12] (as did the two disciples on the

road to Emmaus). An invented story would *never* have made women the primary witnesses.

- The four gospels differ in detail and apparent chronology of the event. A conspiracy among the disciples to propagate a false story would have ensured greater harmony between different accounts. (Note that the differences can be reconciled without undue difficulty.)

- Subsequent eyewitness accounts from different sources and in different circumstances have to be explained. Such a large diversity of eyewitnesses (most of them still alive), and of postresurrection statements, would have been impossible to coordinate and hold together if they were the product of a conspiracy—especially in the face of implacable opposition by Jewish and Roman authorities intent on *disproving* the resurrection. I refer to the testimonies of the disciples walking to Emmaus, of various women at the tomb, of Peter and John at the tomb, of disciples gathered in the upper room, of doubting Thomas, of the fishermen who filled their nets and breakfasted with Jesus on the beach, of the crowd who watched the ascension, of Paul personally on the Damascus Road, and of Paul in his later statement[13] that the risen Christ "was seen by over five hundred brethren at once, of whom the greater part remain to the present, but some have fallen asleep [died]."

I'll leave the reader to ponder these things further, perhaps with the help of recent research by Gary Habermas.[14] But we must now move on—from the evidences to the implications of the resurrection of Christ.

The first implication: justification

Why does the physical resurrection of Christ lie at the heart of historical Christianity and the biblical worldview? There is a simple answer,
as Paul points out to the Corinthians:

> "If Christ is not risen, your faith is futile; you are still in your sins!
> Then also those who have fallen asleep [died] in Christ have
> perished. If in this life only we have hope in Christ, we are of
> all men the most pitiable."[15]

That's clear enough: no resurrection means no forgiveness of sins, no
life beyond the grave, and, in short, no gospel. The New Testament
teaches that resurrection was the divine declaration that Christ's atoning sacrifice had achieved its purpose—that his death in the place of
sinners had been accepted by God the Father as a sufficient payment
for their debt of sin. As Jesus said of himself: "The Son of Man did not
come to be served, but to serve, and to give his life a ransom for many."[16]

This opens up the whole biblical concept of "justification"—of
how God can justify sinners (declare them righteous) while at the
same time satisfying his just demand that sin cannot go unpunished.
As Paul again states:

> "We are ambassadors for Christ, as though God were pleading
> through us; we implore you on Christ's behalf, be reconciled
> to God. For [on the cross] God made him who knew no sin, to
> be sin for us, that we might become the righteousness of God
> in him."[17]

This verse teaches that Christ died willingly to bear the punishment
due to those sinners who would come to believe in him—while at the

same time bestowing on them the innocence that was his own. There was not only a sacrifice; there was an exchange. Christ takes their sin upon himself while imputing his righteousness to them.

Imagine that you have run up a financial debt so large that a lifetime of work will never repay it. In your desperation, you cry out for help, and someone is listening. Suddenly there appears in your bank account an in-payment sufficient to erase all your debts, both now and in the future. For you it means freedom; for the donor there is a huge cost. But the verse just quoted goes further than that, and can be better illustrated from Charles Dickens' novel *A Tale of Two Cities*. In the aftermath of the French Revolution, the hero Charles Darnay, a French aristocrat, is in prison awaiting execution. A waster, Sydney Carton, who bore a remarkable similarity to Darnay, determines to save him for the sake of Darnay's wife. Carton gains entry to Darnay's cell, exchanges clothes with him, and has him carried out, drugged, to safety. Carton himself remains in Darnay's place and suffers death by guillotine. Pronouncing his own epitaph, Carton declares, "It is a far, far better thing that I do, than I have ever done; it is a far, far better rest that I go to than I have ever known."[18]

In this story, the substitute pays not with money but with his life. The condemned prisoner goes free through the grace (free giving) of another, but this is only possible because of their close resemblance. So Jesus took upon himself our full humanity so that he might die in our place: "Christ also suffered once for sins, the just for the unjust, that he might bring us to God."[19] Of course, the illustration falls far short of the reality. Carton was a good-for-nothing until his final days, while Darnay was an innocent man. The roles are reversed in Christ's redeeming work. It is the innocent Son of God who dies, while "good-for-nothing" sinners like ourselves are set at liberty.

We saw earlier that the same principle of "penal substitution" was spelled out prophetically and precisely in Isaiah 53. The letter to the Hebrews explains in detail why the Old Testament sacrificial system, operated under the Law of Moses, could neither remove the guilt of sin nor cleanse the conscience. But it also shows how the Mosaic covenant was always intended to prefigure the high-priestly atoning work of Jesus Christ.

The "old covenant" thus prepared the way for a new covenant under which an *effective* means of reconciling sinners to a holy God would be provided. This new covenant was, in fact, anticipated prophetically by Jeremiah in the sixth century BC.[20] But without the resurrection, all this preparation would have been in vain, for there would be no proof that Christ's self-offering had been accepted. The resurrection provides the missing link, so that Romans 4:25 can declare that "Christ was delivered up because of our offences and *was raised because of our justification*" (emphasis added). Justification is a declaration of innocence, announcing that Christ's righteousness is bestowed freely on those who trust in him for forgiveness. The first implication of the resurrection is, therefore, that those who believe in Christ have their sins forgiven and may be assured of this fact; as Romans 10:9–10 puts it, "If you confess with your mouth the Lord Jesus and *believe in your heart that God has raised him from the dead*, you will be saved. For with the heart one believes unto righteousness, and with the mouth confession is made to salvation" (emphasis added).

The second implication; Christ is alive

The second implication of the resurrection is that Christ is alive today and actively involved in the building of his church and the blessing of his people. His great commission to the church was: "Go therefore and make disciples of all the nations, baptizing them in the name of the Father and of the Son and of the Holy Spirit, teaching them to observe all things that I have commanded you; and lo, *I am with you always, [even] to the end of the age.*"[21] (emphasis added). Indeed, the New Testament teaches that, by the Holy Spirit, Christ actually lives in those who believe. Paul writes to the Galatians, "I have been crucified with Christ; it is no longer I who live, but Christ lives in me; and the [life] which I now live in the flesh I live by faith in the Son of God, who loved me and gave Himself for me."[22] Those who believe in Christ are conscious that he is present with them and has promised "I will never leave you nor forsake you."[23]

Jesus himself is, of course, no longer present bodily on Earth. He has ascended to that nonmaterial realm called "heaven" from which he came. But before he left he made a promise to his disciples:

> "I will pray the Father, and he will give you another Helper, that
> he may abide with you forever, the Spirit of truth, whom the
> world cannot receive, because it neither sees him nor knows
> him; but you know him, for he dwells with you and will be in
> you. I will not leave you orphans; I will come to you."[24]

According to the New Testament, then, Christ "comes to" all who believe in him. He does so in the Person of the Holy Spirit, who works in and through believers, individually and collectively—to carry forward the work of the gospel, to build Christ's kingdom on Earth and to glorify God by bringing sinners to faith in Christ.

This is not the place to develop the Bible's teaching about the "Trinity" of Father, Son, and Holy Spirit—one God in three Persons, but let me add just this note. Many find the doctrine of the Trinity difficult to grasp. That's understandable, but it should really be no surprise that our limited human minds fail to comprehend the nature of the transcendent God. If we could fully comprehend what God is like, he wouldn't be the God of the Bible, "who alone has immortality, dwelling in unapproachable light, whom no man has seen or can see."[25] Unless we accept this teaching, the New Testament as a whole isn't going to make much sense to us.

THE THIRD IMPLICATION: CHRIST WILL RETURN AND JUDGE THE WORLD

The third implication really needs another book to describe it, but I will content myself with stating it simply here. According to the New Testament, the resurrection of Christ guarantees that he will one day return to Earth to judge the living and the dead. Addressing the Athenian philosophers, Paul declares:

"Truly, these times of ignorance God overlooked, but now
commands all men everywhere to repent, because he
has appointed a day on which he will judge the world in
righteousness by the man whom he has ordained. He has
given assurance of this to all by raising Him from the dead."[26]

Not surprisingly, Paul's statement received a mixed response, for:

"When they heard of the resurrection of the dead, some mocked,
while others said, "We will hear you again on this [matter]....
However, some men joined him and believed...."[27]

Not much has changed in 2000 years in the way different people respond to the Christian message: some mock, others sit on the fence, but some believe and put their trust in Christ. What, I wonder, is your own response?

As we contemplate the future of the human race, different people come to radically different conclusions. For some, our race is doomed; we shall either destroy ourselves by one of several means available to us or simply slide gently into extinction like so many species before us. Others take an opposite view and hope that science will not only rescue us from ourselves and from natural disaster, but will also transform us into a race of supermen and superwomen. Either way, they believe with William Henley[28] that:

"It matters not how strait the gate,
How charged with punishments the scroll,
I am the master of my fate:
I am the captain of my soul."

However, the Bible points us in an entirely different direction. Once we are willing to look outside the "two-dimensional" material world of space and time, entirely new possibilities emerge. And these provide answers, not only to our basic question "What is Man?" but to many issues raised by the moral and spiritual dimensions of the human soul. One such issue is, of course, whether or not good will ultimately triumph over evil and justice over injustice. The Bible's answer is positive: there will indeed be a final reckoning, and one in which each of us will be involved. Paul warns the Corinthians:

"For we must all appear before the judgment seat of Christ, that
each one may receive the things done in the body, according
to what he has done, whether good or bad."[29]

Jesus adds ominously: "But I say to you that for every idle word men may speak, they will give account of it in the day of judgment."[30] Such thoughts took even Paul outside his comfort zone, and they will certainly do the same for us. We can, of course, brush them aside as mere superstition, but while we often use words idly, God is not known for doing so. The motto "Be prepared" is never more relevant than when considering the Bible's assertion that "it is appointed for men to die once, but after this the judgment."[31] Introducing the well-known parable of the sheep and the goats, Jesus makes it clear that it's not a matter of "if" he comes in judgment, but "when":

> "When the Son of Man comes in His glory, and all the holy angels with him, then he will sit on the throne of his glory. All the nations will be gathered before him, and he will separate them one from another, as a shepherd divides [his] sheep from the goats. And He will set the sheep on his right hand, but the goats on the left."[32]

No one should be surprised if those who had no time for God in this life find that God has no time for them in the next.

THE FOURTH IMPLICATION: MAN'S DESTINY FULFILLED

The fourth and final implication of Christ's resurrection is that, when he returns, those who believe in him will be changed to be like him. John writes:

> "Behold what manner of love the Father has bestowed on us, that we should be called children of God!... Beloved, now we are children of God; and it has not yet been revealed what we

shall be, but we know that when [Christ] is revealed, we shall be like him, for we shall see him as he is."[33]

In that day, those whom he has called according to his purpose[34] and have put their trust in him will be refashioned into the image of Christ, the perfect man—and will at last fulfill the prophecy of Psalm 8. Being "delivered from the bondage of corruption into the glorious liberty of the children of God,"[35] they will be "crowned with glory and honor" and will be forever with the Lord.[36] They will inhabit "new heavens and a new Earth in which righteousness dwells,"[37] as described in John's great vision of this future world:

> "And he showed me a pure river of water of life, clear as crystal, proceeding from the throne of God and of the Lamb. In the middle of its street, and on either side of the river, was the tree of life, which bore twelve fruits, each tree yielding its fruit every month. The leaves of the tree were for the healing of the nations. And there shall be no more curse, but the throne of God and of the Lamb shall be in it, and his servants shall serve him. They shall see his face, and his name shall be on their foreheads. There shall be no night there: they need no lamp nor light of the sun, for the Lord God gives them light. And they shall reign forever and ever."[38]

Believe it or not, this is the future to which the gospel of Jesus Christ points us, and where human destiny will be realized and fulfilled. It will be the final answer to the question, "What is Man?"

ENDNOTES:

[1] Arnold, Thomas; *Sermons on the Christian Life: Its Hopes, Its Fears, and Its* Close (6th ed., London, 1859) 324.

2   Romans 1:2–4.

3   Acts 2:23–24.

4   Psalm 16:8–11.

5   Acts 2:41–42.

6   Acts 2:41–47.

7   See for example, Wright, N. T.; *The resurrection of the Son of God* (Augsburg Fortress, Minneapolis, 2003)

8   See for example, Morrison, Frank; *Who moved the stone?* (Authentic Media, Milton Keynes, UK, 2006 edition).

9   Blanchard, John; *Jesus: dead or alive?* (EP Books, Darlington, 2009).

10 Mark 14:27, 50–52.

11 John 20:19.

12 Luke 24:11, 24–25.

13 1 Corinthians 15:6.

14 Habermas, Gary; *Resurrection Research from 1975 to the Present: What Are Critical Scholars Saying?"* *Philosophia Christi* http://www.garyhabermas.com/articles/J_Study_Historical_Jesus_3-2_2005/J_Study_Historical_Jesus_3-2_2005.htm.
      See also *The Case for the Resurrection of Jesus* (Kregal, 2004), 60.

15 1 Corinthians 15:17–19.

16 Mark 10:45.

17 2 Corinthians 5:20–21.

18 Dickens, Charles; *A Tale of Two Cities* (1859).

19 ! Peter 3:18.

20 Jeremiah 31:31.

21 Matthew 28:20.

22 Galatians 2:20.

23 Hebrews 13:5. The writer to the Hebrews applies to Christians a promise first made to Joshua in the Old Testament.

24 John 14:16–19.

25 1 Timothy 6:16.

26 Acts 17:30–31.

27 Acts 17:32–34.

28   Henley, William Ernest; *A book of verses* (D. Nutt, London; 1888)
     pp. 56–57.
29   2 Corinthians 5:10.
30   Matthew 12:36.
31   Hebrews 9:27.
32   Matthew 25:31–33.
33   1 John 3:1–2.
34   Romans 8:28–30.
35   Romans 8:21.
36   1 Thessalonians 4:17.
37   2 Peter 3:13.
38   Revelation 22:1–5.

INDEX

A

Abraham viii, x, 235
A Brief History of Time 35, 66, 87, 96,
 109, 224
abstractions 12, 115
Adam viii, 1, 15, 177, 223, 226, 227,
 228, 230-247, 250, 251, 252, 254, 258,
 274, 275, 276, 278
adaptation 147
adapted 122, 162
adoption 246, 258
advocates 299
afterlife 117
age v, 96, 97, 120, 158, 162, 163, 164,
 171, 172, 175, 197, 218, 219, 229, 246,
 261, 304
agnosticism 96
Alexander the Great 91
alien 1, 4, 26, 38, 44-47, 50, 51, 52, 57,
 60, 186
aliens 48, 52, 53, 58, 59, 60
alleles 229, 230, 231
alter egos 108
alternative splicing 132, 136, 145, 146,
 149, 150
amino acids 140
ammonium 56
Analogy 183, 184, 187, 192, 193, 194,
 201, 208

ancestor 112, 121-129, 132, 134, 135,
 137, 140, 149, 151, 156, 162, 165, 167,
 174, 175, 176
ancestry 3, 127, 152, 156, 175
angels 4, 241, 252, 275, 276, 307
Anglo-Saxon 117
animal xii, 9, 10, 12, 14, 15, 110, 114,
 117, 119, 124, 159, 160, 187, 192, 250,
 252, 263
animals 6, 12, 15, 56, 112-116, 129, 153,
 159, 162, 183, 193, 195, 251, 253, 256,
 259, 260, 263, 265, 267
anthropic principle 60, 65
anthropomorphize 116
antirealism 210
ape xii, 1, 123, 124, 127, 129, 151, 152,
 158, 163, 166, 167, 168, 192, 193, 263
apes 5, 6, 10, 15, 112, 120, 123, 140,
 141, 151, 156, 158,-161, 168, 174, 175,
 226, 252, 263, 273
Aping Mankind 11, 128, 192
apocalyptic 232, 285
apple 227
Aramaic 286
archaeology 177, 215, 225
architect 33, 34, 35, 192, 193
Ardipithecus 167, 177, 178

Aristotle 181, 183, 193, 194, 217, 218, 227
arrangement of particles 100
arrow of time 102
art 146, 217, 267
artifacts 12, 115, 117, 118, 160, 174
artificial selection 9
ascension 215, 300
astronomy 22
A Tale of Two Cities 302, 309
atheism 14, 96, 206
Atheists 40, 62, 224

atmosphere 42, 56, 170, 173
atoms 77, 79, 80, 99, 134, 170, 172, 181, 205
attributes 17, 30, 53, 67, 122, 245, 250, 253, 255, 258, 270
A Universe from Nothing 22, 29, 33, 35
Australopithecus 163, 166, 168, 177
awareness vi, 4, 6, 184, 186, 197, 198, 240
axioms 207, 208, 214

B
Babylonian Talmud 276
bacteria 9, 43, 44, 163
baker's yeast 121, 136
Barnes, Luke 62, 67, 68, 69, 72, 73, 88, 93, 109
base 134, 135
basement 94, 182, 185, 194
base pair 134, 135
bat 191, 192
Beatles 268
Beauregard, Mario 199, 203
beekeeping 132, 139, 140, 141
beginning 13, 20, 27, 28, 29, 36, 100, 103, 117, 139, 215, 218, 219, 236, 296
behavior 12, 31, 65, 116, 119, 143, 186, 187, 188, 189, 268, 269, 294
behaviorism 188, 202
being viii, 5, 12, 16, 17, 34, 35, 46, 64, 68, 77, 78, 84, 92, 93, 96, 105, 109, 119, 125, 139, 143, 163, 165, 169, 170, 180, 182, 193, 194, 195, 198, 199, 200, 212, 213, 216, 217, 218, 221, 222, 225, 228, 231, 232, 236, 237, 240, 242, 253-258, 268, 274, 281, 282, 285, 290, 296, 297
belief 1, 38, 51, 90, 96, 116, 118, 141, 152, 156, 175, 180, 186, 188, 190, 191, 197, 200, 205, 207, 208, 211, 214, 216, 219, 234, 291, 295, 299
belief system 207

Beowulf 118
Berkeley, George 123, 210, 211, 212, 216, 224
Bethlehem 284
Bible iv, vi, xii, 2, 3, 10, 20, 22, 30, 204, 212-216, 218, 221, 226, 227, 228, 232, 233, 234, 235, 237, 240, 246, 250, 252, 253, 256, 257, 265, 266, 268, 274, 276, 277, 297, 305, 306
biblical worldview v, vi, 204, 207, 212, 213-217, 221, 222, 223, 227, 233, 234, 236, 237, 239, 241, 246, 256, 277, 286, 301
Big Bang 27, 30, 31, 72, 80, 82, 83, 84, 220
biological function 137
biologists 11, 126, 132
biology ix, 4, 11, 26, 113, 119, 120, 143
biosphere xii, 7, 50, 54, 57, 122, 251
bipedal 120, 125, 162, 167
birth 101, 103, 116, 125, 245, 258, 261, 277, 278, 283, 284, 288
Blanchard, John 297, 309
blind 199, 207, 243, 281
Blomberg, Craig 280, 291
blood 84, 183, 195, 245, 252
body 2, 84, 100, 116, 119, 133, 159, 182, 183, 184, 186, 190, 193, 194, 195, 246, 256, 299, 306
bondage 243, 244, 245, 308

bondage of corruption 245, 308
bone 120, 157, 159, 163, 168, 171
born again 25, 257
bower bird 265
brain 8, 12-15, 18, 106, 127, 162, 163, 180,-183, 185, 186-201, 261, 262
brain states 12, 180, 189
brainwave 197
breath 16, 103, 217, 221, 228, 240, 255, 265, 266

British Museum 118
Brown, Warren 186, 202
brow ridge 120
brute fact 24, 64, 67, 74
Buggs 138, 152, 231, 247
bugs 39, 41, 44, 49, 58, 77
burial chamber 118
butterfly 142
Byzantium 118

C
cancer 121, 148, 153
carbon 42, 54, 56, 66, 79, 170, 171, 178
Carbon 14 163, 170
Carbon dating 170
Carter, Brandon 53, 60
cat 26, 33, 90, 94, 105, 106
caterpillar 142
Cenozoic 171
Chalmers, David 191
chance 9, 17, 39, 51, 53, 54, 58, 62, 67, 70, 76, 82, 161, 171, 270
chaos 219, 220
chemical evolution 10
chemistry 44, 100
Cheshire cat 33
chimpanzee 112, 119, 123, 127, 137, 138, 152, 163, 174, 263
chimpanzee genome 138
chimpanzees 4, 10, 119, 120, 121, 123, 125, 127, 128, 129, 132, 136, 140, 141, 144, 149, 152, 153, 175, 176, 258, 262
Chomsky, Noam 261, 262, 263, 273
Christ iv, vi, vii, 208, 214, 215, 223, 226, 228, 233, 235, 236, 237, 240, 242, 243, 245, 246, 253, 254, 258, 271, 274, 275-290, 294-308
chromosomes 129, 135, 152, 153
church 214, 274, 276, 294, 296, 297, 303
Churchland, Patricia 187, 188, 189, 202
circumstantial evidence 298
city 59, 85, 282, 285, 286, 287
civilizations 47, 50, 52, 57, 114, 117, 218

Civil law 270
claims of Christ 279, 280, 294
clay warriors 117
cleansing 289
Clevenger 133, 152
climate 54, 147
codes 140, 260, 279
commandments 238, 244, 269, 278
common ancestor 112, 121-129, 132, 134, 135, 137, 140, 149, 151, 174, 175
common ancestors 112, 122
common descent 5, 7, 10, 14, 15, 17, 122, 136, 137, 139, 142, 144, 149, 156, 247
communication 52, 259, 260
competence 250, 255, 265, 266, 267
computers 13, 34, 91, 107, 188, 192
condemnation 274
conscience 289, 303
conscious action 188, 198
consciousness 4, 6, 12-15, 181, 183-186, 189, 190, 191, 194, 202, 203
conspiracy 280, 290, 300
constants 62, 64, 65, 67, 69, 70, 73-76, 93, 94, 95, 97
control 10, 120, 132, 142, 143, 147, 150, 161, 185, 199, 222, 238, 266, 299
conversion 79, 296
cookbook 70, 71, 75
Copan, Paul iv, 247, 265, 273
corruption 240, 245, 246, 296, 308
cosmic architect 34

cosmic bubbles 98
cosmic egg 219, 220
cosmic horizon 97, 98, 99
cosmic ocean 218, 219
cosmic origins 20, 22
cosmic radiation 57
cosmological constant 26, 81, 82
cosmologists 20, 22, 27, 28, 30, 62, 69,
   72, 82, 84, 90, 209, 218
cosmology ix, 30, 31, 34, 72, 82, 83, 93,
   101, 102
cosmos xii, 1, 20, 21, 24-27, 29, 32, 35,
   44, 51, 54, 58, 62, 65, 66, 71, 72, 73,
   75, 76, 79, 80, 83, 87, 90, 95, 96, 97, 99,
   100, 101, 215, 217, 218, 222, 243, 252,
   258, 259, 268
cranial volume 162, 166
created order 32, 49, 53, 223, 245
creatio ex nihilo 30, 35, 265
creation xii, 7, 10, 14-18, 20, 21, 23, 30,
   31, 35, 50, 51, 53, 58, 67, 70, 72, 96, 97,
146, 218-222, 225, 226, 227, 230, 232,
   233, 238, 245, 255, 258, 259, 263, 265,
   266, 275
creationism 10
creationists 17
creation stories 218, 219, 220, 233
creativity 250, 255, 265, 266
Creator 3, 17, 20, 62, 64, 65, 67, 88, 217,
   220, 226, 238, 239, 240, 252, 253, 258
credulity 291
Crick, Francis 186, 202
cross 84, 117, 289, 301
crucifixion 215, 233, 276, 278, 286,
   291, 294, 296
cultural mandate 49
cultural norms 118
culture 12, 158, 218
cultures 218, 220, 267
curiosity viii, 4, 26, 48, 49
curse 279, 308
customs 12, 115

D
Daniel 225, 232, 285, 286, 292
dark energy 82, 104
Darwin, Charles 5, 7, 154, 261
Darwin's finches 147
database 70, 71
dating 162, 163, 164, 170-173, 178
David 4, 5, 14, 16, 17, 54, 59, 92, 107,
   108, 109, 110, 191, 213, 287, 288, 295,
   296
Davies, Paul 51, 52, 53, 58, 60, 66, 87
Dawkins, Richard 23, 132, 204
day of judgment 307
death 77, 112-115, 117, 118, 128, 170,
   188, 199, 215, 235, 240, 241, 242, 244,
   246, 256, 276, 277, 282-286, 289, 290,
   291, 296, 301, 302
debt ix, 248, 301, 302
decoherence 106
deism 52
Deists 221
deity 277, 279, 289, 296
density 27, 41, 55, 80, 82, 83
Descartes, René 190, 195, 196
design 8, 76, 85, 154, 188, 189, 265, 266
designer 85, 187
desires 69, 184, 191, 213, 238, 259
destiny v, viii, 58, 192, 307, 308
determinism 6, 100
deuterium 43
Deutsch, David 92, 107, 108, 109, 110
Dickens, Charles 302, 309
diet 124, 144, 148
dinosaurs 91, 107
disciples 256, 270, 274, 276, 279, 280,
   283, 288, 299, 300, 304
disease 9, 148, 153
diseases 120, 148, 149, 281, 282
divine creation 20, 51, 58, 67, 72
divine nature viii, 53
divinity 279, 283

DNA 7, 9, 10, 55, 71, 100, 121, 128, 129, 134-140, 142-147, 152, 153, 154, 160, 177, 186, 230
Dobzhansky, Theodosius 112, 113, 114, 119, 128
doctrines 278
dolphin 116

dominion viii, 16, 49, 251, 253, 275
double helix 134, 135, 186
Drake 45, 51, 58, 59
dualism 180, 191-198, 201
Dubois, Eugene 168
Dyson, Freeman 66, 69, 87

E
Earth viii, 1, 4, 7, 16, 20, 22, 24, 25, 32, 38-44, 48-51, 53-60, 69, 79, 81, 98, 101, 114, 122, 157, 216-222, 229, 236, 246, 250, 251, 253, 254, 266, 274, 280, 283, 294, 304, 305, 308
Eden 226, 237, 241, 245
Edgar, Blake 165, 177
egg 28, 31, 33, 112, 113, 165, 219, 220, 261, 264
Egnor, Michael 193, 194, 203
Einstein, Albert 20, 81, 95
electron 66, 88, 105
emanation 185, 189
emotions 116, 184, 191, 196
empiricism 210
empty tomb 299
ENCODE 137, 139, 142
encoded 201, 202
enemies 269, 278, 283
energy 8, 29, 30, 42, 48, 54, 65, 66, 72, 74, 82, 83, 88, 99, 103, 104, 122, 142, 192, 265
entropy 102
environment 47, 50, 56, 63, 119, 147, 189, 246, 299
environments 122, 128, 147
epigenetic 129, 142-148, 150, 151, 153, 201, 231
epigenetic control 143, 147, 150
epigenetic processes 142-145, 147
epigenetics 136, 142, 151
epiphenomenon 189
eternal 20, 25, 28, 31, 33, 53, 90, 94, 101, 102, 104, 105, 206, 217, 219, 220, 221, 240, 241, 282, 288

eternal inflation 90, 94, 101, 102, 104, 105
eternal life 206, 240, 241, 282
eternity 30
ethical teaching 278
Ethiopia 156, 161, 162, 163
ethos 95, 96
European Space Agency 38, 42
Eve viii, 226, 227, 228, 230-234, 236-243, 246, 247, 250, 251, 252, 254, 258, 259, 274
Everett, Hugh 105, 106
evidence xii, 11, 17, 18, 27, 43, 44, 52, 57, 66, 68, 72, 90, 136, 137, 165, 166, 198, 208, 215, 218, 231, 232, 237, 260, 265, 274, 276, 278, 285, 291, 294, 295, 297, 298
evil 114, 222, 235, 238, 239, 240, 241, 266, 279, 306
evolution 5, 6, 7, 9-12, 14, 16, 17, 38, 46, 60, 69, 113, 120, 122, 123, 124, 126, 127, 129, 133, 142, 148, 151, 163, 166, 174, 177, 180, 186, 187, 188, 192, 231, 232, 237, 261, 264, 267, 273
evolutionary paradigm 134, 137
Evolution from space 16, 19
evolutionists 17, 139, 143, 147, 151, 228, 230
existence vi, 5, 14, 22, 23, 24, 26, 27, 30-33, 35, 48, 49, 50, 52, 55, 56, 58, 62, 64, 65, 67-71, 74, 87, 95, 98, 101, 134, 139, 140, 184, 185, 186, 189, 191, 201, 208, 210-213, 217, 219, 221, 223, 224, 225, 232, 255, 268, 276

ex nihilo 22, 30, 35, 218, 220, 233, 265
ExoMars program 42, 46
exoplanets 40, 48, 50, 53
expanding universe 75, 101, 103
expansion 18, 25, 46, 81, 83, 84, 98,
   103, 129
experiences 161, 191, 199, 200, 210, 212
experimental science 160
explanation 3, 12, 23, 24, 25, 31, 32, 34,
   55, 62, 64, 67-70, 75, 87, 107, 108, 112,
   123, 180, 194, 197, 209, 212, 220, 226,
   233, 266, 290
expression 12, 143, 259
expression of genes 143
extraterrestrial 7, 38, 39, 42, 46, 48, 49,
   50, 52, 55, 57, 60
extraterrestrial organisms 38
eyewitness accounts 300
eyewitnesses 277, 294, 300
Ezra 285, 286, 292

F

faith iv, v, 58, 96, 100, 164, 204, 215,
   216, 258, 280, 294, 296, 301, 304
faith in Christ 294, 296, 304
fall xii, 2, 57, 164, 167, 168, 191, 226,
   227, 234, 236, 237, 239, 241, 243, 245,
   252, 262, 267
families 147, 268
family tree 156, 158, 162, 164, 174, 175,
   235
Faraday, Michael 204
FAST (radio telescope) 47
Father 245, 258, 266, 279, 281, 283,
   287, 289, 301, 304, 307
feelings 100, 191
field 29, 32, 57, 102-105, 160, 185, 190,
   200, 204, 245, 262, 267
final judgment 202, 294
fine-tuned 62-65, 69, 71, 72, 73, 75, 79,
   84, 87
fine-tuning 50, 62, 65, 66, 67, 68, 69,
   70-74, 77, 80, 81, 82, 86, 87, 90, 93,
   109

fixation 126, 147
fixed 74, 80, 124, 126, 127, 144, 148,
   149, 230, 264
flint 164
food chains 56
foreknowledge 296
forgiveness 245, 294, 301, 303
form 1, 10, 11, 14, 30, 33, 69, 77, 78, 80,
   83, 112, 114, 115, 118, 122, 134, 135,
   150, 170, 172, 188, 190, 193, 194, 195,
   204, 213, 219, 253, 283, 287
fossil 15, 122, 156-163, 165-172,
   174-177
fossil record 122, 169, 175, 176
Franklin, Benjamin 112, 113
freedom 203, 270, 288, 302
free will 100, 191, 238, 244, 252
From Nothing to Nature 122, 129, 177
fruit flies 121, 122
fulfilled 214, 215, 236, 276, 282, 283,
   285, 287, 289, 290, 294, 307, 308
functional MRI 198

G

Galactic Diaspora 52
galaxies 38, 40, 77, 80, 83, 84, 98
galaxy v, 42, 98, 109
Garden of Eden 226, 245
Gauger, Ann 178, 231, 247
Gee, Henry 166, 174, 177, 178
Geiger counter 105, 106

gene 124, 125, 132, 136, 137, 140, 141,
   145, 146, 147, 151, 154, 229, 230, 231
genealogies 136, 140, 141, 234, 235
genealogy 141, 235, 254
generations 124, 125, 148, 149, 150,
   229, 235
genes 121, 125-129, 132, 133, 135, 136,

138, 139, 142, 143, 144, 146-149, 152, 153, 159, 191, 195, 230
genetic code 53
genetic engineering 9, 154
genetic information 144, 145
genetic variability 228
gene transfer 151, 154
genome 121, 126, 129, 135, 137, 138, 139-142, 144, 146, 152, 153, 154, 230, 231
genre 232, 233, 285
genres 212, 232
genus 167, 168
geological timescale 158, 164
ghost 100, 185, 189-192
gift 240, 266, 282
glory viii, xii, 3, 4, 67, 243, 275, 276, 281, 307, 308
goats 9, 307
God v-ix, xii, 1, 3-7, 9, 10, 12, 14, 16-24, 26-30, 34, 35, 36, 38, 49, 52, 53, 55, 58, 59, 65, 67, 70, 71, 72, 87, 88, 93, 96, 100, 102, 109, 110, 114, 159, 177, 180, 195, 199, 201-208, 211-218, 220-224, 226, 227, 228, 233-246, 250-260, 263-272, 274, 275, 277, 278, 279, 281-284, 287-290, 294-297, 301-305, 307, 308, 309
Godhead 281
God of the gaps 93
goldilocks 66, 83, 86
Good Samaritan 271
gorilla 123, 174
gospel iv, vi, 224, 242, 243, 255, 278, 281, 283, 295, 301, 304, 308
gospels 276, 300
Gould, Stephen Jay 165, 177
government 46, 286, 287
grammar 261, 262, 263
grave 257, 290, 299, 301
gravity 21, 29, 32, 33, 41, 74, 77, 80, 81, 83, 204
great apes 120, 123, 140, 141, 158, 159, 252
Greene, Brian 94, 97, 99, 109, 110
greenhouse effect 42
greenhouse gas 55
Gribbin, John 87, 91, 92, 107, 109
guilt 240, 303
guilty 289
Guth, Alan 27, 95

H
Habermas, Gary 300, 309
habitability 38, 54
habitable 41, 51, 53, 54, 56, 65, 72, 83, 86
habitable zone 41, 53, 56
habitat 124
Hades 296
Haldane, John 185
Haldane's dilemma 124
Haley, Alex 3
hallucinations 191
hand 20, 21, 38, 64, 72, 83, 84, 112, 120, 159, 175, 187, 208, 220, 222, 223, 228, 241, 252, 278, 281, 282, 287, 288, 290, 307
hard problem 13, 191, 192, 194, 197
Harold, Franklin 134, 152
Hawking, Stephen 6, 18, 21, 22, 28, 29, 33, 35, 48, 66, 87, 90, 93, 96, 109, 209, 210, 211, 224
healing 240, 290, 308
heart viii, 23, 91, 191, 192, 196, 216, 235, 255, 261, 270, 278, 301, 303
heaven 16, 216, 220, 222, 223, 235, 240, 253, 279, 283, 288, 304
heavens 4, 20, 59, 218, 265, 266, 274, 308
Hebrew 228, 255, 272, 284, 286, 287
heir 278, 281, 288
Heisenberg 100, 204
helium 56, 66, 78, 79
hell 223, 235

heresies 265
Higgs bosons 29, 70
High Priest 281
historical documents 277, 294, 298
historical science 160, 168
historicity 226, 227, 234, 236, 246
historiography 215
history viii, 18, 19, 26, 38, 44, 120, 141, 156, 158, 160, 166, 167, 177, 212, 213, 218, 220, 222, 227, 232, 234, 247, 266, 285, 286, 294, 295, 298
Holocene 171
Holy Spirit 213, 214, 257, 258, 304
hominids 124, 158, 164, 174
Homo erectus 168, 178
Homo ergaster 168
Homo habilis 166
Homo naledi 176
Homo rudolfensis 168
Homo sapiens 15, 114, 167, 175, 228, 263
honor 4, 45, 162, 178, 275, 276, 308
hope 31, 43, 72, 95, 96, 116, 157, 160, 182, 205, 206, 208, 217, 245, 246, 266, 301, 306
Hoyle, Fred 16, 19, 63, 65, 66, 87
Hubble, Edwin 20, 81
human genome 136, 138, 141, 142, 146, 154, 230
humanity vii, ix, 1, 2, 4, 12, 14, 15, 20, 38, 46, 49, 50, 67, 158, 174, 204, 213, 231, 232, 236, 243, 250, 254, 255, 274, 276, 302
human race 1, 2, 48, 223, 226, 227, 228, 230, 231, 233, 234, 306
human uniqueness 119
Humpty Dumpty 165
Huxley, Julian 112, 113, 128
Huxley Memorial Debate 132
hybridization 151, 153
hydrogen 43, 45, 56, 66, 70, 78, 79, 83, 134
hydrogen bonds 134
hydroxyl 45
hylomorphism 193, 194, 203
hypnosis 199

I
ideas v, vii, xii, 11, 20, 29, 52, 161, 176, 186, 190, 207, 216, 217, 219, 220, 253, 262, 263, 266, 278
identity vii, viii, 58, 59, 108, 123, 184, 185, 186, 197, 257
igneous rocks 172
ignorance 2, 217, 233, 239, 243, 270, 305
image vii, xii, 1, 3, 5, 12, 14, 16, 18, 52, 180, 195, 223, 228, 236, 237, 238, 241, 246, 250-255, 257, 258, 260, 263, 264, 266, 267, 268, 271, 281, 308
image of God vii, 1, 3, 5, 16, 18, 180, 195, 223, 228, 236, 237, 238, 250, 251, 252-255, 258, 260, 263, 264, 267, 271
imagination 133, 139, 141, 210
immanence 221, 222, 223
incarnation 253, 254, 277
incongruent genealogies 136
indels 121
index fossils 164, 171
infinite regress 23, 24
infinity 12, 64, 65, 75, 102, 110, 115
inflation 90, 94, 101, 102, 104, 105
Inflationary Theory 101
inflaton 102-105
information 17, 51, 88, 100, 133, 134, 135, 144, 145, 160, 161, 200, 201, 202, 214, 232, 259, 260
iniquity 285, 286, 290
innocent 71, 115, 237, 289, 298, 302
inspiration 213, 214
instincts 265
institutions 12, 38, 115
intelligence 7, 13, 20, 38, 58, 60, 183, 255
intelligent life 1, 42, 47, 48, 53, 62, 65, 68, 69

intentionality 196
intentions 259
intercession 290
intermediate forms 122
Interpretations 124
invention 41, 233, 265

ions 55
Isaiah 30, 215, 273, 281, 284, 287, 288,
  289, 303
isochron 173
isotope 42, 172
Israel 159, 276, 284, 285, 288

J
Java Man 168
jaws 14, 165
Jeeves, Malcolm 186, 202
Jesus iv, vi, vii, 208, 214, 215, 223, 226,
  233, 235, 236, 237, 242, 243, 244, 246,
  254, 256, 257, 258, 270, 271, 272, 274-
  291, 294-297, 299-304, 307, 308, 309
Jesus: Dead or Alive? 297, 309
Johanson, Donald 165, 169, 177

Josephus 276
Judah 284
judge 3, 217, 245, 267, 305
judgment 202, 223, 235, 287, 288, 290,
  294, 306, 307
junk DNA 136, 137, 138, 139, 142
Jupiter 41, 56, 57
justification 38, 51, 100, 294, 301, 303
Just Six Numbers 62, 64, 73, 87, 94

K
Kalam 28, 36
Kant, Immanuel 206
kingdom 245, 257, 283, 287, 288, 304

knowledge iv, vi, 6, 27, 58, 132, 191,
  198, 208, 212, 216, 238, 239, 240, 245,
  257, 290
knuckle-walking 123
Krauss, Lawrence 22, 28, 29, 30, 33, 35

L
Lamb 308
landscape 94, 104, 182, 183
language 50, 128, 135, 140, 189, 213,
  233, 250, 254, 255, 258-264, 272, 273
languages 213, 264
last common ancestor 112, 123-127,
  129, 175
law 21, 29, 32, 33, 74, 238, 250, 255,
  267-271, 286, 299
laws 6, 12, 20, 27, 28, 30-35, 50, 51, 53,
  62, 64-67, 69, 70, 71, 73, 75, 91, 93, 94,
  95, 97, 107, 109, 115, 204, 207, 208,
  243, 265-270

laws of nature 6, 20, 27, 28, 30-35, 50,
  51, 53, 62, 64, 67, 69, 71, 73, 93, 94, 95,
  97, 208, 265, 268
laws of science 66
LCA 112, 125, 127
Leakey, Louis 166
Leakey, Richard 166
learning 188, 261
Lewis, C. S. 14, 15, 19, 33, 67, 186, 274,
  278, 291
Lewontin, Richard 165, 177
liberty 245, 269, 281, 302, 308
Libet, Benjamin 197, 198
life vi, vii, 1, 5, 7, 10, 12, 14, 16, 17, 19,
  21, 26, 38-59, 62-66, 68-71, 73, 74,

75, 77, 79, 80, 83, 84, 86, 87, 91, 94, 96, 100, 103, 112, 117, 118, 120, 122, 128, 134, 136, 142, 143, 145, 153, 154, 159, 165, 183, 184, 201, 202, 205-208, 212, 217, 219, 221, 226, 228, 239, 240, 241, 243, 245, 246, 255, 256, 266, 282, 283, 284, 290, 294, 296, 301, 302, 304, 307, 308
life-friendly 71, 80
light v, ix, 11, 21, 39, 41, 42, 43, 45, 56, 74, 80, 88, 92, 98, 101, 103, 109, 144, 157, 161, 194, 204, 233, 243, 258, 270, 305, 308
Lightman, Alan 95, 96, 109

light years 39, 98
likeness xii, 16, 251, 252, 253, 266
lizard 171
lizards 147
logic 33, 34, 49, 94, 208, 224, 250, 255, 258, 263, 264, 294
longevity 120
love 124, 206, 221, 237, 245, 250, 255, 266-271, 278, 307
Lubenow, Marvin 169, 170, 178
Lucky Planet 54, 60, 65
Lucy 169, 177
Luskin, Casey 167, 177, 178
lust 279

M
machinery 182, 183, 185, 189, 194, 195
macroevolution 9, 17, 126, 144, 149, 230
magma 103, 104, 173
magnetic field 32, 57
mammals 116, 159
Man iv-x, xii, 1-7, 10, 11, 12, 14-18, 20, 21, 22, 38, 39, 40, 49, 52, 57, 58, 59, 63, 97, 107, 108, 109, 112, 114, 118, 119, 120, 121, 123, 124, 125, 127, 128, 141, 144, 151, 152, 157-160, 162, 166, 167, 168, 174, 175, 177, 178, 180, 183, 184, 192-195, 204, 205, 215, 226, 227, 230, 236, 237, 239, 241, 242, 244, 245, 246, 247, 250-256, 258, 259, 260, 263, 264, 266, 268, 271, 275, 280, 289, 301, 306, 307, 308
mankind v, viii, xii, 2, 3, 5, 6, 8, 12, 14, 18, 19, 49, 52, 58, 114, 158, 159, 211, 213, 218, 221, 227, 232, 237, 253, 258, 278, 294, 295
Many Worlds 36, 92, 94, 105
marriage 236
Mars 42, 43, 44, 49, 50, 56, 57, 59
marsupials 159
mass media 11, 40, 42, 127
master-chef 71
materialism 96, 185, 194, 206

matrix 5, 18
matter 6, 13, 14, 24, 29, 30, 39, 49, 51, 63, 65, 72, 80, 81, 84, 92, 99, 104, 105, 114, 123, 124, 137, 139, 140, 146, 161, 181, 186, 190, 191, 193, 194, 196, 197, 198, 210, 217, 265, 267, 305, 307
mausoleum 117
Maxwell, Clerk 204
Mayr, Ernst 168, 178
McGrew, Lydia 231, 247
meditation 199, 269
memory 8, 9, 18, 200
mental processes 101, 181
mercy 242, 255
messenger RNA 135, 145
Messiah 214, 283, 286, 288, 296, 299
messianic 288, 289
metaphor 190, 234, 242, 243, 259
metaphysical 52, 187, 210
meteorites 43, 44
methane 42, 43, 56, 59
mice 121, 136, 159
microbes 144
microevolution 9
microwave background 83, 101
microwave radiation 20
Milky Way 24

mind iv, 2, 6, 13, 17, 23, 26, 34, 35, 70, 81, 96, 119, 120, 180,-187, 189-202, 210, 211, 212, 216, 223, 225, 234, 256, 258, 259, 264, 268, 270, 278
mind/body interaction 183
mind of God 96, 201, 211, 212, 216, 234, 268
miracles 6, 17, 233
missing links 10, 168
Mlodinow, Leonard 18, 21, 30, 35, 209, 224
models 5, 25, 90, 120, 187, 209, 210
modern synthesis 7
molecular genetics 135
mongoose 188
monism 185
monkeys 159
moral action 254
moral corruption 240
moral dependence 239
moral nature 267
morals 100, 183

Moreland 203, 253, 272
morphology 123, 147, 153, 158
mortality 226, 229, 241, 242, 246
Moses 215, 221, 283, 286, 303
mountain 49, 103
Mount Everest 49
mourning 116
multiverse 25, 62, 65, 67, 68, 71, 87, 90, 91-94, 96, 97, 99, 101, 104, 105, 107, 108
murder 115, 252, 279
mutation 126, 127, 137, 150, 151, 230, 264
mutation rates 126, 127, 137
mutations 7, 8, 17, 125, 126, 128, 143, 144, 147, 148, 149, 151, 230, 264
MV 67, 92-97, 99, 100, 102, 105, 107, 108
myth 156, 184, 219, 220, 228, 232, 237
mythicists 276, 277
myths 218, 219, 220, 225, 226, 233, 276

N
Nagel, Thomas 191
NASA 40, 43, 44, 45, 80
National Geographic Magazine 167
National Science Foundation 44
natural processes 7, 10, 17
natural selection 7, 126, 128, 129, 142, 144, 147, 149, 151, 187, 230, 261
Nature 122, 129, 166, 174, 177, 178, 217, 231
Nazareth 276, 277, 283, 287, 289
Neanderthal 159
Nebraska Man 160
Nebuchadnezzar 222, 285
negative pressure 102
neighbor 98, 269, 271
neo-Darwinism 7, 10, 144
Neptune 43, 56
nerve cells 186
neurobiology 8, 120
neurochemistry 120

neuro-feedback 199
neurons 8, 12, 13, 186, 188, 190, 191, 198
neuroscientists 182, 186
new covenant 303
New Scientist 190, 191
New Testament 213, 214, 233, 237, 242, 244, 256, 258, 275, 277, 279, 280, 286-291, 296, 298, 299, 301, 304, 305
Newton, Isaac 32, 74, 204
Nietzsche, Friedrich 25, 36, 241
nonmaterial 17, 20, 30, 34, 35, 62, 65, 67, 100, 180, 185, 186, 191-201, 256, 265, 304
nothing viii, 4, 8, 11, 15, 20, 21, 22, 29, 30, 31, 33, 41, 45, 49, 50, 57, 64, 71, 72, 78, 84, 85, 95, 97, 98, 100, 101, 107, 109, 112, 123, 160, 162, 173, 174, 176, 186, 190, 197, 211, 216, 218, 220, 238, 265, 268, 280, 285, 302
nucleotides 134

numbers 40, 63-66, 70, 73, 75, 76, 196, 216, 229

nutrients 56

O

observation 25, 31, 45, 54, 66, 69, 106, 139, 209, 212
observer 3, 97, 98, 106, 211
Occam's razor 58
ocean 29, 116, 218, 219
offering iv, v, 107, 180, 226, 290, 303
offspring 116, 125, 146, 153, 217, 254
Old Testament 159, 213, 214, 215, 222, 232, 239, 255, 278, 283, 284, 288, 290, 303, 309
omnipotence 255
omnipresence 255
omniscience 255
opposable thumb 192

orangutan 160, 174
organism 7, 8, 9, 122, 124, 134, 143, 144, 148, 154, 170
organisms 7, 9, 12, 38, 54, 55, 59, 85, 114, 115, 121, 122, 136, 139, 142, 143, 144, 151, 159, 183, 189
organs 159, 190, 202
origin v, viii, xii, 4, 5, 7, 10, 15, 17, 18, 20, 24, 26, 27, 32, 34, 35, 51, 55, 57, 72, 119, 152, 154, 205, 208, 213, 235, 247, 260, 268, 272
Origin of Species 7
oxygen 43, 54, 55, 56, 79, 170
ozone layer 57

P

PA 129, 157, 159-163, 165, 167, 168, 176, 202
pain control 199
palaeontology 156
paleoanthropologist 157
panspermia 16
pantheism 52
paradigm 134, 137, 154
paradigms 161
particles 29, 30, 78, 79, 99, 100, 104, 106
pathology 120
Patria Potestas 268
Paul (apostle) 53, 195, 214-218, 220-223, 228, 235, 236, 237, 240, 242-245, 248, 255, 257, 258, 266, 280, 295, 296, 300, 301, 304-307
peace 266, 287, 288, 290
penal substitution 303
Penzias, Arno 204
peppered moth 147
person vi, ix, 2, 95, 108, 165, 184, 185, 189, 191, 194, 197, 204, 208, 228, 231,

235, 238, 242, 256, 257, 279, 281, 288, 289
personality 191, 254
Peter (apostle) 213, 220, 277, 296, 300, 309, 310
pharmacology 120
phenome 119
phenotype 119
phenotypes 159
pheromones 260
philosophers 26, 180, 195, 208, 210, 216, 217, 240, 305
philosophy 6, 7, 13, 18, 24, 26, 96, 100, 187, 205, 224, 256
photon 105
photons 29
physicalism 185
physics 28-31, 33, 47, 62, 63, 65, 66, 68, 69, 77, 86, 88, 91, 93, 96, 100, 105, 107
pictograms 264
Piltdown Man 160, 177
Pinker, Steven 48, 263
Pithecanthropus erectus 168

placebo 199, 200
plagiarism 140
planetary systems 40, 84
planet formation 38, 46
planets 7, 21, 38, 40, 41, 47, 50, 51, 64, 77, 83, 84, 219
planning 265
plaster casts 169, 170
pleasure centers 199
Pleistocene 164
Pliny 276
Plutarch 91
point mutation 126
Pope xii, 2, 3, 18
pop idols 274
population 7, 8, 124, 126, 148, 150, 226, 228-231, 247, 264
population genetics 228
population model 231
positivism 6
potassium-argon dating 173
power 5, 8, 17, 23, 32, 53, 82, 102, 139, 185, 189, 198, 223, 229, 243, 244, 258, 261, 265, 268, 271, 280, 281, 282, 289, 294, 296

predictions 75, 108, 215, 225, 289
presuppositions 207, 214, 216
progenitors 15, 148, 226, 231, 233, 234
Project Cyclops 45
Project Ozma 45
promise 304, 309
prophecies 214, 283, 284, 285, 287, 289, 290
prophecy 212, 236, 276, 283, 286, 287, 288, 289, 308
protein 55, 125, 132, 135, 138, 145, 146, 147
proteins 121, 122, 129, 132, 135, 140, 143, 146, 148
proton 66, 78, 79
providence 64, 221, 266
Psalms 213
psychologists 186
punishment 238, 301
purpose vi, viii, xii, 3, 22, 46, 70, 93, 137, 142, 147, 161, 206, 215, 222, 229, 234, 235, 239, 259, 267, 294, 297, 301
purposes of God 294

Q
qualia 196, 197
quantum 28, 31, 90, 94, 100, 105, 106, 107, 108, 204, 220

quantum mechanics 100, 105, 106, 204
quantum strangeness 90

R
Rabbi 276
radial velocity 40, 41
radiation 20, 29, 57, 101, 104, 171, 185, 204
radiometric dating 163, 164, 171, 172, 173
radio telescopes 26, 38, 46
Ramapithecus 166
ransom 301
rationality 95, 109
realism 209, 210, 224

reality v, 5, 23, 24, 25, 27, 43, 66, 69, 92, 93, 97, 106, 107, 108, 156, 167, 182, 183, 205, 208-212, 216, 224, 226, 235, 236, 237, 266, 274, 280, 302
realtor 184, 209, 210
reason 2, 21-24, 31, 49, 54, 57, 58, 69, 72, 76, 91, 99, 106, 117, 142, 151, 175, 181, 230, 236, 237, 239, 250, 254, 269, 298
reconstruction 123, 165, 166, 167
redemption 3, 214, 235, 245, 246, 290

reductionism 185
Rees, Martin 62, 63, 64, 65, 71, 72, 73, 75-81, 83, 84, 87, 88, 90, 93, 94
relativity 20, 25, 30, 32, 81
religion 96, 218, 243, 276, 291
repentance 237
repulsion 56, 78
resonance 66
resonant frequency 66
resurrection 117, 202, 215, 233, 235, 236, 246, 256, 282, 284, 286, 294-301, 303, 305, 307, 309

revelation 213, 214, 257
righteousness 214, 217, 244, 245, 274, 285, 286, 301, 302, 303, 305, 308
RNA 135, 138, 142, 143, 145
robots 182, 188, 189
rock strata 158, 164
roots 3, 4, 58, 95, 96, 212, 235
Roots 3
rule of law 270
rules 32, 70, 100, 209, 259, 267, 268
Russell, Bertrand 25, 36, 205, 206, 208, 224

S
Sabbath 281
sacrifice 271, 301, 302
Sagan 44, 45, 47
saints 274
sanctuary 285, 287
Satan 234, 243, 244
Saturn 56
saved 237, 242, 269, 283, 297, 303
savior 246
scans 70, 198, 199
Schrödinger, Erwin 105, 106
science v, vi, ix, 3, 7, 13, 18, 26, 32, 33, 35, 42, 44, 47, 52, 53, 59, 66, 70, 72, 90-97, 100, 107, 108, 109, 153, 154, 159, 160, 168, 169, 177, 186, 204, 208, 209, 211, 231, 247, 260, 267, 268, 306
Scripture 214, 247, 282
secularism 206
seed 31, 102, 103, 290, 295
selective bias 136
selective pressures 147
self 4, 6, 12, 26, 28, 29, 71, 97, 101, 184, 187, 189, 191, 193, 194, 197, 207, 212, 214, 216, 233, 236, 238, 240, 253, 254, 255, 269, 271, 303
self-awareness 6, 184, 197, 240
self-existence 255
sensations 191, 210
sense organs 190
senses 7, 187, 196, 210

Sermon on the Mount 278
serpents 188
SETI 38, 42, 44-51, 58, 59
Seventy weeks (Daniel) 285
sheep 241, 282, 290, 307
ship burial 118
Shiv, Baba 199
Shklovsky, Losif 45
sign 262, 263, 267, 284, 295
sign language 262, 263
sin 3, 196, 223, 227, 235, 237, 238, 239, 243, 244, 248, 252, 253, 271, 274, 275, 280, 281, 282, 285, 286, 289, 290, 301, 302, 303
singularity 27, 28, 30
sinners 235, 237, 240, 243, 271, 294, 301, 302, 303, 304
skeleton 156, 157, 162, 164, 166, 171, 177
Skeptics 44, 216, 220, 224, 228, 290
skull 120, 160, 162, 163, 166, 167, 168, 177
Smolin, Lee 107, 110
snake 188, 226
Snelling, Andrew 173, 178
snowball 183, 193, 227
social structures 253, 267
societies 114, 118, 160
society 12, 96, 114, 267-270
software 5, 14, 188

solar system 22, 38, 40, 52
solvent 55
son 1, 4, 166, 205, 208, 235, 245, 254, 275, 276, 278, 282, 284, 287, 288, 298
Son of Man 236, 280, 289, 301, 307
soul 6, 184, 185, 191, 194, 202, 240, 250, 255, 256, 257, 270, 278, 290, 296, 306
sovereignty 221, 222
space 16, 18, 23, 25, 29, 30, 32, 34, 42, 43, 45, 52, 57, 60, 67, 72, 82, 84, 85, 91, 93, 97, 98, 99, 101, 102, 103, 109, 152, 194, 196, 199, 265, 268, 283, 299, 306
space-time 29
special creation xii, 17, 18, 263
speciation 150
species 45, 48, 112, 114, 115, 119, 122, 125, 132, 135, 136, 139, 141, 142, 144, 146, 147, 149, 150, 151, 153, 163, 165-169, 174-177, 230, 260, 264, 306
spectroscopy 40
speculation 39, 54, 93, 146, 165, 261

spirit v, xii, 2, 5, 11, 14, 24, 117, 184, 185, 191, 195, 211, 225, 228, 243, 244, 250, 255, 256, 257, 258
Spirit of truth 304
spiritual blindness 243
spiritual death 242
spliceosomes 146, 147
Standard Model 29, 72
Stanford Encyclopedia of Philosophy 25, 189, 210
stars 4, 40, 45, 63, 66, 75, 77, 79, 83, 84, 98
Stenger, Victor 67, 87
substance dualism 195, 197, 198, 201
substances 55, 190, 197, 218
suffering servant 289
sun 32, 40, 85, 98, 219, 279, 308
superposition 105
superstitions 118
surface temperature 41
Sutton Hoo 118, 128
Sweden 118
symbiogenesis 151
symbolism 234, 239
symbols 232, 259, 264
synagogue 281
syntax 263

T
Tacitus 276, 277, 291
Tallis, Raymond 6, 11, 12, 18, 19, 115, 128, 192, 196
Tarter, Jill 47, 48
taxes 112-115
Tegmark, Max 101, 105, 110
Teilhard de Chardin, Pierre 237, 248
teleology 58, 70
telescope 44-47, 60
temperature 27, 41, 54, 55, 56, 82, 83, 101, 102, 189
template 135, 216
temple 285, 287
temptation 244
terracotta army 117

Testaments 212, 214, 216, 226, 234, 256
The Eerie Silence 51, 60
The Fabric of Reality 92, 108, 109, 110
The Grand Design 6, 18, 35, 108, 209, 224
The Hidden Reality 97, 108, 109
The Historical Reliability of the New Testament 280, 291
theism 52, 180, 213
theist 23, 194, 195, 211
theistic evolution 14, 16
Theoretical physics 96
theory of everything 18, 19, 32, 95, 203, 272
The Panda's Thumb 165, 177

The Privileged Planet 54, 60
thermal equilibrium 102
The Wonder of Water 55, 60
thought vii, 2, 4, 6, 8, 11, 14, 18, 34, 43,
    85, 86, 92, 95, 105, 109, 114, 129, 175,
    180, 184, 196, 198, 199, 200, 212, 224,
    225, 236, 244, 259, 263, 264, 265
thoughts 116, 183, 184, 191, 209, 259,
    260, 261, 266, 279, 307
throne 287, 288, 296, 307, 308
Tiberius 277
time iv, viii, ix, x, 11, 18, 25, 26, 29, 30,
    31, 35, 40, 47, 48, 51, 52, 53, 56, 67, 72,
    73, 80, 84, 85, 95, 98, 102, 105, 106,
    114, 116, 117, 125, 126, 127, 144, 147,
    149, 164, 168, 170, 172, 188, 194, 196,
    197, 198, 199, 210, 213, 220, 226, 227,
    230, 237, 240, 241, 254, 258, 261, 265,
    268, 269, 276, 278, 284, 285, 287, 301,
    302, 306, 307
tomb 290, 297, 299, 300
Tomkins, Jeffrey 129, 137, 138, 152
tools 158, 164, 174

tower of Babel 59
transcendent 69, 202, 222, 305
transcribed 135, 142, 145
transcription 142, 143
transgression 237, 285, 286
transgressions 289, 290
transposition 151
tree-dwelling 162
tree of evolution 10
tree of life 122, 226, 239, 240, 241, 308
trees 3, 139, 182, 234, 235, 239
trespass 243, 248
tribes 174, 235, 268
trilemma 274, 278
Trinity 241, 273, 304
trust 2, 18, 245, 271, 274, 279, 303, 306,
    308
truth 3, 13, 34, 48, 72, 107, 139, 157,
    207, 270, 281, 283, 304
turtles 22, 23, 32
Twain, Mark viii, 39, 156, 158, 177,
    250, 251, 252, 271
type 147, 228, 230

U
ultraviolet light 56
uncertainty principle 100
universal grammar 261
universe 7, 17, 20-31, 33, 34, 35, 39, 40,

    45, 47-52, 58, 62-76, 79-88, 90-104,
    107, 108, 206, 211, 212, 217-233, 265
unreality 108
Uranus 43, 56

V
Van Allen 57
Venus 50, 56
vertebrate 125
Vilenkin, Alexander 27, 28, 31, 36

virgin 164, 277, 284
virtual particles 30
volcano 103, 104, 173

W
wages 282
waiting time 126, 149
Waltham, David 54, 60
war 68, 76, 80, 115, 238

Ward, Keith 190, 195, 196, 197, 202,
    203
warranted beliefs 208

water 41, 55, 56, 79, 82, 116, 164, 171, 172, 219, 221, 257, 272, 289, 308
wave function 106, 107
wavelength 101
weather 54, 56
weeks 200, 285, 286, 296, 299
Weinberg, Steven 96
whale 116
Who Made God? vi, ix, 9, 17, 22, 26, 27, 30, 199, 267
will iv, v, viii, x, 2, 4, 5, 6, 9, 10, 13, 14, 18, 20-26, 29, 31, 32, 33, 38, 43, 44, 46, 47, 48, 50, 51, 52, 56, 57, 64, 65, 67, 68, 69, 72, 78, 80, 82, 87, 93, 94, 96, 97, 99, 100, 102, 103, 105, 107, 108, 116, 124, 125, 136, 140, 142, 145, 146, 161, 163, 169, 172, 174, 175, 176, 184, 185, 187, 188, 190, 191, 192, 206, 207, 208, 209, 210, 216, 217, 222, 228, 229, 230, 232, 235, 238, 244, 245, 246, 250, 252, 254, 256, 259, 263, 266, 267, 270, 274, 277, 278, 287-290, 294, 296, 297, 298, 302-308

wisdom ix, 2, 53, 212, 214, 218, 255, 257, 270, 275, 289
word 1, 2, 5, 6, 102, 122, 129, 141, 143, 167, 168, 184, 193, 213, 223, 224, 233, 234, 242, 243, 254, 255-258, 263, 265, 270, 277, 281, 284, 285, 289, 307
world iv, vii, xii, 2, 3, 4, 6, 12, 26, 38, 49, 53, 55, 77, 80, 81, 84, 85, 95, 106, 109, 115, 117, 118, 128, 151, 158, 167, 182, 183, 187, 191, 205, 206, 207, 209, 210, 212, 216, 217, 218, 219, 220, 221, 223, 225, 226, 236, 237, 238, 242, 243, 245, 246, 253, 256, 258, 261, 264, 274, 304, 305, 306, 308
worlds 67, 92, 106, 107, 110
worldview iv, v, vi, vii, 25, 31, 183, 204, 206-210, 212, 213, 214, 216, 217, 220-223, 227, 233, 234, 236, 237, 239, 241, 246, 256, 277, 286, 301
worldwide web 8, 52
worship 216, 238, 286
wounded 289
Wow! signal 45

X

Y

Z
zebra fish 121

zombie 195

CPSIA information can be obtained
at www.ICGtesting.com
Printed in the USA
LVHW051016180419
614654LV00006B/32